THE TRISTAN LEGEND
A Study in Sources

HE TRISTAN LEGEND

A Study in Sources *By Sigmund Eisner* Northwestern University Press: 1969 *Evanston* Illinois

Sigmund Eisner is Professor of English
at the University of Arizona.

To Nan, Tom, Chip, Nicky,
Tory, Halley, and Cassie,
who have borne with me "in
much patience, in afflictions,
in necessities, in distresses."

2 Corinthians 6:4

Contents

List of Maps

List of Charts

List of Abbreviations

ALMA	*Arthurian Literature in the Middle Ages,* ed. Roger Sherman Loomis (Oxford, 1959).
BBCS	*Bulletin of the Board of Celtic Studies.*
BBSIA	*Bulletin Bibliographique de la Société Internationale Arthurienne.*
EC	*Études Celtiques.*
EETS	*Early English Text Society.*
FF	*Folklore Fellows.*
ITS	*Irish Texts Society.*
MLQ	*Modern Language Quarterly.*
PMLA	*Publications of the Modern Language Association of America.*
RC	*Revue Celtique.*
RP	*Romance Philology.*
SATF	*Société des anciens textes français.*
THSC	*The Transactions of the Honourable Society of Cymmrodorion.*
TJDGNA	*Transactions and Journal of Proceedings of the Dumfriesshire and Galloway Natural History and Antiquarian Society.*
ZCP	*Zeitschrift für celtische Philologie.*
ZFSL	*Zeitschrift für französische Sprach und Litteratur.*
ZRPh	*Zeitschrift für romanische Philologie.*

Acknowledgements

In 1958, in accordance with an agreement between the Conference Board of Associated Research Councils of Washington, D. C., and An Bord Scolaireachtai Comalairte of Dublin, Ireland, I was awarded a Fulbright grant to do research at the School of Celtic Studies of the Dublin Institute for Advanced Studies. The courtesy, hospitality, and kindnesses of the Director and the professors whom I met at the Institute far exceeded the basic needs of our relationship. Only there and only with their help was I able to assemble the nucleus of this study.

Now at the pleasant moment of offering acknowledgments I wish first to thank the staffs of the various libraries where I have studied: the Library of the Dublin Institute for Advanced Studies; the Library of Trinity College, Dublin; the Royal Irish Academy; the National Library of Ireland; the Library of the University of California at Berkeley; the Library of Dominican College of San Rafael, California; and the Library of the University of Arizona.

To certain people I owe an especial acknowledgement of appreciation for indirect yet substantial aid. The late Professor Roger Sherman Loomis would have disagreed with some of my conclusions here. I am, however, forever indebted to Professor Loomis not only for awakening my interest in Arthurian studies but also for schooling me rigorously in the disciplines which resulted in this study. Secondly, Gary Mac Eoin of Nutley, New Jersey, long ago led me to an appreciation of Celtic studies and has kindly offered council and wisdom ever since.

Many others have helped me along the way, some unwittingly, and all graciously offering encouragement, advice, and basic information. A few of these people are mentioned below. Professor James P. Carney of the Dublin Institute for Advanced Studies first suggested the topic to me, guided me to the proper sources during my period of initial research, and continued with useful advice and comment as the work progressed. Sister M. Nicholas Maltman, O. P., Chairman of the Department of English at the Dominican College of San Rafael, California, was continually stimulating in her quiet and knowledgeable way. Professor Charles W. Jones of the University of California at Berkeley encouraged me far more than I suspect he knew at the time. Professor George Michael Evica of Hartford University in Connecticut suggested valuable paths of inquiry to me. Professors A. Laurence Muir, Richard Hosley, and Oliver Sigworth of the

University of Arizona read the manuscript and offered valuable comments, some of which they may recognize in the pages below. To Mrs. Janice Feldstein of Northwestern University Press and to Michael R. Peed, a graduate student in English at the University of Arizona, I owe gratitude for wise and painstaking work in editing and proofreading. Finally my wife, Nancy Fereva Eisner, has patiently read the manuscript more times that I can remember or count and has criticized both what appears in this study and what was rejected from it.

S. E.

Tucson, Arizona
February, 1969

Harp of the North! that mouldering long hast hung
   On the witch-elm that shades Saint Fillan's spring,
And down the fitful breeze thy numbers flung,
   Till envious ivy did around thee cling,
Muffling with verdant ringlet every string,—
   O Minstrel Harp, still must thine accents sleep?

The Lady of the Lake
Sir Walter Scott
Canto First, lls. 1–6

THE TRISTAN
LEGEND
A Study in Sources

Chapter One ✳ ✳

KING ARTHUR IN HISTORY & LEGEND

STORYTELLING, so far as anyone can tell, is as old as mankind and as new as today. Any tale is old to someone who knows it and new to someone who does not. The number of plots, of course, is limited, and much old wine has been redecanted into the expected new bottles. Sometimes two or more different vintages are combined to delight the palate of a new age with presumably a new taste. Still the connoisseur can distinguish the older tastes now partially hidden in the new. A student of stories does much the same. He takes a tale as it comes to him, a tale which possibly exists only because someone had the time and ability to write it down. Then with much detective work, that is with exhaustive trial and repeated error, he perhaps recognizes other tales told by other cultures. For a story is much like all of us in that it has ancestors. And just as we are enriched by knowledge of our ancestors that goes deeper than the mere fact of their existence, so can a good tale be better appreciated if we know and understand its antecedents.

For years ancestral tales were all but ignored. Great artists retailored what they knew and let it go at that. As literacy became more widespread in Western civilization, some people paused to wonder where a tale came from but, shrugging off the problem with a vague reference to the misty past, began merely to recreate it and to build a history in its own image. One of the most recent of such fictions is based on the nineteenth-century idea of evolution, not a bad one really, as far as ideas go, but still one which brought with it some unworkable corollaries. Thus, for years it has been assumed that the further back in time a storyteller existed, the more primitive he was. The subtleties of a tale were believed to be recent acquisitions, while any direct action or statement was believed to be old. It is only in the past few decades that we have been able to escape such a fiction and arrive at a point where we can conceive of earlier cultures, different from our own, yet quite capable of structuring a literary masterpiece of which only tantalizing fragments survive.

This new approach is exciting and revealing. It combines literary studies with an exacting examination of factual history—as factual anyway as can be discovered. Guesswork is eschewed or properly labeled as guesswork, and builders try to create their edifices not on sand but rock. All this is an ideal, but it is an honest one, and once in a while it leads to new discoveries to be added to the ever-expanding repository of scholarship. In recent years we have learned more than we ever knew of how stories grow. We have learned that great authors, unknown to us yet, lived in the past, and although only bits and pieces of their masterpieces survive, they created and audiences assembled to absorb these creations. As we learn more about historical circumstances, we learn how tales develop: how one plot suitable for a given age must be altered for the next, and then the next, until the popular tale known to us becomes the surviving product.

This study is concerned with the sources of the Tristan story, an old tale, popular in the Middle Ages and popular today. Why a new book about the sources of the Tristan story? Gertrude Schoepperle did such a book in 1913,[1] and her findings have withstood time so well that her work must be highly recommended to any student of either the Tristan or the Arthurian legends. But more than half a century has passed since Miss Schoepperle published her excellent and original research. Discoveries about the actual history of the

---

1. Gertrude Schoepperle, *Tristan and Isolt: A Study of the Sources of the Romance*, 2 vols. (Frankfurt and London, 1913; reprinted, New York, 1959).

peoples who first talked of Tristan have given us new points of departure so that it is possible now to attempt answers to questions which were beyond the capabilities of the scholar of half a century ago.

RELATIONSHIP OF THE TRISTAN AND ARTHUR LEGENDS

The relationship of the Tristan story to the Arthurian legends has been demonstrated repeatedly, although critics have disagreed as to when the tale was actually incorporated into Arthurian romance. Miss Schoepperle says that Arthurian incidents were the stock in trade of the French storytellers, that they originally united the previously independent Tristan and Arthurian cycles by bringing the Arthurian knights into the Tristan story:

These [Arthurian] incidents are stories universally current in mediaeval fiction. The treatment of Arthurian tradition in them is characteristic of French romance of the [twelfth-century] period of extant redactions. It would seem, therefore, that we owe them to French redactors. The purpose of introducing them into the narrative seems to have been to associate Tristan with a popular cycle with which his story had a certain affinity.[2]

According to Miss Schoepperle, the writers of French romances, interested in the surface similarities of the separate Tristan traditions and King Arthur traditions with which they were familiar, combined them. She was persuaded that the Tristan and Arthurian traditions were never united until the twelfth-century writers of French romances effected the combination.

Since the time of Miss Schoepperle, however, scholars have revealed not only that the period of the French redactors was later than the time of much of the Welsh body of Arthurian fragments but also that in these early Welsh fragments may be found Arthur's and Tristan's names united in their traditional relationship. The Welsh stories, with the exception of a few which are closely parallel

2. *Ibid.*, I, 222–23.

to French tales,[3] were mostly completed before 1100. The French narrators did not flourish until after that date.[4] Yet King Arthur himself appears in Welsh fragments of the Tristan story. In one such example, known as the Welsh *Ystoria Trystan*, Arthur acts as a referee between Mark and Tristan, who have been quarreling over the possession of Isolt.[5] The *Ystoria Trystan*, which is preserved in a sixteenth-century manuscript,[6] includes both prose and verse. The prose passages are explanatory glosses and might be later redactions of an earlier story. The verse is made up of a series of *englynion* (singular: *englyn*), which are short stanzas of three or four lines. The *englynion*, according to Sir Ifor Williams, date back to the earliest stages of the Tristan tradition, long before the influence of the twelfth-century writers.[7] Here are the relevant *englynion*:

> Trystan, worthily renowned,
> Dost thou know not, has not found,
> Arthur's host that hems thee round? . . .

> Trystan, thy repute is clear,
> And thy blow can cleave a spear.
> Spurn not Arthur's friendship dear.[8]

3. Later Welsh Arthurian tales which are similar to Continental versions include *The Lady of the Fountain, Peredur,* and *Gereint Son of Erbin.* See J. Loth, *Les Mabinogion,* 2 vols. (Paris, 1913), II, 1–185; Gwyn Jones and Thomas Jones (trans.), *The Mabinogion,* Everyman's Library No. 97 (London, 1949), pp. 155–273, and especially the Introd., p. x. Current agreement is that the Welsh and Continental versions are based on lost tales known to the authors of both and that the Welsh versions were written later. See Rachel Bromwich, "The Character of Early Welsh Tradition," *Studies in Early British History,* ed. Nora K. Chadwick (Cambridge, Eng., 1954; reprinted, 1959), p. 110, n. 4; Roger Sherman Loomis, *Arthurian Tradition and Chrétien de Troyes* (New York, 1949), p. 23; and Thomas Parry, *A History of Welsh Literature,* trans. H. Idris Bell (Oxford, 1955), p. 87.

4. Loomis, *Arthurian Tradition,* pp. 14 ff.; "The Oral Diffusion of the Arthurian Legend," *ALMA,* pp. 52 ff.

5. For a translation of the *Ystoria Trystan* see Roger Sherman Loomis (ed. and trans.), *The Romance of Tristram and Ysolt,* new rev. ed. (New York, 1951), pp. xxi–xxvi. The *Ystoria Trystan* has also been edited and translated by Tom Peete Cross, "A Welsh Tristan Episode," *Studies in Philology,* XVII (1920), 93–110. See also: J. Loth, "L'Ystoria Trystan et la question des archétypes," *RC,* XXXIV (1913); Sir Ifor Williams, "Trystan ac Esyllt," *BBCS,* V (Cardiff, 1930), 115–29.

6. Sir Ifor Williams, *Lectures in Early Welsh Poetry* (Dublin, 1954), p. 18.

7. *Ibid.,* pp. 22 f. See also Rachel Bromwich, *Trioedd Ynys Prydein—The Welsh Triads* (Cardiff, 1961), p. 332.

8. Loomis, *The Ystoria Trystan,* pp. xxi–xxvi.

Thus we see Tristan and Arthur together in a Welsh verse old enough to be entirely free of the twelfth-century Continental Arthurian influence.[9]

A second such example is selected from the body of Welsh triads: [10]

Three Mighty Swineherds of the Island of Britain. Drystan mab Tallwch who guarded the swine of March ap Meirchiawn, while the swineherd went to ask Essyllt to come to a meeting with him. And Arthur kept trying to get one pig from among them, either by deceit or by force, but he did not get it. . . .[11]

Here we have Mark, Tristan, and Isolt, albeit their names are spelled in the Welsh manner, engaged in their traditional triangle and also involved with Arthur. These Welsh fragments could not have been influenced by any extant French Arthurian literature.[12] Contrary to the statement by Miss Schoepperle, the association of the Tristan story with Arthurian legend was evidently an early historical development, earlier, certainly, than the time of the French redactors of the story.[13] This study is based on the conclu-

---

9. Thomas Parry records no Continental Arthurian influence on Welsh poetry before the twelfth century. See *A History of Welsh Literature,* passim, and especially pp. 86 ff.

10. The Welsh triads, as discussed in this study, were a literary device popular among Celtic peoples in the early and later Middle Ages. They consisted of easily memorized groups of three objects, persons, or events and were concerned with oral traditions of law, history, legend, and the mechanics of poetic composition. They were probably used in the Welsh bardic schools as an aid in memorizing whatever lore was judged worthy of preservation. See Rachel Bromwich, "The Welsh Triads," *ALMA,* pp. 44–51; *Trioedd Ynys Prydein,* pp. lxiii ff.

11. This triad is No. 26 in the manuscript known as the Peniarth 16 collection. See J. Rhŷs and J. Gwenogvryn Evans, *Text of the Mabinogion from the Red Book of Hergest* (Oxford, 1887), p. 307; Loth, *Les Mabinogion,* II, 270, No. 63; Joseph Bédier (ed.), *Le Roman de Tristan par Thomas, SATF,* No. LIII, 2 vols. (Paris, 1902–5), II, 115. For commentaries on this and other triads see Rachel Bromwich, "Some Remarks on the Celtic Sources of 'Tristan,' " *THSC,* Session 1953 (London, 1955), p. 33; "The Character of Early Welsh Tradition," p. 114; "The Welsh Triads," p. 48; and *Trioedd Ynys Prydein,* passim, especially p. 45.

12. So agrees Mrs. Bromwich, "Celtic Sources of 'Tristan,' " p. 34; *Trioedd Ynys Prydein,* p. 332.

13. Thus Mrs. Bromwich says that the fitting of the Tristan story in "the Arthurian complex is an insular development which had begun in Wales before the possibility of French influence need be considered." See "The Character of Early Welsh Tradition," p. 116.

sion that the story of Tristan and Isolt was attracted to the Arthurian orbit during the period of its insular, pre-Continental development.

The association of the Tristan story with the Arthurian corpus
dates, then, from the period when Arthur was barely known outside
of the British Isles. A discussion of this body of Arthurian material
and an outline of the sources and transmissions of the Matter of
Britain will be useful to the reader so that when he sees that the
Tristan legend, although genuinely a part of the Arthurian corpus,
deviates from the accepted pattern of Arthurian transmissions, he
will have enough knowledge to appreciate the significance of the
deviation.

THE HISTORICAL ARTHUR ▨

Who was King Arthur, what was his story, where was it first
told, and how did it develop into that tremendous body of literature
so popular during the Middle Ages and so appealing ever since?

We all have a vague idea of the answer to such a question. We
remember tales in which King Arthur was a wise monarch of the
Britain of the indefinable past. He ruled in splendor, and with him
was associated a group of figures known as the Knights of the
Round Table. Each one of them embodied the acme (or occasionally
the nadir) of chivalry. But this world of faëry and magic was not
British. It introduced an Arthur of medieval French romance, the
great leader of a fictional land created from the highest Christian
and courtly ideals of the twelfth-century French. But when we ask
ourselves who Arthur really was and when the luminous court
existed, we run into problems. It is easy enough to place someone
like Alexander in time. We know enough about him so that we can
locate him, the Macedonians, and his other contemporaries in the
period where they belong. The same applies to Charlemagne: we
know from contemporary records when he lived, who his family
was, and what he did. But Arthur is another matter. We can say
that he lived during the height of chivalry, but the height of chivalry
was the twelfth century, the time of other English heroes, the
Plantagenets. So we must conclude that although Arthur is por-
trayed as a powerful monarch of the twelfth century, there is no
room for him in actual twelfth-century history.

A number of people, Mark Twain for one, place him in the sixth century. It is a historical fact that in the sixth century the British provided some fighting forces that for a time challenged the invading Germanic tribes. And it is a historical possibility that one successful British leader of the sixth century could have been named Arthur. But as far as I can see few if any of the tales about him have any concrete basis in fact. Whether he did or did not exist, it seems obvious that as Anglo-Saxon military success augmented, the British, in a natural desire for self-esteem, developed in their defeat a psychological need for a great hero. After reading numerous repetitive tales written about him, we become familiar with many legends about Arthur but few if any historical facts about him.

Although we are left with little factual information, we still have a plethora of educated guesses. Apparently the first mention of Arthur was in a Welsh poem, attributed to one Aneirin, called the *Gododdin,* which scholars now say was written in or about the year 600.[14] The poem, which evidently was composed shortly after the event,[15] tells of a small British force annihilated near what is now Edinburgh by the Germanic peoples of Bernicia and Deire, kingdoms that occupied the area around present-day Yorkshire. In the *Gododdin* a hero is praised "though he was not Arthur." Still the passage does not prove the historicity of Arthur because, as Professor Jackson has pointed out, there were some later interpolations to the *Gododdin,* and this particular passage might have been one of them.[16]

The next significant references to Arthur were those by the South Welsh priest, Nennius, in his *Historia Brittonum* (c. 800).[17] Nennius mentions Arthur enough times that one may rightly believe that to a ninth-century British audience Arthur was a familiar name. In the *Mirabilia* appended to the *Historia Brittonum,* Nennius describes a cairn called *Carn Cabal,* topped by a stone bearing a foot-

14. Sir Ifor Williams (ed.), *Canu Aneurin* (Cardiff, 1938). Reviewed by Kenneth Jackson, *Antiquity,* XIII (1939), 25–34. Trans., in part, by Gwyn Jones, *Cymmrodor,* XXXII (1922), 4–47. For further comments see Williams, *Lectures on Early Welsh Poetry,* pp. 65–70; Kenneth Jackson, "The Arthur of History," *ALMA,* pp. 3, 7.
15. Bromwich, "The Character of Early Welsh Tradition," p. 88.
16. "The Arthur of History," p. 3.
17. F. Lot, *Nennius et l'historia Brittonum* (Paris, 1934). See also A. W. Wade-Evans, *Nennius's History of the Britons* (London, 1938).

print once made by Arthur's dog, Cabal, while hunting the pig Troit. This particular hunt is a central incident in the Welsh fairy tale *Culhwch and Olwen,* which was probably written before 1100.[18] Also in the *Mirabilia* Nennius mentions the tomb of Arthur's son, Amr, about whom we know nothing else. In the *Historia Brittonum* proper, Nennius refers to Arthur not as a king but as a leader in twelve great battles. He names the sites of these engagements, and much has been written to identify their localities.[19] There is little more to establish the Arthur of history as a factual person. Nennius says that his chief battles were fought around the year 500,[20] and if we knew that he actually lived, we would place him in the late fifth century.[21]

THE LEGEND OF ARTHUR ▒

So much for the historical Arthur. His career pales when it is compared with the legend of Arthur, which, as is usually the case with legends, is another matter entirely. As one would expect, it was the Welsh who were the early propagators of this legend. Arthur, if he existed, was either a Briton, that is, a member of the native race of the island, or a Roman, fighting beside the Britons. His opponents were largely the Anglo-Saxons, although it is certainly conceivable that he fought against Britons too. As the Britons were squeezed into smaller and smaller acreage by the invaders,[22] they recalled their ancient heroes and described them to each other with more and more luster. Accordingly, in written British literature the figure of Arthur developed into a companion of the Celtic deities, and it was only natural that as the years went on he shared godlike

18. Gwyn Jones and Thomas Jones (trans.), *Culhwch and Olwen* in *The Mabinogion,* pp. 95–136. Idris Llewelyn Foster, "*Culhwch and Olwen* and *Rhonabwy's Dream,*" *ALMA,* p. 32.

19. The leading attempts include Arthur G. Brodeur, "Arthur, Dux Bellorum," *University of California Publications in English,* III (1939), 237–83; Kenneth Jackson, "Once Again Arthur's Battles," *Modern Philology,* XLIII (1945), 44–57; and Jackson, "The Arthur of History," pp. 4 ff.

20. Gildas, who lived shortly afterwards, mentions some of the battles but not Arthur himself.

21. Professor Jackson, who brings convincing arguments to the problem, suggests this date, although he too is not completely convinced that Arthur existed. See "The Arthur of History," p. 10.

22. See Maps 1–4, pp. 20–21.

adventures. In these tales [23] Arthur becomes more than a battle leader; he is a worker of magic. Accompanied by his earliest retainers, Cei (later Sir Kay) and Bedwyr (later Sir Bedivere),[24] he roams the Welsh countryside killing a witch,[25] undertaking expeditions to the Welsh otherworld,[26] and accumulating miraculous possessions.[27] Even the location of his tomb is as nebulous as the graves of mythical figures and other national heroes whose graves are mysteries; in a passage from the twelfth-century *Black Book of Carmarthen* we read:

> A grave for March, a grave for Gwythur,
> A grave for Gwgawn of the red sword;
> An eternal wonder is the grave of Arthur.[28]

The implication is, of course, that he will one day return: other twelfth-century writers state that to the Welsh—and indeed to the Bretons—Arthur never died.[29] The magic associated with his name over the years absorbed the magic associated with others. Arthur and his retainers gradually joined other heroes of Celtic mythology, and more and more they were placed into stories which were much older than any historical Arthur ever could have been.

The placing of a given character into a story much older than he

23. These legends are listed by John Rhŷs in his introduction to Malory's *Morte d'Arthur*, Everyman's Library No. 45 (London and New York, 1906; reprinted, 1941), I, xix–xxv. See also Kenneth Jackson, "Arthur in Early Welsh Verse," *ALMA*, pp. 13 ff.

24. See Bromwich, "Celtic Sources of 'Tristan,'" p. 33, n. 8.

25. The witch incident occurs in *Culhwch and Olwen*, *The Mabinogion*, p. 136; and in Loth, *Les Mabinogion*, I, 344 f.

26. The expedition occurs in *The Spoils of Annwn*. See Roger Sherman Loomis, "*The Spoils of Annwn*, An Early Welsh Poem," *PMLA*, LVI (1941), 887–936, reprinted in *Wales and the Arthurian Legend* (Cardiff, 1956), pp. 131–78.

27. These may be found in *The Dream of Rhonabwy*, *The Mabinogion*, pp. 137–52, and in Loth, *Les Mabinogion*, I, 347–77. For a commentary see Idris Llewelyn Foster, "*Culhwch and Olwen* and *Rhonabwy's Dream*," *ALMA*, p. 32.

28. Thus translates Kenneth Jackson. See "Arthur in Early Welsh Verse," p. 13. Mrs. Bromwich suggests for the last line: "difficult to find is the grave of Arthur" ("The Character of Early Welsh Tradition," p. 112). The difficulty of the line is also recognized by Parry; cf. *A History of Welsh Literature*, p. 42.

29. Roger Sherman Loomis, "The Legend of Arthur's Survival," *ALMA*, p. 64; "The Oral Diffusion." (In these pages *Briton* means a native of the Island of Britain while *Breton* is a noun or an adjective pertaining to a person from Continental Brittany.)

is, whether the character be historical or fictional, is a standard and common method of story building. Someone looks at a hero of history or fiction and says that a certain good story might have happened to him. If it might have happened to him, it could have happened to him, and here we go. Thus the same adventure may happen to many heroes, as, for instance, most slayers of dragons, after similar difficulties, invariably win the king's daughter.[30]

The earliest authors in the Arthurian complex brought together two distinct traditions. One was the national memory of a hero named Arthur. The other was the old Celtic mythology which presumably was a weakening one, since a strong mythology is jealous and does not readily admit new figures to its pantheon.

In the Arthurian situation we are fortunate because the myths that were associated with the Arthurian complex were also known to the Irish although, of course, the heroes were different; a given adventure would occur to one of Arthur's knights and to one of the traditional Irish heroes as well.[31] The Irish stories are useful, for they show us variations in the original. Thus scholars have been able to deduce the contributions of the various groups of authors of the Arthurian tales. Such is the task that I wish to attempt in this book.

In general the combination of myths and heroic names provided the nucleus for the Matter of Britain. The Welsh, remembering stories known to their pre-Christian ancestors, attached the plots of these tales to the name Arthur, who in early medieval Wales was believed to be a successful hero of a happier past.

30. Cf. below, pp. 125 ff.

31. Irish reflections of Arthurian tales have been observed by many. See lists in Sigmund Eisner, *A Tale of Wonder—A Source Study of the Wife of Bath's Tale* (Wexford, Ire., 1957), pp. 14 f.; and Helaine Newstead, *Bran the Blessed in Arthurian Romance* (New York, 1939), p. 4, n. 7. See also Loomis, *Arthurian Tradition;* "The Origin of the Grail Legend," *ALMA*, pp. 274–94; Roger Sherman Loomis (ed.), and K. G. T. Webster (trans.), *Lanzelet* by Ulrich von Zatzikhoven (New York, 1951), pp. 157–232; Lucy Allen Paton, *Studies in the Fairy Mythology of Arthurian Romance* (Cambridge, Mass., 1903; reprinted, New York, 1960), especially the "Survey of Scholarship since 1903" and Bibliography appended by R. S. Loomis to the 1960 edition, pp. 280 ff; and Cecile O'Rahilly, *Ireland and Wales* (London, 1924), pp. 147 ff. For convincing evidence that the Irish and Welsh shared different versions of similar myths the reader is referred to, among many, C. O'Rahilly, *Ireland and Wales;* and W. J. Gruffydd, *Math Vab Mathonwy* (Cardiff, 1928).

Arthur, of course, was not the only Welsh hero so treated. Actual Celtic kings of the sixth century, Urien and his son Owain among them, found their way into the Matter of Britain. To them also were attached old stories.

Nor did all of the plots come from Celtic mythology; there were travelers during the post-Roman period, and a good story on one side of Europe was just as good on the other. We shall see in this study that the heroes of the Tristan story were also known Celtic leaders and that the plot outlines of the Tristan story were excavated from the rich mines of the many European mythologies. Foreign plot and local heroes were combined and dovetailed into the Arthurian complex before the story ever left the British Isles. Like other Arthurian romances, the Tristan story evolved its essential form in a Welsh-speaking land. From there, as did the rest of the Matter of Britain, it traveled to Brittany.

In the second half of the fifth century, the natives of Britain, harassed by the invading Germanic tribes,[32] sought new homes. Some fled to the west of their island, and many traveled overseas to Galicia in Spain and Armorica in France.[33] A century later that section of Armorica in which they had settled bore their name and has been called Brittany ever since.

The migrations of the Britons to Brittany began in the fifth century and continued into the seventh. Among the migrants were many ecclesiastical figures who went to Brittany as missionaries and later became local saints.[34] The Bretons wrote stories about their lives and included in them miraculous material similar to the Arthurian legends.[35]

There is evidence that these Bretons were even more conscious of the mystery and wonder of Arthur than were the people whom they had left behind. By the twelfth century Bretons were referred

32. Actually the reasons for the migrations were not so simple, although the problem is not one of great concern here. Linguistic evidence shows that the migrants were from Cornwall and Devon, yet those parts of Britain were not at that time menaced by the invaders. See Kenneth Jackson, *Language and History in Early Britain* (Edinburgh, 1953), pp. 16 ff.

33. A. W. Wade-Evans, *The Emergence of England and Wales* (Cambridge, Eng., 1959), p. 41; C. O'Rahilly, *Ireland and Wales*, pp. 15 f.

34. Jackson, *Language and History in Early Britain*, pp. 12–30.

35. See below, pp. 56 ff.

to as those who would fight if one proposed that Arthur were dead.[36] In 1125 the Anglo-Norman William of Malmesbury said that even at that date the Bretons still revered Arthur; [37] Wace, in the *Brut* (1125), said that the Bretons told many stories about the Round Table; [38] and Giraldus Cambrensis in about 1216 credited the Bretons with the story of Arthur's eternal life.[39] Further evidence for the popularity of the Arthurian tales among the Bretons is the fact that so many Arthurian stories, in the forms we now have them, contain Breton proper nouns. For instance in the Tristan story we find the Breton name Rivalen used for the hero's father instead of the insular Tallwch. Then, too, many native Breton poems or *lais* contain Arthurian episodes,[40] and Breton folktales, even those which have developed in recent centuries, reflect Arthurian motifs.[41] Evidently the Bretons preserved the old Welsh tales for a time when Europe was ready for the next great popular demand for the Matter of Britain.

Scraps of evidence here and there demonstrate that the Bretons, or people familiar with Breton versions of Arthurian tales, roamed Europe telling of the adventures of Arthur and meeting receptive audiences in many lands.[42] These tellers of tales we know as Breton *conteurs,* and evidence of their presence is found wherever French was understood. Among such lands was England, where after the

---

36. E. K. Chambers, *Arthur of Britain* (London, 1927), pp. 109 f., 265; Loomis, "The Oral Diffusion," p. 54.

37. William of Malmesbury, *De Gestis Regum Anglorum,* ed. William Stubbs, 2 vols. (London, 1887–89), I, 11. Chambers, *Arthur of Britain,* p. 250. Loomis, "The Oral Diffusion," p. 55. E. Faral, *La Legende arthurienne,* Pt. 1, *Bibliothèque de l'école des haute études,* CCLV–CCLVII (Paris, 1929), 244–50. H. Zimmer, "Beitrage zur Namenforschung in den altfranz Arthurepen, 'Tristan, Isolt, Marc,'" *ZFSL,* XIII (1891), 58–86. E. Brugger, "Ueber die Bedeutung von Bretagne, Breton in mittelalterlichen Texten," *ZFSL,* XXI (1898), 92 f.

38. Wace, *Le Roman de Brut,* ed. Ivor Arnold, *SATF,* No. LXXXIII (Paris, 1938–40), Vol. II, vss. 9747–60. G. Huet, "Le Témoignage de Wace sur les 'fables' arthuriennes," *Le Moyen Âge,* XXVIII (1915), 234–49. Charles Foulon, "Wace," *ALMA,* pp. 94–103. Loomis, "The Oral Diffusion," p. 55.

39. Chambers, *Arthur of Britain,* p. 272; Loomis, "The Oral Diffusion," p. 55.

40. Ernest Hoepffner, "The Breton Lais," *ALMA,* pp. 112–21; *Les Lais de Marie de France* (Paris, 1955). See also K. Warnke, *Die Lais der Marie de France,* 3d ed. (Halle, 1925), Introd. For a further bibliography see Hoepffner, "The Breton Lais," p. 112, n. 2.

41. Loomis, "The Oral Diffusion," pp. 56 f.; *Arthurian Tradition,* pp. 479–89.

42. Loomis, "The Oral Diffusion," pp. 60 f.

Conquest of 1066 Norman French was the usual language among those who had the leisure to listen to Arthurian tales. One who listened well and who wrote well was Geoffrey of Monmouth.

With Geoffrey the Arthurian tales return home again. His name tells us that he lived in or near Wales. During the early twelfth century, possibly before 1136,[43] he wrote the *Prophetae Merlini* or *Libellus Merlini,* which he later included in his masterpiece, *Historia Regum Britanniae.*[44] Geoffrey, obviously influenced by the *Aeneid,* began his history of Britain with a mythical eponymous hero, Brutus, the conventional Trojan refugee, who in this case migrated to a convenient western island which he named Britain after himself. Brutus, in the usual manner of such heroes, sired a race of kings which was to culminate in Geoffrey's favorite, the attractive and popular King Arthur, who occupied most of Geoffrey's *Historia* as the all-time hero of Christendom. Geoffrey is the first to tell us about the tragic legend of the conventional King Arthur. Although much of Geoffrey's information is obviously borrowed, we owe thanks to him for being the compiler of the earliest book which has survived to give us today much of the corpus of the Arthurian romance. His other contribution was the *Vita Merlini,*[45] which is based on the Welsh traditions of Merlin's battle-born madness and his prophetic ability.[46]

Geoffrey's stories include traditional material that once had been exclusively Welsh but by his lifetime had had Welsh, Cornish, Breton, and Norman French infusions. The dispute over the source of the *Historia Regum Britanniae* rises from Geoffrey's own state-

43. John J. Parry and Robert A. Caldwell, "Geoffrey of Monmouth," *ALMA,* p. 73.

44. A convenient English edition is Geoffrey of Monmouth, *History of the Kings of Britain,* trans. Sebastian Evans, rev. Charles W. Dunn (New York, 1958). A. Griscom has printed one manuscript and recorded the variants of two others (London and New York, 1929). For other editions and commentaries see Parry and Caldwell, "Geoffrey of Monmouth," p. 79, n. 10.

45. John J. Parry (ed.), *University of Illinois Studies in Language and Literature,* X, No. 3 (Urbana, Ill., 1925). For other editions and commentaries see Parry and Caldwell, "Geoffrey of Monmouth," p. 89, n. 8.

46. For further commentary on Merlin's madness see James Carney, " 'Suibne Gelt' and 'The Children of Lir,' " *Studies in Irish Literature and History* (Dublin, 1955), pp. 129 ff., originally printed in *Éigse,* VI, Pt. II (1950), 83–110. See also A. O. H. Jarman, *The Legend of Merlin* (Cardiff, 1960), especially the Bibliography, pp. 29–31.

ment that he received his information in a British book from "Brittania." [47] If to Geoffrey "Brittania" meant Brittany, then like others Geoffrey received his material from the Bretons,[48] who, presumably, had come to Geoffrey's part of the world with their friends, the Normans. If Geoffrey were depending upon Breton lore for his material, one would have to presuppose a large body of Arthurian tradition in circulation before his time. It is this point that the late Professor Tatlock denied, stating that much of what we read in Geoffrey was invented by Geoffrey.[49] Professor Loomis replied that the legends were known before Geoffrey.[50] What preceded the *Historia Regum Britanniae* has thus been a matter of dispute; what followed it has not.

Even if Geoffrey depended upon traditions which had been transmitted by the Bretons, he was not unaware of local tradition. The Welsh of the Middle Ages lived within the approximate boundaries of today's Wales, but traditionally their people came from the North, from Strathclyde, that part of western Britain lying approximately between the modern cities of Carlisle and Glasgow.[51] A story which originated in either Strathclyde [52] or a neighboring land [53] is that of the madman whose unfortunate condition was brought on by battle fright and who later became an accurate prophet. This is the tale which Geoffrey evidently utilized in writing his *Vita Mer-*

47. So believed the late Professor Parry. See Parry and Caldwell, "Geoffrey of Monmouth," p. 81.

48. Geoffrey in his text means Armorica when he says "Brittania" and Wales when he says "Gauliis," according to Professor Loomis and others. See Roger Sherman Loomis, "The Arthurian Legend before 1139," *Romanic Review,* XXXII (1941), 3–38, reprinted in *Wales and the Arthurian Legend* (Cardiff, 1956), p. 186, n. 50. See also Parry and Caldwell, "Geoffrey of Monmouth," p. 81.

49. "The Dates of the Arthurian Saints' Legends," *Speculum,* XIV (1939), 357 f.

50. "The Arthurian Legend before 1139."

51. Nora K. Chadwick, "Early Culture and Learning in North Wales," *Studies in the Early British Church,* ed. Nora K. Chadwick (Cambridge, Eng., 1958), pp. 32 ff., 118 ff.; Bromwich, "The Character of Early Welsh Tradition," pp. 83 ff., 121; Williams, *Lectures on Early Welsh Poetry,* pp. 50 ff.

52. Carney, " 'Suibne Gelt' and 'The Children of Lir,' "; "The Origin of *Suibne Gelt," Studies in Irish Literature and History,* pp. 385 ff.

53. Kenneth Jackson, "The Motive of the Threefold Death in the Story of Suibhne Geilt," *Essays and Studies Presented to Professor Eoin Mac Neill,* ed. John Ryan (Dublin, 1940), pp. 547 ff.; "A Further Note on Suibhne Geilt and Merlin," *Éigse,* VII (1954), 112–16.

lini.[54] Apparently Geoffrey did not confine himself to single groups of sources. Evidence today shows that he was a well-read man living at a time when the Arthurian legends were in the air. In the Wales of his day the people remembered great racial heroes who had lived and fought in the North. Secondly, they were aware of legends of a near-mythical or mythical hero named Arthur. Third, the Bretons, who themselves had nurtured the traditions of Arthur, were spreading Arthurian tales throughout Europe. The three streams, Strathclyde, Wales, and Brittany, all carrying fragments of the Arthurian legend, crystallized in the consciousness of Geoffrey of Monmouth. From the mid-twelfth century on, the Arthurian legend varied only slightly from the pattern used by Geoffrey. Stories, of course, were added and subtracted, but the mold had set, and Geoffrey of Monmouth had much to do with its shape.

The popularity of Geoffrey's *Historia Regum Brittaniae* was immediately apparent. In 1154, the year of Geoffrey's death, Wace [55] wrote a Norman paraphrase of the *Historia* called the *Roman de Brut.*[56] Wace introduced a number of innovations to the extant Arthurian corpus; the most striking was the Round Table. We do not know the ultimate source of the Round Table, although Wace says that the Bretons had much to say about it.[57]

Wace was followed by the first English poet to write of Arthurian matters, Layamon,[58] who also called his version the *Brut.* Ac-

54. Although Professor Carney is convinced that Geoffrey's source of the *Vita Merlini* was the Strathclyde source of *Suibhne Geilt, Studies,* pp. 385 ff., Parry and Caldwell show some skepticism: "Geoffrey of Monmouth," p. 91; and Loomis points out some Breton influences upon the *Vita Merlini:* "Morgain la Fée and the Celtic Goddesses," *Speculum,* XX (1945), 183–203, reprinted in *Wales and the Arthurian Legend,* pp. 105–30; "*The Spoils of Annwn:* an Early Welsh Poem," *PMLA,* LVI (1941), 887–936, reprinted in *Wales and the Arthurian Legend,* pp. 131–78.
55. A recent study of Wace is Charles Foulon, "Wace," *ALMA,* pp. 94–103. Others are Gaston Paris, "Comptes-rendus," *Romania,* IX (1880), 592–614; Robert Huntingdon Fletcher, *Arthurian Material in the Chronicles* (Boston, 1906; reprinted, New York, 1958), 127–43; J. H. Philpot, *Maistre Wace* (London, 1925).
56. Ivor Arnold (ed.), *SATF,* 2 vols. (Paris, 1938–40), LXXXIII.
57. *Ibid.,* II, vss. 9747–60. For more about the Round Table see Loomis, *Arthurian Tradition,* pp. 61–68.
58. For a recent discussion of Layamon see Roger Sherman Loomis, "Layamon's Brut," *ALMA,* pp. 104–11. See also H. C. Wyld, "Layamon as an English Poet," *Review of English Studies,* VI (1930), 1–30; "Studies in the Diction of

cording to the wording of his dedication, Layamon completed his
Brut after the death of Henry II, that is, after 1189. Linguistically
the book appears to be twelfth century,[59] and thus an approximate
date would be in the last decade of that century. Layamon, too,
brought contributions to the legend, many of which may be traced
to the omnipresent Breton *conteurs*.[60] One was that Arthur after his
death was taken to Avalon, where he still lives.[61]

The twelfth and thirteenth centuries were the time of the great
writers of the Arthurian legends. The Breton *conteurs* and Geoffrey
of Monmouth had reactivated a most popular genre. The romances
about Alexander, Thebes, Aeneas, Troy, and Roland were all present,
but the romances about Arthur stimulated the greatest artists: Gottfried von Strassburg, Chrétien de Troyes, Wolfram von Eschenbach,
and the author of *Gawain and the Green Knight*.[62] In every country
where people could pause and listen to the local storyteller someone
was reciting an adventure of King Arthur or of the people associated with him. The English, who walked the very ground associated with him, produced much less literature about Arthur than
did their admiring contemporaries on the Continent. Aside from
some minor poems, until the time of Malory the only notable English-language Arthurian compositions were *Gawain and the Green
Knight* and Chaucer's *Wife of Bath's Tale*.

In the late fifteenth century Sir Thomas Malory[63] gave to the

---

Layamon's *Brut*," *Language*, IX (1933), 47–71, 171–91; X (1934), 149–201;
F. L. Gillespy, "Layamon's *Brut*: a Comparative Study in Narrative Art," *University of California Publications in Modern Philology*, III (1916), 361–510;
Fletcher, *Arthurian Material*, pp. 125–66; J. S. P. Tatlock, *Legendary History
of Britain* (Berkeley and Los Angeles, 1950), pp. 472–531; Dorothy Everett,
Essays on Middle English Literature (Oxford, 1955), pp. 28–45; W. F. Schir-
mer, *Die frühen Darstellungen des Arthurstoffes* (Cologne, 1958), pp. 54–82;
Brut, ed. Sir Frederic Madden (London, 1847). A new edition is in preparation
for *EETS*.

59. Loomis, "Layamon's *Brut*," p. 104; Tatlock, *Legendary History of Britain*, pp. 511–14; J. Hall (ed.), *Layamon's Brut* (Oxford, 1924), p. vii.

60. Loomis, "Layamon's *Brut*," pp. 109 f.

61. This, of course, is the famous Breton hope hinted at by Geoffrey and
actually expressed by Layamon.

62. Space does not permit a lengthy discussion of each of these writers. The
reader is referred to *ALMA*, which contains a chapter on each along with rep-
resentative bibliographies of other significant works.

63. Thomas Malory, *Le Morte d'Arthur*, Everyman's Library Nos. 45 and
46, 2 vols. (New York and London, 1941). See also Eugène Vinaver (ed.), *The*

English-speaking world its permanent concept of King Arthur, yet he relied upon French romances for his sources. When we think of King Arthur today we think of Malory. When Tennyson, Mark Twain, or T. H. White takes us to Arthur's court, we visit a court familiar to the readers of Malory. Even a twentieth-century musical drama, *Camelot,* was ultimately based on his version. Malory re-created the Arthurian world for the English reader, but, if we wish to find the ultimate answers to the Tristan problem, we must look beyond Malory and beyond the other great writers mentioned above. As great as they all were, neither they nor any known figures were the creators of the tradition.

The Tristan story is and always has been an Arthurian tale. Wherever the Tristan story was told, Arthur was mentioned. Realizing how the Arthurian stories were built, author upon author, we can understand how the Tristan legend also developed.

Works of Sir Thomas Malory, 3 vols. (Oxford, 1954); (ed.), *The Tale of the Death of King Arthur by Sir Thomas Malory* (Oxford, 1955); "Sir Thomas Malory," *ALMA,* pp. 541–52.

THE BRITISH ISLES FROM THE SIXTH THROUGH THE NINTH CENTURY

c. 600

Picts

Scots

Dalriada

Bernicia
Deire
Angles
Rheged
Strathclyde
Cumbria

Saxons

Jutes

Cymry
(Welsh)

Saxons

Cornwall

Scots

Irish

MAP 2

c. 550

Picts

Scots

Dalriada

Bernicia
Deire
Angles
Rheged
Strathclyde
Cumbria

Saxons

Jutes

Cymry
(Welsh)

Cornwall

Scots

Irish

MAP 1

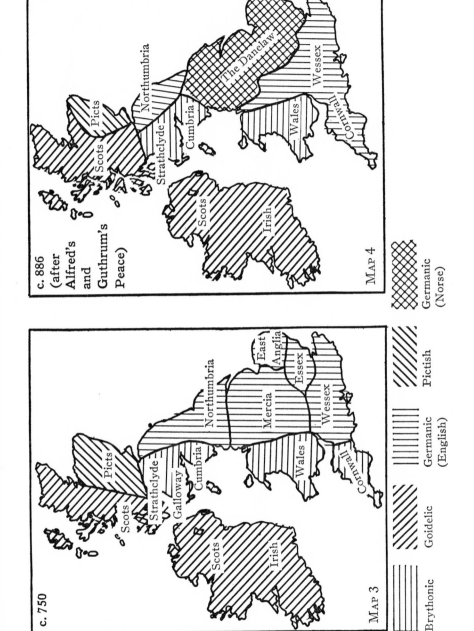

c. 886
(after
Alfred's
and
Guthrum's
Peace)

Picts

Northumbria

Strathclyde

Scots

Cumbria

The Danelaw

Scots

Wales

Irish

Wessex

Cornwall

MAP 4

Germanic
(Norse)

c. 750

Picts

Scots

Strathclyde

Galloway

Cumbria

Northumbria

East
Anglia

Mercia

Essex

Scots

Wales

Wessex

Irish

Cornwall

MAP 3

Brythonic

Goidelic

Germanic
(English)

Pictish

Chapter Two ✸ ✸

THE TRADITION OF TRISTAN & ISOLT

HE TRADITION of Tristan and Isolt, by virtue of its recurrent fascination, has appealed to so many redactors and to so many fresh audiences that it is difficult to know what the story was to begin with. The Tristan legend, that of the young man, who, enchanted by a love charm, loves his uncle's bride but unhappily settles for another lady with the same name, is unquestionably old and had obviously undergone many changes before the appearance of our earliest versions. Its many strands have each presented a complex problem of identification; and as with many Arthurian tales, each discovery has posed further questions.

The following synopsis of the Tristan story is not a translation and is not a rendition of any single source. Rather, it is a composite of that material which is particularly important to my thesis and is taken mainly from Thomas of Britain and Eilhart von Oberge. The spellings of the proper nouns are, of course, arbitrary. A more detailed examination of each relevant episode of the story will be presented when the given episode is discussed.

SYNOPSIS OF THE TRISTAN LEGEND ✸

When King Arthur ruled in Britain, the king in Cornwall was Mark, who had neither wife nor heir. His only sister Blanchefleur

was married to King Rivalen of Loonois and had had by him one
son named Tristan. Blanchefleur died at Tristan's birth and Rivalen
not long afterward, when one Duke Morgan attacked his land and
usurped his crown. Tristan, now an orphan, grew up under the
harsh rule of Morgan and as a young man came to the court of his
uncle, King Mark. In Cornwall Tristan soon distinguished himself
as a clever hunter, an accomplished harpist, and an adroit swords-
man. He was young, personable, and extraordinarily intelligent;
everyone loved him.

At the time of Tristan's arrival Mark was under threat by the
King of Ireland, who was demanding that Mark send young men
and women to Ireland in the charge of a villainous giant, the Morholt of Ireland. The Morholt, who was the brother of the Queen of
Ireland, would visit Cornwall annually, claim the tribute, and return to the Irish court. On the particular anniversary after Tristan
came to Cornwall he determined to put an end to the tribute. He
planned to be included among the young people of the tribute, challenge the Morholt to single combat, kill him, and rid Cornwall of
the unfortunate obligation. Mark begged him not to go, but Tristan
was adamant. Eventually Mark agreed, and the Morholt accepted
the challenge. Mark then pressed upon Tristan the gift of a new
and beautiful sword. Tristan did kill the Morholt but broke the tip
of his sword, leaving a small fragment of steel in the Morholt's
head. The tribute was ended; the Morholt's body was returned to
Ireland. There the Princess Isolt, daughter of the King, removed
the steel fragment and kept it for her own as a reminder of her
uncle's defeat.

Although Tristan conquered the Morholt, he was badly injured
by his enemy's poisoned sword. The wound festered, would not heal,
and the stench became so offensive that Tristan was forced to retire
to an isolated hut by the sea. Like all heroes, Tristan hated inac-
tivity. Anything would be better than stagnating in a hut. He persuaded Mark to push him out to sea in a small rudderless boat.
Taking only his harp, he resolved to remain away from Cornwall
until he could be a more fit member of the court.

Tristan's wound was curable by only one person in the world—
Princess Isolt of Ireland. The niece of his recent antagonist, she had
learned medical skill from the Queen, her mother. Fortunately his
boat took him directly to the Irish harbor. Tristan, clever enough

to land without giving his name, was cured by the Princess, although some versions say that the Queen herself gave him the medicine. Then, when he had recovered his strength, he returned to the Cornish court.

Tristan was now a personal favorite with King Mark, so much so that the jealous Cornish barons urged Mark to provide himself with an heir. And then a curious event occurred. A swallow bearing a bright golden human hair in its beak flew into a window. Mark seized the hair and, hoping to forestall the barons, vowed that he would marry only that woman whose hair matched the single strand he held in his hands.

The barons were delighted. Here was an excellent way of disposing of Tristan. Let him seek the owner of the hair. If he were successful, Mark would marry; if he were not and failed to return, so much the better.

When Tristan saw the strand of hair, he knew that only Isolt the Fair, Princess of Ireland, had hair that would match the King's sample. In spite of the contempt of the barons, whom he ignored, he vowed to find the lady and persuade her to become King Mark's bride.

In Ireland things had changed since his last visit. A fire-breathing dragon, a kidnapper of maidens, was devastating the country. In desperation the King had offered his daughter and half of the kingdom to any hero who would kill the monster.

Instead of going to the court to announce the purpose of his mission, Tristan went directly to the lair of the dragon. The monster came roaring out of its cave, breathing fire and sulphurous smoke. Tristan's companions fled, and armed only with his chipped sword he faced the dragon. He plunged the sword through flames into the mouth of the beast and killed it. He cut the tongue from the dragon, took it with him, staggered a few feet away, and collapsed behind a small hill.

The King's seneschal, who had long loved the Princess Isolt, came by. Seeing the dead dragon, he ran back to the court shouting that he had killed the monster and that he wanted to marry the Princess. But Princess Isolt hated the seneschal. Refusing to believe that he could have killed the dragon, she went to see for herself. She found the unconscious Tristan and brought him back to the castle for medication. Tristan responded to the treatment and as usual did not reveal his identity. Nor did Isolt recognize him, not having had a close look at him when he was previously in Ireland. Because he still had the dragon's tongue, he soon proved that the seneschal was a liar.

While the unidentified Tristan was bathing, Isolt casually examined his sword. She saw the broken tip, and the shape of the notch was familiar. She ran to where she kept the steel fragment taken from the Morholt's skull. The piece fitted Tristan's sword exactly. The nameless hero was that very Tristan who had slain her uncle, the Morholt. Isolt, whose temper was short under the best of circumstances, ran to the bath waving the sword and prepared to avenge her uncle on the spot. Tristan acknowledged his own identity and soothed her by explaining that he wooed her not in his own name but in King Mark's. Pacified by the thought of becoming a queen, Isolt agreed to go to Cornwall and there to marry King Mark. Arrangements were soon made, and a ship was ordered.

Before the ship sailed, Isolt's mother visited Brangien, Isolt's personal maid, and gave her a small bottle containing a love charm. Were a man and a woman to drink the charm together, no matter what their previous feelings or commitments had been, they would be lovers. Brangien was told to guard the charm and give it to Mark and Isolt on their wedding night. She agreed, and the ship sailed as scheduled.

The weather on the Irish Sea was hot. Tristan and Isolt, thirsty and seeking refreshment, found the love charm and drank it together. Before the ship landed they were lovers; the damage had been done.

Isolt, no longer a maiden, was faced with the obvious wedding night problem: how to hide her indiscretion from King Mark. She persuaded Brangien to take her place, and thus not for the last time was King Mark deceived. But the game was a dangerous one, and Isolt reasoned that the fewer people who knew the secret the better. Accordingly she employed servitors to lure Brangien into the woods in order to kill her. But Brangien presented such impassioned pleas that she was released to face, as it turned out, a repentant and forgiving Isolt.

Now came a long period of deception. Information was passed between the lovers in all sorts of surreptitious ways. Chips of wood floating down a stream into the castle became secret messages. Pine trees became hiding places. Tristan and Isolt were helpless before the magic of the charm, yet neither wished to shame King Mark.

Tristan's old enemies, the jealous and contemptuous barons, did. Eager to disgrace the hero, they revealed the secret to Mark. The King had Tristan imprisoned in a cell high on a cliff. But Tristan, ever an athlete, escaped from his cell with a fantastic leap and fled to banishment in the nearby Wood of Morois. There Isolt joined him, and the lovers continued their life in a hut, eating the game which Tristan killed.

They slept with Tristan's sword between them, and once when they were so sleeping King Mark discovered them. The gullible King, seeing the sword between the lovers, was convinced of their innocence and left believing that he had wronged his nephew and his wife.

Still the barons accused Tristan to Mark. And the King, now in doubt, said he would reaccept Isolt as his queen if she could pass an ordeal or trial by hot iron. A person suspected of lying was asked to touch a hot iron. If he were innocent, he would not be burned; if he were guilty, he would be.

Isolt agreed to the experiment and gave Tristan his instructions. On the day of the ordeal the King and his nobles assembled by a stream. Interested witnesses of the trial included King Arthur himself and a number of the Knights of the Round Table. Isolt appeared on a horse by the other shore. Tristan was nowhere to be seen, for no one knew that the ragged beggar loitering across the stream from the assembled court was the King's nephew. As Isolt rode her horse into the stream in order to cross, the disguised Tristan sprang forward to guide her. Half way across she slipped from her horse into the water. The apparent beggar picked her up from the river and replaced her on her saddle. On the other bank Isolt presented herself for the ordeal of iron. She was asked by the presiding magistrate if ever she had been unfaithful to the King. Her truthful answer was that she had never been in the arms of any man save the King and, oh, yes, that ragged fellow who had picked her out of the water. Then she touched the iron, which of course did not burn her. The King and his nobles were satisfied. Isolt was exonerated and welcomed back to the court. Tristan remained in the woods except for occasional nocturnal visits with Isolt.

The strain of all this deception was too much for Tristan. He decided to go abroad, to travel the world, and above all to escape the conflict of love for Isolt and loyalty to Mark. To forget Isolt the only answer was flight.

In Wales he entered the service of a young duke troubled by a giant named Urgan. The duke owned a magic dog named Petit Crû, which was so beautiful that no one could tell what color it was. It wore a bell which made such a lovely sound that Tristan immediately coveted the dog. Tristan challenged and killed the giant Urgan, cutting off Urgan's right hand as a trophy. The grateful duke offered Tristan any reward he wished, and Tristan, turning down offers of gold, half the dukedom, and the duke's sister, chose the dog, which he immediately sent by secret courier to Isolt. She was not as easy to forget as he had hoped.

He continued wandering; on one adventure he killed Morgan, the usurper of his father's kingdom. In Brittany he entered the service of Duke Hoël and soon became friends with Hoël's son, Kaherdin. Again he defended his new friends against their enemies, and again he was offered the duke's daughter as his reward.

For years Tristan had been turning down the nubile daughters and sisters which were continually being offered him. His only love was Isolt, the wife of Mark. But he changed his mind when he met Hoël's daughter, for she was also named Isolt, Isolt of the White Hands. They were married, but Tristan, unable to forget Isolt the wife of Mark, refused to consummate his marriage.

One day Tristan, Kaherdin, and Isolt of the White Hands were riding across some puddles left by a recent rain. The water kicked by the horses' hooves splashed up, some of it high under the skirt of Isolt of the White Hands, who broke into laughter. Kaherdin was puzzled by her laughter. She said that the water had been bolder with her than ever her husband had been. Kaherdin was furious. If Tristan had refused to touch his sister, the family was insulted. Tristan could do no more than beg for a chance to explain.

So Tristan told Kaherdin all about the love charm and the long affair with Mark's wife. Kaherdin now understood but wished to take a secret voyage to Cornwall to see for himself.

Once again Tristan in disguise approached the court of King Mark and Isolt the Fair. And once again his disguise allowed him to resume his affair. This time Kaherdin was with him and on seeing the beauty of Queen Isolt sympathized with Tristan. Kaherdin was further won by his admiration for Isolt's maid and became her lover.

Back in Brittany Tristan and Kaherdin were faster friends than ever. Only Isolt of the White Hands, still the untouched bride, was unable to share their happiness. Tristan and Kaherdin fought against common enemies and on one occasion were challenged by a fierce baron named Bedalis. Tristan killed Bedalis (of course) but in the battle received a poisoned wound very similar to those he had received from the Morholt and the dragon years before.

Only Isolt the Fair had cured the wound made by the Morholt and only Isolt the Fair had cured the wound made by the dragon. Tristan knew that only she could help him now. He sent her a secret message to come to him. The captain of the ship was given Tristan's own ring for identification and two sets of sails, one black, one white. He was to return with white sails if Isolt the Fair was with him and black sails if she was not. The captain agreed and set off. Unfortunately Isolt of the White Hands had overheard the plan. Each day Tristan asked if a ship were approaching the harbor. Each day she answered that there was none. Then one day she told him that a ship was in sight. Tristan asked what the sail color was. The sail color was white, but Isolt of the White Hands, remembering her grievance, falsely reported the sail as black. Heartbroken, Tristan, believing that his own Isolt had deserted him, turned his face to the wall and died. When Isolt the Fair arrived, she learned she was too late. On viewing Tristan's corpse, she too died.

King Mark had the two bodies buried side by side. From the grave of Tristan grew a vine and from the grave of Isolt a rose. These met, and no man could ever part them.

VERSIONS OF THE LEGEND

The familiar versions of the Tristan legend are really no older than the other major Arthurian romances such as those by Chrétien de Troyes, Geoffrey of Monmouth, or other twelfth-century story-tellers. But like the other Arthurian legends, the germs of the Tristan story are much older than any full account of it. Only by detective work, by a comprehensive analysis of all clues, of anything that we know of the history, legend, or myth that seems to be significant to the existing story, can we guess where the tale came from. The stories which we have are only the visible points of an iceberg in a dark sea. What lies under these points is the object of the detective work and the subject of this study.

We know the names of three twelfth-century poets who wrote of the romance of Tristan. The German Eilhart von Oberge [1] probably translated a lost French version.[2] Thomas of Britain [3] wrote a rendition in French at the court of Henry II of England during the mid-century. Most of this poem is lost, but it may be reconstructed from its derivatives, the *Tristram und Isolt* of Gottfried von Strassburg [4] and the Norse *Tristrams Saga* translated from Thomas in 1226 by one Brother Robert.[5] The third was the Norman Béroul, who late in the century composed a *Tristan* of which only a fragment of about 4500 lines is extant.[6] In addition to the above three [7] we have the thirteenth-century prose *Tristan*,[8] and other twelfth- and thirteenth-

1. Eilhart von Oberge, *Tristrant*, ed. Franz Lichtenstein, *Quellen und Forschungen zur Sprach- und Culturgeschichte*, Vol. XIX (Strasbourg, 1877); ed. K. Wagner, *Reinische Beiträge*, Vol. V (Bonn, 1924).

2. So suggested Gertrude Schoepperle, *Tristan and Isolt: A Study of the Sources of the Romance*, 2 vols. (Frankfurt and London, 1913; reprinted, New York, 1959), pp. 108–11 (my references use the pagination of the 1959 edition). I have found no information to the contrary.

3. Joseph Bédier (ed.), *Le Roman de Tristan par Thomas, SATF*, No. LIII, 2 vols. (Paris, 1902–5), II, 115. B. H. Wind (ed.), *Fragments du Tristan de Thomas* (Leiden, 1950). For a convenient English translation see A. T. Hatto (ed. and trans.), *Gottfried von Strassburg Tristan with the Surviving Fragments of the Tristan of Thomas* (Harmondsworth, Middlesex, and Baltimore, 1960), pp. 301 ff. Roger Sherman Loomis (ed. and trans.), *The Romance of Tristram and Ysolt*, new rev. ed. (New York, 1951), is based whenever possible on Thomas and supplemented by Brother Robert.

4. Gottfried von Strassburg, *Tristram und Isolt*, ed. A. Closs, 2d rev. ed. (Oxford, 1947); also ed. F. Ranke (Berlin, 1930). See also Hatto, *Gottfried von Strassburg Tristan*. For a commentary and bibliography see W. T. H. Jackson, "Gottfried von Strassburg," *ALMA*, pp. 145–56.

5. Eugen Kölbing (ed.), *Die nordische und die englische Version der Tristansage*, 2 vols. (Heilbronn, 1882), Vol. I.

6. A. Ewert (ed.), *The Romance of Tristran by Beroul* (Oxford, 1953). E. Muret (ed.), *Le Roman de Tristan par Béroul, SATF*, No. LII (Paris, 1903), rev. L. M. Defourques, *Les Classiques français du moyen age* (Paris, 1947).

7. For a commentary on Eilhart, Thomas, and Béroul see Frederick Whitehead, "The Early Tristan Poems," *ALMA*, pp. 134–44.

8. E. Löseth (ed.), *Le Roman en prose de Tristan* (Paris, 1891). For commentaries on the prose *Tristan* see Eugène Vinaver, *Études sur le Tristan en prose, les sources, les manuscrits, bibliographie critique* (Paris, 1925); "The Prose Tristan," *ALMA*, pp. 339–47.

century renditions and fragments including the English metrical romance *Sir Tristrem;* [9] *Le Chèvrefeuil,*[10] a Breton *lai* by Marie de
France based on an episode in Eilhart; [11] the Berne *Folie Tristan,* a
fragment apparently based on Béroul and the Oxford *Folie Tristan,*
a fragment apparently based on Thomas; [12] and some others.[13]

To encourage familiarity with the story of Tristan and Isolt, I
recommend (to the English-language reader) the following modern
renditions of the legend: Eilhart's *Tristant* was outlined by Gertrude
Schoepperle; [14] Bédier published a version compiled from Eilhart,
Thomas, Gottfried, and Béroul, and this has been translated into a
convenient English form; [15] Roger Sherman Loomis' sensitive translation follows Thomas and Brother Robert; and A. T. Hatto has
translated the version of Gottfried along with what is surviving from
Thomas.

TRANSMISSIONS OF THE LEGEND 🏵

As was stated in the previous chapter, the Tristan legend is and
always has been an Arthurian tale and will be treated as such in
the pages of this study. Arthurian tales are stories about King Arthur
and the many figures whom we know as the Knights of the Round
Table. Malory in the late fifteenth century compiled the best known

9. Kölbing, *Version der Tristan-sage,* Vol. II.

10. K. Warnke (ed.), *Die Lais der Marie de France,* 3d ed. (Halle, 1925),
pp. 181–85. Marie de France, *Lais,* ed. A. Ewert (Oxford, 1944), pp. 123–26.
Marie de France, *Lais,* ed. Ernest Hoepffner (Strasbourg, 1921).

11. For a commentary on the relationship between *Le Chèvrefeuil* and the
episode in Eilhart see Ernest Hoepffner, "The Breton Lais," *ALMA,* p. 117;
Les Lais de Marie de France (Paris, 1955); Schoepperle, *Tristan and Isolt,* I,
138–47. For further studies of *Le Chèvrefeuil* see Roger Sherman Loomis, "A
Bibliography of Tristan Scholarship after 1911," appended to the 2d ed. of
Gertrude Schoepperle's *Tristan and Isolt* (New York, 1959), II, 592.

12. Bédier, *Le Roman de Tristan par Thomas,* II, 282–96, 372–79; *Les Deux
Poèms de la Folie Tristan, SATF,* No. LIV (Paris, 1907). Ernest Hoepffner (ed.),
Folie Tristan de Berne, 2d ed., (Paris, 1949).

13. For an outline of some of these minor poems see Frederick Whitehead,
"The Early Tristan Poems," *ALMA,* p. 144; and Loomis, "A Bibliography of
Tristan Scholarship after 1911."

14. *Tristan and Isolt,* I, 11–65.

15. Joseph Bédier, *Le Roman de Tristan et Iseut* (Paris, 1918); *The Romance of Tristan and Iseult,* trans. Hilaire Belloc and Paul Rosenfeld (Garden
City, New York, 1956; reprinted, New York, n.d.). Page references are to the
later edition.

book of Arthurian legends, but as everyone knows, these tales are much older than Malory.[16] They are also older than the twelfth-century romances of Chrétien de Troyes, Wauchier, Marie de France, Geoffrey of Monmouth, and other authors who delighted the French and English courts of the time. Sources of these romances have been acknowledged to be Welsh. Arthur, if he lived at all, was a Welshman or one of a people who became Welsh.[17] Of course the Welsh did not invent all the tales of Arthur, nor did they record factual history. Those tales later associated with Arthur were early myths, some Welsh, some Irish, and some pan-Celtic.[18] Some even were derived from myths of the Greeks and Romans, as we shall see.

The currently accepted theory of the transmission of these tales is as follows: analogous Irish and Welsh tales depended upon a hypothetical earlier pan-Celtic myth. Both the Irish and Welsh attached these stories to folk heroes who may or may not have existed as real people. The Irish *senachies,* throughout Irish history, sang stories of Cú Chulainn, Lugh, and Fionn.[19] The Welsh told similar stories about some of the same [20] heroes, and about others, like Arthur, as well.[21]

The Welsh and their Continental relatives, the Bretons, spoke similar languages and told each other the same stories. From about

16. Eugène Vinaver, "Sir Thomas Malory," *ALMA,* pp. 541–52.

17. Kenneth H. Jackson, "The Arthur of History," *ALMA,* pp. 1–11.

18. For example see Helaine Newstead, *Bran the Blessed in Arthurian Romance* (New York, 1939). Professor Newstead demonstrates that Bran, the ancestor of many French Arthurian figures, is a development of a Celtic mythological figure. My own study, *A Tale of Wonder—A Source Study of The Wife of Bath's Tale* (Wexford, Ire., 1957), concerned with the Arthurian tale of the loathly lady, reached similar conclusions.

19. Cú Chulainn, the Irish Achilles, defended Ulster singlehandedly against an invading army. See Myles Dillon, *Early Irish Literature* (Chicago, 1948), pp. 1 ff. Lugh was an Irish solar deity derived from an early Celtic Continental god. See my *Tale of Wonder,* pp. 32 f. Fionn was the legendary leader of a band of hunters called the Fianna. We shall see more of him when we discuss an Irish tale called *The Pursuit after Diarmaid and Gráinne.* For more about Fionn and the Fianna see T. F. O'Rahilly, *Early Irish History and Mythology* (Dublin, 1946), pp. 271–81.

20. For a comparison of the Irish Lugh and the Welsh Llew see W. J. Gruffydd, *Math Vab Mathonwy* (Cardiff, 1928).

21. An example of a hero related to Celtic deities is Lancelot, as his ancestry has been deduced by Professor Loomis. See "The Descent of Lancelot from Lug," *BBSIA,* III (Paris, 1951), 67 ff.

the seventh century on the Bretons, who were slowly developing their own language,[22] concentrated many of their story themes on the adventures of Arthur and his retinue. And it was the Breton *conteurs,* those bilingual story tellers of the twelfth century, who carried these old Celtic Arthurian tales to the courts of France,[23] where the final polish of courtly love was given to the now stock characters of old King Arthur, faithless Queen Guenevere, wily Merlin, invincible Sir Lancelot, noble Sir Gawain, faithful Sir Perceval, amorous Sir Tristrem, virginal Sir Galahad, and others.[24]

The fruitful Tristan scholarship of our times dates from the excellent work of Gertrude Schoepperle and has continued through, among others, the studies of J. D. Bruce,[25] Roger Sherman Loomis,[26] Rachel Bromwich,[27] James Carney,[28] and Helaine Newstead.[29] Although full agreement has not been reached, it is now generally recognized that the French, German, and other extant Tristan stories had a British prototype. In surviving fragments of medieval Welsh may be found Mark, Tristan, and Isolt, their relationship to each other, and their connection with Arthur.[30] It is agreed that Tristan's name is an evolution of the name Drust, a name borne

22. The Welsh dialect began to differentiate itself from the Cornish-Breton dialect approximately during the sixth century. But similarities and traffic between Britain and Brittany continued well into the seventh century. See Kenneth H. Jackson, *Language and History in Early Britain* (Edinburgh, 1953). Nor did traffic between Britain and Brittany completely cease after the seventh century. See Roger Sherman Loomis, *Arthurian Tradition and Chrétien de Troyes* (New York, 1949), pp. 21 f.

23. Loomis, *Arthurian Tradition,* pp. 21–24. Hoepffner, "The Breton Lais," pp. 112–21.

24. *ALMA,* passim.

25. *Evolution of Arthurian Romance,* 2d ed. (Baltimore, 1928), I, 177–85.

26. "Problems of the Tristan Legend," *Romania,* LIII (1927), 82–102. *The Romance of Tristram and Ysolt,* introd. *Wales and the Arthurian Legend* (Cardiff, 1956), pp. 15 f., 187, 194.

27. "Some Remarks on the Celtic Sources of 'Tristan,' " *THSC,* Session 1953 (London, 1955), pp. 32–60. "The Character of Early Welsh Tradition," *Studies in Early British History,* ed. Nora K. Chadwick (Cambridge, Eng., 1954; reprinted, 1959), pp. 122 f.

28. *Studies in Irish Literature and History* (Dublin, 1955), pp. 189–242.

29. "King Mark of Cornwall," *RP,* XI, No. 3 (1958), 240–53; "The Origin and Growth of the Tristan Legend," *ALMA,* pp. 122–33.

30. Bromwich, "Celtic Sources of 'Tristan,' " p. 33; *Trioedd Ynys Prydein— The Welsh Triads* (Cardiff, 1961), pp. 329 ff., 349 f. and 443 ff.; Loomis, "Problems of the Tristan Legend," pp. 82–102; *Tristram and Ysolt,* pp. xxi–xxvi.

by a number of Pictish kings.[31] A connection between the Tristan story and the Irish tale of elopement, *The Pursuit after Diarmaid and Gráinne*, has long been recognized.[32] As is often the case with Arthurian tales,[33] the Irish version, in this instance *Diarmaid and Gráinne*, is believed to be older than a source of some episodes of a British version which served as a prototype of the surviving tales.[34] The agreement is that the Tristan legend was molded by several authors from a number of countries, from different periods of time, and dependent upon a variety of sources.[35] Here I wish to discuss the reasons that have led me to a conclusion differing somewhat from the consensus.

HISTORICAL BACKGROUND ▩

A brief statement of historical background followed by my conclusions will enable the reader to follow an argument which is necessarily complex. The names and characters of Tristan and Mark are, I believe, evolved from historic northern figures of the sixth century. By 400 to 800 the north of Britain was a land of conflicting cultures. The first known occupants had probably spoken a Brythonic dialect of Celtic, and the mysterious Picts had lived close by.[36] The Romans invaded the island of Britain under Julius Caesar in 55–54 B.C. but withdrew. Later they returned and by 127 had occupied the country

31. This equation was first demonstrated by H. Zimmer, "Beitrage zur Namenforschung in den altfranz arthurepen, 'Tristan, Isolt, Marc,'" *ZFSL* (1891), XIII, 67. For recent comments see Bromwich, *Trioedd Ynys Prydein*, pp. 329 ff.

32. J. F. Campbell, *Popular Tales of the Western Highlands* (London, 1893), IV, 240. Schoepperle, *Tristan and Isolt*, pp. 289–90, 395 ff. Loomis, "Problems of the Tristan Legend," p. 95.

33. Loomis, *Arthurian Tradition*, pp. 25–27; Introd. to *Lanzelet* by Ulrich von Zatzikhoven (New York, 1951), pp. 15 ff. Eisner, *A Tale of Wonder*, pp. 135 ff.

34. Schoepperle, *Tristan and Isolt*, II, 396 ff. Loomis, "Problems of the Tristan Legend," pp. 82 ff.; *Tristram and Ysolt*, p. xxi. Newstead, "The Origin and Growth of the Tristan Legend," pp. 122 ff., and especially p. 127.

35. Loomis, *Tristram and Ysolt*, pp. xv ff. See also Loomis, "A Survey of Tristan Scholarship after 1911," pp. 565–87. For a different opinion see Carney, *Studies in Irish Literature and History*, pp. 189 ff.

36. The language of the Picts is not known for certain, although it is believed to differ from the other languages of the area. For an excellent recent study see Kenneth H. Jackson, "The Pictish Language," *The Problem of the Picts*, ed. F. T. Wainwright (Edinburgh, 1955), pp. 129 ff.

as far north as Hadrian's Wall, which ran from the mouth of the Tyne to Solway Firth. In 143 they built the Wall of Pius or Antoninus, extending from the Firth of Forth to the Firth of Clyde. Warfare continued on both sides of this wall until the Roman withdrawal from Britain in the fifth century.

When the power of the Empire dwindled, the north of Britain became a land of fluid cultures. The Brythonic Celts held power in the west, roughly between the present cities of Carlisle and Glasgow. A Gaelic or Goidelic speaking group of Celts, the Dalriadic Scots, were invading from Ireland and setting petty kingdoms along the west coast north of the Clyde. These new invaders brought with them a monastic form of Christianity which had come to them ultimately from the Near Eastern deserts by way of Gaul. The guiding precepts of this type of Christianity were intellectual discipline inherited from the Greeks and asceticism inherited from the Egyptians and Syrians. What had developed in the fourth century in Gaul, the fifth century in Ireland, the sixth century in North Britain, and later in Continental Europe was a tradition of monastic scholarship which was to outshine any comparable group in Europe for centuries.[37] Irish learning remained a major force in North Britain until the seventh and eighth centuries. The Scots increased their political power until by the eleventh century the Brythonic-speaking Celts of northern Britain had become politically unimportant. Meanwhile the Angles had settled in neighboring lands along the east coast, where they formed the kingdoms of Bernicia and Deire, later to be united as the Kingdom of Northumbria; and after the eleventh century the Normans became a menace. These changing cultures, Brythonic, Roman, Goidelic, Anglian, and Norman, each left some stamp upon the land.[38] The effects of the Goidelic invasions upon the Brythonic and Germanic cultures of the area will be studied in later chapters.

The outstanding cultural offering of the Goidels was Irish Christianity, brought to North Britain by St. Columba in 563. By the time of his death in 597 St. Columba had converted much of North Britain to Irish Christianity, and thriving monasteries were scattered throughout all kingdoms north of the Humber. We know that these

37. Nora K. Chadwick, *The Age of the Saints in the Early Celtic Church* (London, 1961), pp. 6 ff.
38. See Maps 1–4, pp. 20–21.

ROMAN BRITAIN

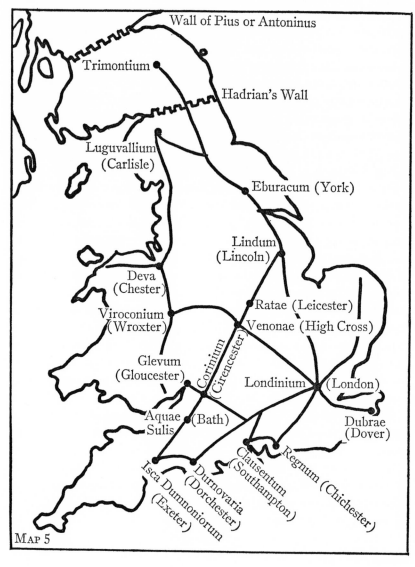

MAP 5

monasteries produced learned men, and in this study I shall suggest that one of these savants about the seventh or eighth century borrowed some names from local history and attached to them classical tales, thus forming a nucleus for *Tristan and Isolt.*

In the course of this study I propose to comment especially on Tristan and Mark and to advert to the standards of learning that we can assume existed in the monasteries of the North during the period in question. We have seen that Tristan's name is known to be a development of a local Pictish name, Drust, and I shall suggest that Mark's name also was taken from an actual figure who lived in North Britain.

Secondly, after comparing *Tristan and Isolt* to certain Greek myths, mainly from the legends of Theseus and of the Trojan War, I shall advance the thesis that these Greek tales were known to someone who altered them to fit the story of Tristan.

I shall conclude that there was one original story composed by one literate author; and as far as is possible I shall reconstruct the original author's version. This reconstruction will be based upon both the extant stories and the tales which are evidently the ultimate sources of the Tristan story.

In conclusion, the author of the first Tristan story used the names and some of the traditions of local heroes of his own recent past. To these figures he attached adventures which had been handed down from Roman and Greek mythology. He lived in the north of Britain, was associated with a monastery, and started the first rendition of the Tristan story on its travels to wherever it has been found.

Before examining the Tristan story itself, let us look at the monasteries in order to understand that cultural environment that evidently was the source of much ecclesiastical and some non-ecclesiastical literature.

Chapter Three ▨ ▨

CELTIC MONAS-
TICISM

ECAUSE THE NATURE of Celtic monasticism is important to this study, I wish briefly to describe it here so that when I assert that certain cultural levels were unique to seventh-century North British monasteries, the reader will understand the reason for my opinions.

Monasticism itself is older than Christianity. According to the Dead Sea Scrolls, Jewish groups practiced monasticism at Qumrân from the second century B.C. into the first century A.D. Perhaps even earlier than that hermits endured their lonely yet spiritually gratifying lives on the Syrian and Egyptian deserts. Two groups emerged from this period: the anchorites and the cenobites. The anchorites lived in semieremitical communities, each monk in his individual cell practicing continence, living in poverty, and engaging in study. They would meet for common prayer only periodically and were not bound by community rules. Anchorite monasticism was the common form in the Egyptian desert areas. The cenobite monastery was a later development, wherein monks lived in a community according to a general set of rules and obeyed a superior, while occupying themselves with religious exercises and manual labor.

MONASTICISM IN WESTERN EUROPE ▨

Eastern monasticism was first brought to the attention of the inhabitants of Gaul by St. Athanasius of Alexandria, who went from Egypt to Gaul in the early fourth century, and then by St. Martin of Tours, who in the fourth century established the first monastery in Gaul. The major fifth-century Gaulish monastery was at Lérins, an island near Cannes, where monks lived the semieremitical life of the Egyptian monasteries.[1]

The tradition is that early in the fifth century Irish Christianity was brought from the European continent through Britain by St. Patrick. The date of the arrival of St. Patrick has presented a number of problems, which I shall make no attempt to settle here.[2] Suffice it to say that when we are talking about the advent of monasticism in Ireland, we must talk about fifth-century Gaul.

Gaul in the fifth century was the outpost of a crumbling empire. The Church settlements, which originally were designed to be governed much like Roman cities, in time came to resemble armed camps standing against the barbarian onslaughts.[3] The spiritual approach, which had been inherited from the Egyptian ascetics, became increasingly attractive, not only to Christians but also to the followers of pagan cults dedicated to Cybele and Isis.[4] The picture one has of fifth-century Gaul is one of much political instability tempered by a rising interest in the asceticism of the Near East, both Christian and non-Christian.

Standing against the monastic influence in Gaul were the earlier episcopal elements, which were usually grouped around cities and were more dedicated to the active than the contemplative life. A hostility between the two groups rose and manifested itself in the election of bishops. St. Patrick, who has been given credit for being the first great Christian leader in Ireland, belonged to the episcopal

1. Rev. John Ryan, *Irish Monasticism* (Dublin, 1931), pp. 8–56.
2. To say that St. Patrick flourished in Ireland during the fifth century is sufficient for the purposes of this study. Here is no place to enter into the Patrician controversy, where, as Professor Carney puts it, the spectators all too often become participants. The question of whether Patrick landed in Ireland in 432 or in 457 is posed in a tidy summary of the problem entitled *Saint Patrick*, ed. Rev. John Ryan, The Thomas Davis Lecture Series, No. 4 (Dublin, 1958). See also T. F. O'Rahilly, *The Two Patricks* (Dublin, 1942); and James Carney, "Comments on the Present State of the Patrician Problem," *Irish Ecclesiastical Record*, 5th ser., XCII (July 1959); *The Problem of St. Patrick* (Dublin, 1961).
3. Nora K. Chadwick, *The Age of the Saints in the Early Celtic Church* (London, 1961), pp. 9 f.
4. Olwen Brogan, *Roman Gaul* (London, 1953), p. 194.

group. Nowhere in his writing does he mention monasticism.[5] Whatever else he did, Patrick did not bring the monastic movement to Ireland. Still, when we read about Irish Christianity of the sixth century, we read about monasticism.

Mrs. Chadwick suggests that the reason why monasticism spread from Gaul to Ireland was that Ireland had never had a Roman occupation and consequently had no cities. It was the cities that attracted the episcopal elements and the rural areas that were hospitable to monasticism:

> In Ireland, where there were no cities, the monastery served as the natural gathering point for the scattered rural population, and the monastic system of the Celtic Church was essentially adapted to a pastoral people, the only recognized unit being the *túath*, with its centre in the royal *rath*.[6]

The point is that after the time of Patrick, whose death date was traditionally 461 [7] yet believed by another school of thought to be almost a half century later,[8] Irish monasticism developed. By the sixth century it existed with its traditions of ascetic piety and, very important for our purposes, intellectuality.[9]

INTELLECTUAL NATURE
OF MONASTICISM

The intellectual activity in the sixth-century Celtic monasteries is a lineal descendant, through the Gaulish monasteries, of the intellectual activity found in the ascetic semieremitical communities of the Near Eastern deserts. The monks of the Egyptian and Syrian deserts carried on a lively correspondence with the world leaders of

5. Chadwick, *The Age of the Saints*, pp. 23, 31.

6. *Ibid.*, p. 33.

7. Ryan, *Irish Monasticism*, p. 97. See also his essay, "The Traditional View," in *Saint Patrick*.

8. O'Rahilly, *The Two Patricks;* Carney, *The Problem of St. Patrick*, p. 118.

9. See James F. Kenney, *Sources for the Early History of Ireland*, Vol. I, *Ecclesiastical* (New York, 1929), p. 142, where he quotes a sixth- or seventh-century Gaulish statement complaining that by that time, because of the barbarian invasions, the intellectual classes had fled the country, mainly to Ireland.

their own time. They were familiar with Greek literature and of course spent much time not only copying the Scripture but disputing in writing its arguable points.[10] This intellectuality followed anchorite, and later cenobite, monasticism wherever it developed, including Ireland.

Literary activities were not the only signs of culture passed from the Near Eastern deserts to the Irish monasteries. Irish artifacts and manuscript designs demonstrate a similarity to those from the Egyptian and Syrian monasteries, and the implication of some sort of a cultural dependence is inescapable.[11] These objects show independence from Continental influence; both sculpture and manuscript illumination are apparently related to the Coptic and Syrian.[12]

Although the monasteries retained some of their anchorite traditions, by the sixth century each monastery was under the governance of an abbot. The activity of the members of the community, aside from their devotions, consisted of both manual and intellectual labor. The monasteries they built and maintained were used to carry on their intellectual pursuits, such as copying, reading, writing, and teaching.

The intellectual level in the sixth- and seventh-century Irish and North British monasteries has significance to the reader of these pages. Therefore, let us look at one such place closely rather than deal only in the generalities of the previous paragraph. St. Columbanus (543–615) of Bangor, Ireland, who later was to bring Irish Christianity to Central Europe, had access not only to works written by the fathers of Christian monasticism but to those of the classical writers as well. He gives evidence of being well read in Horace, whose works were barely known on the Continent in his time; he frequently quotes Virgil; he knows Ovid, Juvenal, and Martial; [13] and he may have known Statius, Persias, and Lucan.[14] He shows an extensive knowledge of classical mythology which was ingrained so deep within him that it was not an affectation but a

10. Chadwick, *The Age of the Saints*, pp. 36 ff.
11. Françoise Henry, *Early Christian Irish Art*, trans. Máire Mac Dermott (Dublin, 1954–55), p. 24.
12. Chadwick, *The Age of the Saints*, p. 51.
13. G. S. M. Walker (ed.), *Sancti Columbani Opera* (Dublin, 1957), p. lxvii.
14. Kenney, *Early History of Ireland*, I, 191.

determining factor in his literary taste,[15] and he may have known some words of Greek and Hebrew.[16] Where was Columbanus so well trained? The answer is at the Bangor monastery in sixth-century Ireland. There the library contained a fantastic number of authorities, both ecclesiastical and lay, Christian and pagan.[17]

Nor was the library at Bangor the only such collection. Irish monasticism expanded across the North Channel of the Irish Sea when in 563 St. Columba (521–97), not to be confused with St. Columbanus, sailed from Derry to found a monastery at Iona or Hii, an island on the west coast of Scotland, his purpose being to bring the benefits of Irish monasticism to the Britons of Strathclyde, the Scots of Dalriada, and the Picts beyond the mountains.[18] Columba brought the tradition of classic scholarship with him.[19] St. Adamnán (624–704), the ninth abbot of Iona and the biographer of St. Columba, was equally well schooled in classic material.[20] From Iona the tradition of scholarship passed on to the daughter monasteries,[21] where new libraries were collected so that St. Cuthbert could study at Melrose, St. Bede at Jarrow, and any number of Northumbrian youths at Lindisfarne.[22]

Such a tradition of scholarship also flourished at Whithorn in Galloway, where the monastery of Candida Casa had been founded, presumably by St. Ninian, years before St. Columba had come to Iona.[23] I have more to say about Whithorn and its tradition of scholarship in the next chapter, where I discuss St. Finnian of Moville (Ireland), who, according to one tradition, traveled to Whit-

15. Walker, *Sancti Columbani Opera*, p. lxvii.

16. So suggests Walker, *ibid.*, p. lxvii. Kenney, on the other hand, says that he did not (*Early History of Ireland*, I, 191).

17. Walker, *Sancti Columbani Opera*, pp. 221 f.

18. John A. Duke, *The Columban Church* (Edinburgh and London, 1932; reprinted, 1957), pp. 66 ff. For the location of these people and their areas, see Maps 1–4 above, pp. 20–21; maps 6, 7 below, pp. 65, 113.

19. Kenney, *Early History of Ireland*, I, 433.

20. *Ibid.*, pp. 285 ff.

21. Ramona Bressie, "Libraries of the British Isles in the Anglo-Saxon Period," *The Medieval Library*, ed. J. W. Thompson (New York, 1957), p. 106.

22. Kenney, *Early History of Ireland*, I, 224 f. Gareth W. Dunleavy, *Colum's Other Island* (Madison, Wis., 1960), pp. 2, 28 ff.

23. For more about Whithorn see *TJDGNA*, Whithorn Volume, 3d ser., XXVII (1950).

horn to receive instruction from one St. Mugint. The monastery at Whithorn, which was said to be patterned after the monastery founded by St. Martin of Tours, was one place where traditionally the Irish Christians learned the details of the monastic life.[24]

Wherever we look we discover evidence that the North British monasteries, both Columban and others, during the sixth through eighth centuries were cultural centers, much like today's universities, where a man could visit and could study from the best collections of books in northern Europe.[25] Since the tradition of these Irish and British monasteries, with their particular style of manuscript illumination, their types of artifacts, and most important their emphasis on scholarship is related to the Gaulish and the earlier Coptic and Syrian monastic centers; and since the desert monasteries housed men familiar not only with the Scripture but also apparently with Greek, and presumably with Egyptian, tales, it appears that if we wish to find the source of a tale with classic or Coptic echoes set in North Britain in the seventh or eighth century, we should look to these very monasteries as being the only British places capable of providing an environment for such a composition.

When we look further and discover that such tales contain heroes whose names would be known to a North British audience, the location of the origin of such a tale is further enforced. I believe that Tristan, Mark, and others received their names and some of their characteristics from actual persons living in North Britain. Let us look first at Tristan, or, as he was formerly known, Drust.

24. Duke, *The Columban Church,* pp. 25 ff. St. Columba is said to have been the pupil of St. Finnian of Moville, who was said to have received his own instruction at Casa Candida.

25. For the location of these monasteries see Map 7, below, p. 113.

Chapter Four

DRUST

THE TASK of this study is to search for the time, place, and some of the structure of the parent tale, that story which we can say was the progenitor of the Tristan legend and of all its analogues. Some proper names are traditionally associated with the leading figures of the legend. Tristan's own name, fortunately, appears frequently in the medieval Welsh triads.

TRISTAN IN THE WELSH TRIADS

A triad is a literary device in which lists of three corresponding heroes, heroic actions, or objects are briefly noted, sometimes with an explanation of their correspondences. Since the Middle Ages or earlier,[1] the triad has been a favorite mnemonic aid for the Welsh, who included in it legal and historical facts which had to be memorized as well as material from their own heroic and legendary past. Mrs. Bromwich explains that the triads became necessary when the eleventh- and twelfth-century Welsh bards realized that the oral tradition was no longer satisfactory for preserving the national heroic legends. Those triads surviving in manuscript form reflect oral traditions and legends which had been the property of the pre-medieval professional Welsh storytellers or *cyfarwyddiaid*[2] (singular: *cyfarwydd*). Their subject matter included myths which are preserved in *The Four Branches of the Mabinogi*[3] and legends of

1. Rachel Bromwich, "The Welsh Triads," *ALMA*, p. 44. See also Rachel Bromwich, *Trioedd Ynys Prydein—The Welsh Triads* (Cardiff, 1961), pp. lxvii f.

2. See Kenneth H. Jackson, "Arthur in Early Welsh Verse," *ALMA*, p. 12, for a description of the *cyfarwyddiaid*.

3. For a convenient English translation see Gwyn Jones and Thomas Jones (trans.), *The Mabinogion*, Everyman's Library No. 97 (London, 1949). See also J. Loth, *Les Mabinogion*, 2 vols. (Paris, 1913).

the semi-historical and historical North British ancestors of the
Welsh. The composers of the triads, who had to be brief in order
to memorize quantities of material, presented only an outline of any
particular story. Thus the picture of a figure taken from the triads
alone barely projects whatever it was that made the figure interesting to the medieval Welsh.

In spite of the condensed presentation, some of the character and
tradition surrounding Tristan is apparent in the triads. He is briefly
mentioned as an enemy-subduer, a battle-diademed man, a powerful
swineherd, a lover, a stubborn man, a peer and one of the enchanter
knights of Arthur's court.[4]

In summation: Tristan was traditionally a leader in battle (but
then, what legendary hero wasn't?), a lover, and a trickster. In
some triads, such as the first two quoted below, his customary relationship to his uncle, King Mark, and to King Mark's wife appears:

Three Powerful Swineherds of the Island of Britain:

. . . .

And the second, Drystan son of Tallwch, tending the swine of March
son of Meirchyawn, while the swineherd went with a message to Essyllt.
Arthur and March and Cai and Bedwyr were (there) all four, but they
did not succeed in getting so much as one pigling—neither by force,
nor by deception, nor by stealth. . . .[5]
Three Lovers of the Island of Britain:

. . . .

and Drystan (son of Tallwch, for Essyllt, the wife of his uncle
March).[6]

And again:

Three Enchanter Knights were in Arthur's Court: Menw son of
Teirgwaedd, and Trystan son of Tallwch, and E(i)ddilig the Dwarf;

4. Bromwich, *Trioedd Ynys Prydein*, Triad 19, p. 33; Triad 21, p. 37; Triad
26, pp. 45 ff.; Triad 71, p. 189; Triad 72, p. 192; Triad 73, p. 193; and "The
Twenty-Four Knights of Arthur's Court," p. 252. For a discussion of the name
Tristan in the triads see pp. 329 ff.
5. This is Triad 26W, a rendition from the *Red Book of Hergest* of No. 26 in
Peniarth MS. 16, which is approximately the same but does not mention Cai or
Bedwyr. The translation is Mrs. Bromwich's, *Trioedd Ynys Prydein*, p. 48.
6. This is Triad 71 from Peniarth MS. 47. The translation is Mrs. Bromwich's
(*ibid.*, p. 189).

since they changed themselves into the form they wished when they were hard-pressed, and therefore no one could overcome them.[7]

Thus in the medieval Welsh traditions of Tristan:

1. He was known as Drystan son of Tallwch.

2. He was associated with the world of Arthur and Arthur's most constant companions, Cai and Bedwyr,[8] who, of course, are the Sir Kay and Sir Bedivere of later Arthurian romance.

3. He was the lover of the wife of his uncle, King Mark.

4. He was accustomed to a world of deception and disguise.

DRUST SON OF TALORC

All of these points, except the name of Tristan's father, may be found in the later Continental tales about him. It is the name of this father that gives us whatever clues we have to Tristan's original identity. Zimmer,[9] who was supported by many later scholars,[10] first suggested that the name of the Welsh Tristan (or Drystan) son of Tallwch was a development of the Pictish name Drust son of Talorc. We know that a Pictish king, Drust son of Talorc, died about 780.[11] Of all the known Pictish kings named Drust, only that Drust who died in 780 was a son of a Talorc; consequently that date has been accepted for the introduction of the name into the Tristan story,[12] although the name Drust was frequently used by Pictish kings.[13]

7. This is one triad in the series entitled "The Twenty-Four Knights of Arthur's Court," from Peniarth MS. 127 (*ibid.*, pp. 250, 252).

8. See Rachel Bromwich, "Some Remarks on the Celtic Sources of 'Tristan,'" *THSC*, Session 1953 (London, 1955), p. 33, n. 8.

9. "Beitrage zur Namenforschung in den altfranz Arthurepen, 'Tristan, Isolt, Marc,'" *ZFSL*, XIII (1891), 67.

10. J. Bédier (ed.), *Le Roman de Tristan par Thomas, SATF,* No. LIII, 2 vols. (Paris, 1902–5), II, 105–8. J. Loth, "Le Noms des Tristan et Iseut," *RC,* XXXII (1911), 407 ff. Roger Sherman Loomis (ed. and trans.), *The Romance of Tristram and Ysolt,* new rev. ed. (New York, 1951), pp. xx f. H. Newstead, "King Mark of Cornwall," *RP,* XI, No. 3 (1958), p. 242.

11. A. O. Anderson, *Early Sources of Scottish History,* 2 vols. (Edinburgh, 1922), I, cxiii, cxxvii, 253. H. M. Chadwick, *Early Scotland* (Cambridge, Eng., 1949), p. 19.

12. Loomis, *Tristram and Ysolt,* p. xx. Cf. Newstead, "King Mark of Cornwall," p. 242; and "The Origin and Growth of the Tristan Legend," *ALMA,* p. 125. This acceptance is not universal. See Bromwich, "Celtic Sources of 'Tristan,'" pp. 35 f.; *Trioedd Ynys Prydein,* p. 512.

13. Anderson, *Early Sources,* I, cxix–cxxviii.

THE *WOOING OF EMER* ▨

That someone named Drust was traditionally involved with adventures reminiscent of the Tristan tales was demonstrated long ago by Deutschbein [14] and reaffirmed by Thurneysen. [15] Deutschbein pointed out that in the Irish *Wooing of Emer* Cú Chulainn anonymously slew a giant and was identified as the hero during his bath; similarly Tristan's identity as the slayer of the Morholt was revealed while he was bathing. [16] In the adventure of Cú Chulainn, which took place in the Hebrides near the land of the Picts, he was accompanied by a retainer named Drust son of Seirb, who is unknown elsewhere in the body of tales about Cú Chulainn. [17] Both Deutschbein and Thurneysen suggested that an original story about Drust was transferred to Cú Chulainn and that in the transference the name *Drust* was retained to apply to a mere follower. Neither Deutschbein nor Thurneysen considered it remarkable that the name of the father of Cú Chulainn's retainer was given as Seirb instead of Talorc.

THE PREFACE TO ST. MUGINT'S *HYMN* ▨

A second episode concerned with the name *Drust* has not previously, so far as I know, been adverted to in reference to the Tristan legend. [18] This is an adventure which is used in the Preface

14. Max Deutschbein, "Eine irische Variante der Tristan-sage," *Beiblatt zur Anglia*, XV (1904), 16–21.

15. R. Thurneysen, *Die irische Helden- und Königsage bis zum siebzehnten Jahrhundert* (Halle, 1921), p. 392, n. 2.

16. Tristan's identification in the bath followed his dragon fight although he had been identified as the slayer of the Morholt. The dovetailing of Tristan's two combats and two identifications is discussed elsewhere. See below, Chapter Eight.

17. For English versions of this tale see Kuno Meyer, "The Wooing of Emer," *Archaeological Review*, I (1888), 68–75, 150–55, 231, 235, 298–307; Eleanor Hull, *The Cuchullin Saga* (London, 1898), pp. 81 f.; Tom Peete Cross and C. H. Slover, *Ancient Irish Tales* (London, n. d.), pp. 168 ff. In the latter two for *Durst* read *Drust*. For a synopsis see below, pp. 128 ff.

18. Mrs. Bromwich mentions it but only as another example of a British king named Drust. See "Celtic Sources of 'Tristan,'" p. 35; *Trioedd Ynys Prydein,* p. 329.

to a *Hymn* attributed to St. Mugint and included in *The Irish Liber Hymnorum.*[19]

Finnian of Moville, with his disciples Rioc and Talmach, went from Ireland to Whithorn in Galloway [20] to receive instruction from St. Mugint. At this time the King of the Britons of the North was Drust, and he had a daughter named Drusticc. Drust had sent Drusticc to Mugint of Whithorn so that she too would receive instruction. Drusticc fell in love with Rioc and told Finnian that she would give him all the books St. Mugint had written were he to persuade Rioc to love her. Finnian agreed, but instead of sending Rioc he sent Talmach in Rioc's shape. Thus was conceived Lonan of Treoit.[21] Drusticc claimed that Rioc was the father of her son, but he was not. St. Mugint was angry with Finnian and planned to have him attacked when he entered the church that night. Unfortunately for St. Mugint he himself was assaulted when he entered. Then St. Mugint composed a *Hymn,* or rather a prayer for protection, to which this tale is a Preface.

The manuscript is Irish and dates from the eleventh century or slightly earlier.[22] The action is concerned with characters who flourished in the sixth century.[23] Finnian belonged to the royal dynasty of the Ulaid, and he died, according to the Annals of Ulster, in 579.[24] Drusticc is mentioned in *The Book of Leinster* as the mother of Lonan, Talmach's son.[25] St. Mugint is difficult to identify. Todd attempts to equate him with the Welsh St. Meigant, who died

---

19. J. H. Bernard and R. Atkinson, *The Irish Liber Hymnorum* (London, 1898), I, 22 f. For an English translation see Anderson, *Early Sources*, pp. 7 f. The incident also appears in *The Martyrology of Oengus*, ed. and trans. Whitley Stokes (London, 1905), p. 239.

20. The site of the action is identified as Galloway in the commentary on the Preface. See Bernard and Atkinson, *Liber Hymnorum*, II, 113. For more about Whithorn see *TJDGNA*, Whithorn Volume, 3d ser., XXVII (1950).

21. Anderson, *Early Sources*, I, 8, n. 1, says that Treoit was a place in Galloway.

22. *Ibid.*, I, xii.

23. James F. Kenney, *Sources for the Early History of Ireland*, Vol. I, *Ecclesiastical* (New York, 1929), pp. 172, 177, 263.

24. Anderson, *Early Sources*, I, xii.

25. *Ibid.*, p. 7, n. 3. The phrase "Britons of the North" usually means people of Strathclyde and Pictland, where the name Drust was customarily found. But since the Picts were probably Britons of a sort and certainly of the North, the point is not significant.

in the sixth century,[26] but there are no records of such a person in
the North.[27] As we have seen, Whithorn, his abbey, also known as
Candida Casa, was a noted Celtic ecclesiastical center in Galloway.[28]
Rioc, according to Todd, was Irish, but he flourished too early to
have a contemporary who died in 579.[29] Talmach fits chronologically,[30] and as we have seen there have been a number of Pictish
kings named Drust, any one of whom could or could not have been
the father of Drusticc.

There is little in this story which is credible. Finnian certainly,
and Rioc, Talmach, Drust, and Mugint probably, lived in the
British Isles in the sixth century. What is important is that here we
have a tale from an eleventh-century manuscript concerning the
adventures of sixth-century figures in Galloway, a tale in which
the name *Drust* and a substitution in a bridal bed appear. If a
Pictish Drust is the source of Tristan, it is likely that adventures
of the Tristan type were told about him. The substitution in the
bridal bed is possibly one of these. It is, of course, reminiscent of
Isolt, who wishing to conceal her loss of virginity, persuaded
Brangien to replace her in Mark's bridal bed.[31]

26. James H. Todd, *The Book of Hymns of the Ancient Church of Ireland*
(Dublin, 1855), I, 107 f.
27. One wonders if Mugint could be a form of Mungo, another name for St.
Kentigern, who also flourished in that area in the sixth century. For discussions
of the name Mungo see Kenneth Jackson, "The Sources for the Life of St.
Kentigern," *Studies in the Early British Church*, ed. Nora K. Chadwick (Cambridge, Eng., 1958), pp. 300 f., and James Carney, *Studies in Irish Literature
and History* (Dublin, 1955), p. 162.
28. Nora K. Chadwick, "St. Ninian: a Preliminary Study of Sources,"
TJDGNA, Whithorn Volume, 3d ser., XXVII (1950), 9 ff.; "Early Culture and
Learning in North Wales," *Studies in the Early British Church*, ed. Nora K.
Chadwick (Cambridge, Eng., 1958), pp. 60 ff.
29. Todd, *The Book of Hymns*, pp. 109 f. The name *Rioc* or *Riacatus* appears
in Patrician tradition. See Whitley Stokes (ed.), *The Tripartite Life of St.
Patrick* (London, 1887), I, 82, 84, 152; II, 502, 550.
30. Todd, *The Book of Hymns*, I, 117 ff.
31. Gertrude Schoepperle suggests as a source an old folktale called *The
Forgotten Bride*. See *Tristan and Isolt: A Study of the Sources of the Romance*,
2 vols. (Frankfurt and London, 1913; reprinted, New York, 1959), I, 206. Cf.
Ingen Ríg Gréc—The Daughter of the King of the Greeks, an Old Irish story,
probably based on a Latin *exemplum*, in which a Greek princess persuades her
maid to take her place as a virgin on the princess' bridal night and later kills
the maid to keep the secret. For the Irish version see Standish Hayes O'Grady,
Silva Gadelica (I–XXXI), 2 vols. (London, 1892), I, 413 ff.; Latin translation,
II, 449 ff. For a synopsis and commentary see Carney, *Studies*, pp. 230 f.

That the Tristan legend inspired these incidents in the Preface seems likely, for many elements of the legend are present here: geographical location in North Britain; the name *Drust;* a bridal substitution concerning Drusticc, whose name is a feminine form of the name *Drust;* and lastly, Rioc who plays the reluctant lover, an important figure in the Tristan story and one discussed elsewhere in this study.[32] In early Irish material when monks and ecclesiastics act out of character, it is reasonable to suspect the influence of tales with a secular background.[33] Thus we have another Tristan-type adventure given a North British setting and told in association with a figure named Drust, just as we had in the episode in *The Wooing of Emer.*

DRUST ELSEWHERE

The name *Drust* or its derivatives was not confined, of course, to the Picts, although the name was most frequently recorded in the Pictish royal genealogy.[34] A sixth-century Pictish saint bore a form of the name; [35] on a sixth-century Cornish stone appeared another form of the name;[36] and strangely enough, at the Swabian

32. See below, Chapter Seven.
33. The reality is seen in Adamnán's *The Life of Columba,* ed. William Reeves (Dublin, 1857); E. J. Gwynn and W. J. Purton, "The Monastery of Tallaght," *Proceedings of the Royal Irish Academy,* XXIX, Sec. C., No. 5 (Dublin, 1911), 115 ff.; and G. S. M. Walker (ed.), *Sancti Columbani Opera* (Dublin, 1957), pp. xii ff.
34. Anderson, *Early Sources,* I, cxiii, cxix ff. See also T. F. O'Rahilly, *Early Irish History and Mythology* (Dublin, 1946), pp. 366 f. William F. Skene in *Celtic Scotland,* II (Edinburgh, 1886–90), 113, calls *Drostan,* a form of *Drust,* "a thoroughly Pictish name."
35. This saint, Drostan son of Cosgrach, was originally believed to be a disciple of St. Columcille, the founder of the monastery at Iona and the Columban branch of the Catholic Church. Scholarship during this century has disclosed that St. Drostan antedated St. Columcille and that the anachronism existed because St. Drostan was accompanied by three followers, one bearing the name Colm. See W. Douglas Simpson, *The Historical Saint Columba,* 3d ed. (Edinburgh and London, 1963), pp. 48–53; Alexander B. Scott, "S. Drostan of Buchan and Caithness," *Transactions of the Gaelic Society of Inverness,* XXVII (1908–11), pp. 110–25; William Mackay, "Saints Associated with the Valley of the Ness," ibid., pp. 150 f. In the *Martyrology of Oengus,* ed. and trans. Whitley Stokes (London, 1905), p. 251, mention is made of "Drusus cona thriur," "Drusus with his triad."
36. For discussions of this stone see Ralegh Radford, *Journal of the Royal Institution of Cornwall,* n. s., I (1951), Appendix. Bromwich, "Celtic Sources

Abbey of St. Gall in 807 a witness to a legal document, who must have been born in the late eighth century, bore the name Tristan.[37] Whether he was named after St. Drostan, King Drust, or an unknown Pict journeying to Rome by way of St. Gall, there is no telling. The spelling of his name coincided with Swabian pronunciations of Celtic names, for we know that at St. Gall the Irish *Dubhtach* and *Demri* became *Tubthac* and *Temeri*.[38] Still other examples of the name appeared in what is today Scotland.[39]

At this point enough *Drusts* and allied names have been mentioned to generate some confusion. There is Drust son of Talorc, whose death is recorded in 780; Drust son of Seirb, an unknown; Drusticc, daughter of Drust, also an unknown; St. Drostan of sixth-century Pictland; a ninth-century Swabian named Tristan; and a name on a sixth-century Cornish stone. When we look at the list of the Pictish kings, the confusion is not lessened. Between c. 400 and c. 850 we find forty-five kings; ten are named Drust and eight Talorc(an). That is, forty percent of the Pictish kings were named either Drust or Talorc(an).

WHICH DRUST?

I mentioned earlier that the Tristan of the romances was believed to have received his name from that Drust son of Talorc who died in 780, but for reasons which I shall give below, I feel that the date 780 is late for the death of whatever Drust gave his name to the original Tristan. One earlier possibility is Drust son of Seirb, who was mentioned in *The Wooing of Emer*. There was a Drust son of Erp who was reigning, according to the Pictish Chronicle, when

of 'Tristan,' " pp. 47 f.; *Trioedd Ynys Prydein*, pp. 445 f. Newstead, "King Mark of Cornwall," p. 241. See also below, pp. 56 f.

37. Wilhelm Hertz (ed. and trans.), *Tristan und Isolde von Gottfried von Strassburg*, 3d ed. (Stuttgart and Berlin, 1901), pp. 283–84.

38. St. Gall Abbey, which was founded about 613 near Lake Constance by an associate of St. Columcille, was an important way station during the seventh century for British pilgrims bound for Rome. See J. M. Clark, *The Abbey of St. Gall* (Cambridge, 1926), pp. 2, 18, 21, 26.

39. Perhaps it was still another Drust for whom Trusty's Hill in Scotland was named. See R. C. Reid, "Trusty's Hill Fort," *TJDGNA*, XIV (1930), 366–72. For further examples and discussions of the name see O'Rahilly, *Early Irish History and Mythology*, pp. 366 ff. The author also discusses *Talorc(an)* and other Pictish names.

St. Patrick came to Ireland in the fifth century. Since the Pictish Chronicle, which is the source of this list of kings, was written in Latin, and since Erp was spelled in a variety of ways including Irb and Yrb, it is easy to see how *Drustfiliusirb* became *Drustfiliusseirb* or Drust son of Seirb.[40]

But now we must consider whether that Drust who was the source of Tristan's name was a king or a king's son. For in Pictland he could not be both,[41] no matter how many guises he appropriated in his later career as Tristan. As the Continental Tristan, of course, he was the son of Rivalen, king of Loonois.[42] The traditional Tristan is never a great king. Rather, he is the son of a king and of course the antagonist of a king. In such a society as the Picts, where a king's son never became a king, a hero antagonistic to an old king could very naturally be the son of a king.

Thus the possibility exists that a Drust son of Talorc was a king's son but never a king. It has been stated that by the common consent of scholars the name of Tristan was derived from the name of that Drust son of Talorc whose death is recorded in 780.[43] This identification, at best an attractive suggestion, should not be allowed to crystallize into certainty.[44] We have seen that forty percent of the Pictish kings were named either Drust or Talorc. Under these circumstances it is mathematically certain that many of the known Talorcs had unrecorded sons named Drust. It is equally certain that many of the Drusts had unrecorded sons called Talorc. But there is, or should be, consent among scholars as to the following: when a son's name is X and a father's Y, X and Y both being common names, we cannot conclude without further evidence that a given X son of Y is identical with another. With three generations in most cases identity may be established, but in rare cases four or even five are necessary. With such an effusion of the names *Drust*

40. Chadwick, *Early Scotland*, p. 8. Anderson, *Early Sources*, I, cxix.

41. In the list of Pictish kings, no king is a Pictish king's son.

42. Eilhart von Oberge, *Tristrant*, ed. Franz Lichtenstein, *Quellen und Forschungen zur Sprach- und Culturgeschichte*, XIX (Strasbourg, 1877), ll. 75 f.

43. Loomis, *Tristram and Ysolt*, p. xx. Newstead, "King Mark of Cornwall," p. 242; "The Origin and Growth of the Tristan Legend," *ALMA*, p. 125.

44. Mrs. Bromwich says: "At present there does not seem to be sufficient evidence to identify Drystan or his father with any known Pictish rulers" ("Celtic Sources of 'Tristan,'" p. 35). See also her *Trioedd Ynys Prydein*, p. 512.

and *Talorc,* it is not only likely but probable that there existed a Drust son of Talorc whose name was not recorded among the Pictish kings. We know that a Talorc son of Muircholach is recorded as having reigned for eleven years during the sixth century.[45] If this Talorc had a son whose name was the source of Tristan's name, it is quite possible that when the Irish borrowed part of the story for inclusion in *The Wooing of Emer* they changed Drust son of Talorc to the more familiar Drust son of Erb. I suggest that an unrecorded Drust son of Talorc is our best candidate for the one who gave his name to Tristan. It is too easy and very tempting to assert that all factual people who were the progenitors of folk heroes were also kings. The king's son, although his name was not recorded in a genealogy of kings, could also have been a hero.

Thus in conclusion I think it is fair to agree with previous scholars that Tristan's name was derived from the Pictish name *Drust* and that the particular Drust known for his Tristan-like adventures was the son of one Talorc. But the Drust who is under consideration here was associated with so many sixth-century figures that I cannot believe he was that Drust son of Talorc whose death was listed as occurring in 780. More likely he was an unrecorded Drust, son of a *King* Talorc, a contemporary of the people in the Preface to St. Mugint's *Hymn* and, as we shall see shortly, a contemporary of the man whose name was given to the legendary King Mark.

45. Chadwick, *Early Scotland,* p. 13. Anderson, *Early Sources,* I, cxxiii.

Chapter Five ▩ ▩

KING MARCH

HERE IS MUCH to be said about King March or Mark. In the Tristan story as we have it, he is King Mark of Cornwall, yet it has been pretty well established that wherever Mark was king, it was not Cornwall.[1] In the Welsh versions he is known as King March ap Meirchiawn, but the name of his father does not occur in any French or German version. Rhŷs proposed that Mark and Meirchiawn are forms of the same name,[2] and none of my findings has given me reason to reject the suggestion. March mab Meirchiawn appears in the Welsh Triads from MS. Peniarth 16, formerly MS. Hengwrt 536, as one of the three fleet owners, or seafarers, of the Island of Prydein,[3] as the owner of swine kept by Trystan mab Tallwch, and as the husband of the unfaithful Essyllt.[4] In the Welsh *Dream of Rhonabwy* he is at the head of a group of men from Llychlyn and is

1. H. Newstead, "King Mark of Cornwall," *RP*, XI, No. 3 (1958), 241. Rachel Bromwich, "Some Remarks on the Celtic Sources of 'Tristan,'" *THSC*, Session 1953 (London, 1955), 46 ff. Note that there is a Mote of Mark in Scotland, which may or may not refer to the Mark of the Tristan story. The point of interest is that this mote is not in Cornwall and is in Scotland. See R. C. Reid, "Trusty's Hill Fort," *TJDGNA*, XIV (1930), 366–72.

2. John Rhŷs, *The Hibbert Lectures, 1886* (London and Edinburgh, 1888), p. 271.

3. Rachel Bromwich, *Trioedd Ynys Prydein—The Welsh Triads* (Cardiff, 1961), Triad 14, p. 25. The word *llyghessavc* is translated as "fleet owner" by Professor Newstead, "King Mark of Cornwall," p. 243. Mrs. Bromwich translates the word as "seafarer, pirate, exile" and equates it with the Irish *loingsech*. See *Trioedd Ynys Prydein,* p. 25 n. For a suggestion concerning this equation see below, pp. 63 f., 68 f.

4. Bromwich, *Trioedd Ynys Prydein,* Triad 26, pp. 45 ff. For another examination of these triads see William F. Skene, *The Four Ancient Books of Wales* (Edinburgh, 1868), II, 458 f.

presented as the first cousin of Arthur.[5] The sixteenth-century
Welsh *Ystoria Trystan* says that March son of Meirchion is the
husband of the faithless Essyllt, uncle of Trystan son of Tallwch,
and cousin-german to King Arthur.[6] In a twelfth-century poem the
Welsh Cynnddelw, singing the praises of his patron Owain Gwyn-
edd, says that Owain rules the Cymri as honorably as March did
after Meirchiawn.[7] Evidently, as indeed one would expect, King
March had a history apart from the part he played in the Tristan
legend. He was an honorable and a powerful Brythonic king.

BRITISH TRADITIONS OF MARCH

The earliest extant reference to a King Mark is in the Latin
Life of St. Paul Aurelianus, written in 884 by Wrmonoc, a Breton
monk.[8] At one point the fame of St. Paul reached the court of
King Mark, or as he is also known in this text, Quonomorius, who
was king over people who spoke four languages. In no other extant
text is King Mark equated with Quonomorius or Cunomar, who
appears as the oppressor in the lives of a number of Breton saints.[9]
However, on a sixth-century stone found at Castle Dôr near Fowey
in Cornwall there is a barely decipherable inscription, which reads
or may read: [10] DRUSTAUS HIC IACIT CVNOMORI FILIUS. Some

5. Llychlyn or Lochlann and the Irish Lothind or Lochlainn are names for
Scandinavia. See W. J. Gruffydd, *Rhiannon* (Cardiff, 1953), p. 26, n. 2. See also
Gwyn Jones and Thomas Jones (trans.), *The Mabinogion,* Everyman's Library
No. 97 (London, 1949), p. 143; J. Loth, *Les Mabinogion,* 2 vols. (Paris, 1913),
I, 361.
6. Roger Sherman Loomis (ed. and trans.), *The Romance of Tristram and
Ysolt,* new rev. ed. (New York, 1951), pp. xxi–xxvi. See also Tom Peete Cross,
"A Welsh Tristan Episode," *Studies in Philology,* XVII (1920), 93–110; J. Loth,
"L'Ystoria Trystan et la question des archétypes," *RC,* XXXIV (1913); Sir
Ifor Williams, "Trystan ac Esyllt," *BBCS,* V (Cardiff, 1930), 115–29.
7. Bromwich, "Celtic Sources of 'Tristan,'" p. 48; *Trioedd Ynys Prydein,*
p. 444.
8. Ch. Cuissard (ed.), "Vie de Saint Paul de Léon," *RC,* V (1881–83), 413–
60, and especially p. 431.
9. Bromwich, "Celtic Sources of 'Tristan,'" p. 48; *Trioedd Ynys Prydein,*
pp. 44 f.
10. Ralegh Radford, *Journal of the Royal Institution of Cornwall,* n.s. I
(1951), Appendix. Bromwich, "Celtic Sources of 'Tristan,'" p. 47; *Trioedd Ynys
Prydein,* p. 445. Newstead, "King Mark of Cornwall," p. 241. For different
readings and opinions about this stone see R. A. S. Macalister, *Corpus Inscrip-*

have enthusiastically cried that because Mark was once equated with Cunomar, here we have the headstone that was placed over the original Tristan, who was in fact a son of King Mark.[11] But Mrs. Bromwich, although she agrees that *Drustaus* is a sixth-century form of the Welsh *Drystan,* after reviewing all possibilities rejects the stone as a possible source, instead of the Pictish *Drust,* for the name *Drystan.*[12] Nor is there any real evidence that the Cunomorius of the inscription is King Mark, although the suggestion might be made that the stone itself, because it mentions the name *Drustaus,* is the reason for Wrmonoc's ninth-century equation of Mark and Cunomar. Without further proof I must agree with Professor Newstead, who says that the stone only tells us that a Drustaus (or someone with a similar name) was a sixth-century son of a Cunomorius.[13]

But then is there any connection between the King Mark of *The Life of St. Paul* and the King Mark of the Tristan legend? Two items may be noted: that Mark was king over people who spoke four languages, and that Mark at one time refused to give St. Paul a bell. I shall return to the matter of the four languages later and comment now about the bell. The gift of a bell occurs in the lives of a number of southern British saints and also in the Tristan legend,[14] where it is found around the neck of the dog Petit Crû.[15] Were the bell in *The Life of St. Paul* alone, it would be un-

---

tionum Insularum Celticarum (Dublin, 1945–49), I, 465 f.; *Archaeologia Cambrensis,* LXXXIV (1929), 181; J. Rhŷs, *Archaeologia Cambrensis,* V (1875), 369. For a sketch of the stone see No. 4 among the illustrations in Arthur G. Langdon and J. Romilly Allen, *Archaeologia Cambrensis,* XII, No. 45 (1895), 50 ff.

11. See Jon Manchip White, "Tristan and Isolt," *History Today,* III, No. 4 (April, 1953), 233–39. A slightly abridged form of the same essay appears in *Myth or Legend,* ed. G. E. Daniel (London, 1955), pp. 69 ff.

12. "Celtic Sources of 'Tristan,' " pp. 47 f.; *Trioedd Ynys Prydein,* pp. 444 ff.

13. "King Mark of Cornwall," p. 242.

14. Presumably in Thomas and actually in the texts of his followers, Brother Robert and Gottfried von Strassburg.

15. A suggestion for a parallel of the Petit Crû name is proposed by Professor James P. Carney, *Studies in Irish Literature and History* (Dublin, 1955), p. 241, n. 2, who equates Petit Crû with *Cnú Deróil,* the dwarf harper of Fionn, on the grounds that *deróil* equals *petit* equals *small* and that *Cnú* may have been *Cru.* See also Vernon J. Harward, Jr., *The Dwarfs of Arthurian Romance and Celtic Tradition* (Leiden, 1958), pp. 8, 107 ff. Miss Schoepperle suggests an Irish story about Cormac. See *Tristan and Isolt: A Study of the Sources of the*

important, but in the twelfth-century *Life of St. Illtud*[16] there is an incident involving King Meirchiawn which recalls both *The Life of St. Paul* and the Tristan bell. St. Illtud left the court of King Meirchiawn because he was denounced by a wicked servitor. He was living in the woods when a messenger appeared carrying a bell as a gift from St. Gildas to St. David. The sound of this bell was so beautiful when St. Illtud handled it that he coveted it, though he did not request it. However, when St. David received the bell, it failed to make a sound. Because the bell was silent St. David understood that St. Illtud had desired the bell, and he sent it to him as a gift. If *Meirchiawn* and *March* are two forms of the same name, as Rhŷs proposed,[17] we have two incidents involving the similarly named kings and a gift of a bell. Tristan, too, was delighted by the bell around Petit Crû's neck; and although he did not request it, it was given to him later as a gift. Tristan was also denounced by a servitor at King Mark's court and was forced to live in the woods. Evidently some incidents in *The Life of St. Illtud* were modeled on the Tristan story. Admittedly none of this evidence conclusively proves that King Mark Cunomorus of *The Life of St. Paul*, King Meirchiawn of *The Life of St. Illtud,* and King Mark of *Tristan and Isolt* are the same. But it does disclose a body of somewhat similar southern British tradition surrounding the name of King Mark, and there, for the moment, the matter may stand.

According to certain traditions King Mark was cursed with horse's ears. Among all the Tristan stories this information appears only in Béroul's version,[18] although it is a widespread tale outside the Tristan legend and is told of others including King Midas as well.[19] The story was that a king had the ears of a horse and to

Romance, 2 vols. (Frankfurt and London, 1913; reprinted, New York, 1959), II, 320 ff.

16. A. W. Wade-Evans (ed.), *Vitae Sanctorum Brittaniae et Genealogiae* (Cardiff, 1944), pp. xii, 194 ff.

17. *Hibbert Lectures, 1886*, p. 271.

18. E. Muret (ed.), *Le Roman de Tristan by Béroul, SATF*, No. LII (Paris, 1903), rev. L. M. Defourques, *Les Classiques français du moyen âge* (Paris, 1947), vss. 1303 ff.

19. Schoepperle, *Tristan and Isolt*, II, 269–72. See also Antti Aarne and Stith Thompson, *The Types of the Folktale*, FF Communications No. 184 (Helsinki,

conceal his deformity had each of his successive barbers slain. A
youth escaped death on promising to keep the secret, but he was so
burdened by his knowledge that he told it to an inanimate object.
Later the object in one way or another became vocal and revealed
the secret. King Mark's name means *horse,* and it has been agreed
that the connection between Mark and the story lies in Mark's
name.[20] The story survived in Welsh folklore to the end of the
nineteenth century [21] and still may not have disappeared.

Thus, in the Welsh traditions of Mark we see: that he was
married to Essyllt, who betrayed him with Trystan; that he was a
powerful king, occasionally tyrannical; that he was a fleet owner
or seafarer; that he was connected with Llychlyn; that he ruled
where four languages were spoken; and that he had horse's ears.

THE *BONHED GWYR Y GOGLED*

Many Welsh kings traced their ancestors to a small group of
subreguli who reigned in the North, that is in Strathclyde, the land
between present-day Glasgow and Carlisle. Genealogies of the
Strathclyde ruling kindreds, the *Bonhed Gwyr Y Gogled* or the
Descent of the Men of the North [22] have survived in MS. Peniarth
45, fo. 291[v] (formerly MS. Hengwrt 536). Since these pedigrees
are important to the discussion that follows and are not always
readily available, I shall give the entire substance of the text in
tabular form in Chart 1.

1961), Type 782; Stith Thompson, *Motif-Index of Folk Literature,* rev. ed., Vol.
II (Bloomington, Ind. 1956), D.1316.5, F.511.2.2, N.465; Tom Peete Cross,
Motif-Index of Early Irish Literature (Bloomington, Ind., 1952), p. 274; J. J.
Jones, "March ap Meirchion, A Study in Celtic Folklore," *Aberystwyth Studies,*
XII (1932), 21–33; W. Stokes, "Mythological Notes—VII. Labraid Lorc and
his Ears," *RC,* II (1873–75), 198; W. Crooke, "King Midas and his Ass's Ears,"
Folk-Lore, XXII (1911), 196 f.; Myles Dillon, *The Cycles of the Kings* (Oxford, 1946), pp. 9 f.; J. Rhŷs, *Celtic Folklore, Welsh and Manx,* 2 vols. (Oxford, 1901), I, 232 ff., 197; II, 572–74.

20. Newstead, "King Mark of Cornwall," p. 246; Schoepperle, *Tristan and Isolt,* II, 269 ff.; Bromwich, *Trioedd Ynys Prydein,* pp. 446 f.

21. Rhŷs, *Celtic Folklore,* I, 232 ff.

22. Skene, *Four Ancient Books,* II, 454 f. The Welsh is on p. 454, and an
English translation is on the following page. See also Bromwich, *Trioedd Ynys Prydein,* pp. 238 f.

THE DESCENT OF THE MEN OF THE NORTH (*Bonhed Gwyr Y Gogled*)

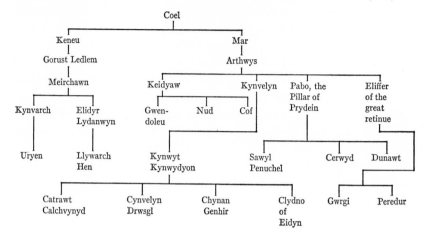

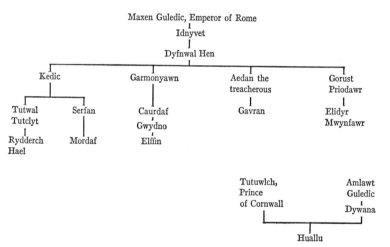

CHART I

From other sources we know that many of the names in the *Bonhed Gwyr Y Gogled* refer to actual people. According to Nennius in Chapter 63 [23] Uryen and Rydderch Hael were allied with Gaullanc and Morcant (all four being descendants of Coel,[24]) against King Hussa of the Bernician Angles about the year 600; [25] later Uryen and his sons fought Hussa's brother Deodric. Various histories refer to a number of the Men of the North as actual figures, although the various dates do not always coincide. Aedan the Treacherous, who was the son and not the father of Gavran, is said to have died in 605,[26] 606,[27] 607,[28] and 608.[29] Dunawt, son of Pabo the Pillar of Prydein, died in 595; [30] Dyfnwal Hen (Domangart), son of Idnyvet, in 506; [31] Gavran between 557 and 559; [32] Gwendoleu, son of Keidyaw and loser of the Battle of Ardderyd, in 573; [33] and Gwrgi and Peredur, the sons of Eliffer of the Great Retinue, in 580.[34] The triad which refers to the love of Drystan son of Tallwch for Essylt wife of March also tells of the love of the son of Clydno of Eidyn for the daughter of Uryen.[35] The Men of the North were celebrated in triads and in Welsh poetry down through the centuries.[36] There seems to be no question of their

23. F. Lot, *Nennius et l'historia Brittonum* (Paris, 1913), p. 202. See also A. W. Wade-Evans, *Nennius's History of the Britons* (London, 1938), pp. 80 f.

24. A. O. Anderson, *Early Sources of Scottish History,* 2 vols. (Edinburgh, 1922), I, 13, n. 4.

25. Anderson dates Hussa's reign from 599 to 605 or 606 (*ibid.,* n. 3). Lot admits the difficulty of dating the reign of Hussa exactly and places it at about the end of the sixth and beginning of the seventh century (*Nennius,* p. 74). Adamnán, *The Life of St. Columba,* ed. William Reeves (Dublin, 1857), p. 44, offers 601 as the date of the death of Rhydderch Hael.

26. *Annals of Ulster,* ed. and trans. William M. Hennessy (Dublin, 1887), I, 84 f.

27. *The Life of St. Columba,* p. 438.

28. *Annales Cambriae,* ed. John Williams ab Ithel (London, 1860), p. 6.

29. Anderson, *Early Sources,* I, cxii.

30. *Annales Cambriae,* p. 5.

31. Anderson, *Early Sources,* I, cxii.

32. *The Annals of Ulster,* pp. 54–57, gives the date as 557 and 559; the *Annales Cambriae,* p. 4, dates Gavran's death as 558; and Anderson, *Early Sources,* I, cxii, says 559.

33. *Annales Cambriae,* p. 5.

34. *Ibid.*

35. Bromwich, *Trioedd Ynys Prydein,* Triad 71, p. 189.

36. Bromwich, "The Character of Early Welsh Tradition," *Studies in Early British History,* ed. Nora K. Chadwick (Cambridge, Eng., 1954; reprinted,

existence, and evidently some of the order of their kings is preserved in the *Bonhed Gwyr Y Gogled*.[37]

That the activities of and stories about the Men of the North were sources of many Welsh traditions has not gone unobserved.[38] We have already seen that the source of the name *Tristan* is agreed to be the name *Drust,* which was held by a number of Pictish kings who were much closer geographically and chronologically to the Strathclyde Celts than to those Celts who inhabited the southern parts of the Island of Britain. What, then, about the name of King Mark? Could it too have a northern origin?

On turning back to the chart of the *Bonhed Gwyr Y Gogled,* we see a Meirchawn or Meirchiawn, great grandson of Coel and grandfather of Uryen. This Meirchiawn was probably born c. 450–70 and may have been named after the Roman Emperor Marcianus, who reigned from 450–57.[39] Meirchiawn, we remember, was (1) the name of the father of Mark in the Welsh sources, and (2) in *The Life of St. Illtud* the name of a king who like Mark in the Tristan story employed a servitor who served his master by forcing an important figure in the court into forest exile. Furthermore, because of the similarity of names Rhŷs says that Meirchiawn and Mark are one.[40] Could this Meirchiawn of the North be the Meirchiawn who was the father of King Mark? There is nothing to connect Meirchiawn of the North with Meirchiawn of the South except their names and their sons. The son of Meirchiawn of the South was Mark or March. Looking at the *Bonhed Gwyr Y Gogled* we see that the son of Meirchiawn of the North was Kynvarch.

1959), pp. 83 ff., and especially p. 121. See also Sir Ifor Williams, *Lectures on Early Welsh Poetry* (Dublin, 1954), pp. 50 ff.

37. Cf. H. M. Chadwick, *Early Scotland* (Cambridge, Eng., 1949), pp. 143 ff.

38. Williams, *Lectures on Early Welsh Poetry,* 50 ff. Nora K. Chadwick, "Early Culture and Learning in North Wales," *Studies in the Early British Church,* ed. Nora K. Chadwick (Cambridge, Eng., 1958), pp. 63–65, 75–93; "The Lost Literature of Celtic Scotland," *Scottish Gaelic Studies,* VII (1953), 115–83. Bromwich, "The Character of Early Welsh Tradition," pp. 121 f.; "The Celtic Sources of 'Tristan,'" p. 49. Roger Sherman Loomis, *Arthurian Tradition and Chrétien de Troyes* (New York, 1949), p. 24. Carney, *Studies,* pp. 150 ff., 197. Mrs. Bromwich gives a good analysis of the *Bonhed Gwyr Y Gogled,* indicating its faults and virtues from the modern scholar's point of view, *Trioedd Ynys Prydein,* pp. cxvii ff.

39. Chadwick, *Early Scotland,* p. 143.

40. *Hibbert Lectures, 1886,* p. 271.

Kynvarch, as it is written in the pedigrees, is merely a late spelling of the Old Welsh *Cinmarch.* The *v* is a mutated *m,*[41] although the earlier spelling, *Cinmarch,* has survived in some of the genealogies.[42] The word *cyn* or *cin* was a term of honor; in the *Bonhed Gwyr Y Gogled* alone it is found in *Kynvelyn, Cynvelyn, Kynwyt Kynwydyon,* and *Chynan.* Its meaning was "hound," and to the Celts this word had meliorative overtones, appearing, for instance, in the Irish *Cú Chulainn* (Hound of Culann) and the Welsh *Maelgwn* (Princely Hound).[43] *Cinmarch,* then, probably means "Hound-like Mark." Because Kynvarch is son of a Meirchiawn, I propose tentatively that the Welsh March son of Meirchiawn bears a name that is borrowed from the northern Kynvarch (Cinmarch) son of Meirchiawn, whose existence is preserved in the *Bonhed Gwyr Y Gogled.*[44]

The proposal is tentative because the names *March* and *Meirchiawn* were common among the Welsh; [45] and, as I have said before, positive identity of common names may not be established when one is dealing with only two generations. However, other matters which are shortly to be discussed support this identification.

MARCH IN THE NORTH

If Mark received his name and some of his reputation from Kynvarch, it is not surprising that he was remembered as a fleet owner or seafarer. That British ships raided Irish shores searching for slaves we know from an indignant letter written by St. Patrick

41. I am indebted to Miss Cecile O'Rahilly for the confirmation of this information. See also Kenneth Jackson, *Language and History in Early Britain* (Edinburgh, 1953), pp. 482 ff., and note the relationship of the modern *Devon* to the early British *Dumnonii.*

42. Loth, *Les Mabinogion,* II, 334. See also Bromwich, *Trioedd Ynys Prydein,* p. 322.

43. Kenneth Jackson, "The Sources for the Life of St. Kentigern," *Studies in the Early British Church,* ed. Nora K. Chadwick (Cambridge, Eng., 1958), p. 298.

44. Rhŷs also noted the similarity between *Kynvarch* and March son of Meirchiawn but said that the former (whom he evidently believed to be non-existent) was derived from the latter. See John Rhŷs, *Studies in the Arthurian Legend* (Oxford, 1891), p. 238.

45. J. Gwenogvryn Evans and John Rhŷs, *The Text of the Book of Llan Dâv* (Oxford, 1893), Index. Jackson, *Language and History in Early Britain,* p. 571.

to the soldiers of Ceretig (Coroticus), a North British king, during the fifth century complaining of such a raid.[46] Any Strathclyde king would have found a fleet useful, and Kynvarch may have been remembered for his.[47] Furthermore, the particular epithet meaning "seafarer," as we shall see shortly, was attached to an Irish figure some of whose adventures apparently were related to the Tristan complex and who himself, like Mark, had horse's ears.[48]

The reference to Llychlyn, which as we have seen meant Scandinavia, probably recalls a vague association with the North. To the Welsh who wrote the triads, Kynvarch was from the North and, because transportation by sea was easier than by land, from over the sea.[49] Also, since Llychlyn refers to a land over the sea, there may be a connection between Mark's fleet ownership and his association with Llychlyn.

As we have seen, in the ninth-century *Life of St. Paul Aurelianus* Mark is described as a king over people who spoke four languages. Bede, whose *Ecclesiastical History* was finished in 731, says in two places that, besides Latin, four distinct languages were used on the Island of Britain: British, Scottish, English, and Pictish.[50] By British he means Brythonic or that branch of Celtic which is the ancestor of present-day Welsh. In Bede's day Brythonic was spoken not only in today's Wales but also in Strathclyde. By Scottish Bede means the eighth-century form of Goidelic or Scottish-Irish Gaelic. Scottish and Irish Gaelic are today mutually understandable and obviously were when Bede was writing. In the sixth through eighth centuries this language was spoken in Ireland and in Western Scotland by people known as the Dalriadic Scots, who came from Ireland to settle in Galloway and to the North. The English language

46. John A. Duke, *The Columban Church* (Edinburgh and London, 1932; reprinted, 1957), pp. 27 f. For more about this letter see James P. Carney, *The Problem of St. Patrick* (Dublin, 1961), pp. 54, 93 f., 113 f., and 180.

47. The Picts, who were near neighbors of the Strathclyde Britons, were also known as fleet owners. See Nora K. Chadwick, "The Name Pict,"*Scottish Gaelic Studies*, VIII, Pt. 2 (1958), 172.

48. See below, pp. 68 ff.

49. For a further statement that the Welsh looked to their northern ancestors as sea rovers, see A. W. Wade-Evans, "Prolegomena to a Study of the Lowlands," *TJDGNA*, Whithorn Volume, 3d ser., XXVII (1950), 58.

50. *Venerabilis Baedae*, ed. Carolus Plummer (Oxford, 1896), Book I, Chap. 1; Book III, Chap. 6.

in the sixth, seventh, and eighth centuries in Bede's area meant the language of Bernicia and Deire, two kingdoms on the east coast of present-day Northumbria. The Pictish language, which was still alive in Bede's time, was spoken by people north of the Firth of Forth to the east of those areas occupied by Brythonic and Goidelic speakers.[51]

Although Brythonic and English were spoken in both the northern and southern parts of the Island of Britain, Goidelic and Pictish were used principally in the North. The best candidate in the British Isles for a quadrilingual land, the only area where all four languages came together, would be somewhere near the Clyde-Forth isthmus, that is the Strathclyde area, as may be seen on Map 6.

THE FOUR LANGUAGES

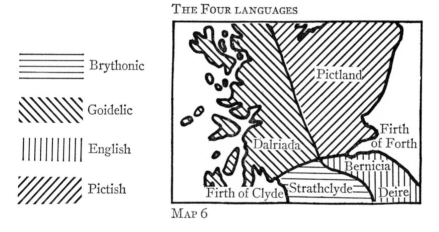

Brythonic

Goidelic

English

Pictish

MAP 6

THE KING WITH HORSE'S EARS

The question of the horse's ears is more complex. If Mark existed as a person at all (and the evidence is that he did) it seems likely that the story was attached to Mark because his name, although ultimately derived from the Latin *Marcianus*, meant "horse" in the language of the Brythonic people who first listened to tales about him. The story was earlier told about King Midas and other classical figures.[52] The possibility that the Tristan story was attached to

51. Kenneth Jackson, "The Pictish Language," *The Problem of the Picts,* ed. F. T. Wainwright (Edinburgh, 1955), pp. 129–66.
52. Thompson, *Motif-Index of Folk Literature,* F.511.2.2, N.465, D.1316.5.

Mark *because* his name meant "horse" will be considered shortly.[53]

The tale is of particular interest to students of the Tristan problem when it is associated with either a man whose wife loves another man or with a lover who sends a harpist to woo a potential spouse. The Béroul account of Mark and his horse's ears mentioned above is one example of the former, and others include an Irish tale of King Eochaid of the Hui Failgi (*Eochaid* meant "horse" in Old Irish) and an episode from *The Pursuit after Diarmaid and Gráinne*. An example of the latter appears in the Irish traditions of Labraid Loingsech.

The King Eochaid example[54] is from the Stowe MS. D IV 2. (Royal Irish Academy), fo. 32b1–53b2. Meyer assigns the story to the tenth century.

King Eochaid of the Hui Failgi wore a golden crown to conceal his horse's ears. Each barber who shaved him was slain to preserve the secret. The King had a nephew, Mac Dichoime, a talented youth who was accustomed to shaving the members of the court, grooming their horses, and repairing their war equipment. He was an accomplished musician, a poet, a swimmer, and a hunter. With women he was a favorite, and Eochaid's Queen so loved him that only the presence of her husband prevented her from declaring her love.

The Queen looked with such favor upon Mac Dichoime that King Eochaid, becoming jealous, invited him to a lonely house to serve as royal barber. There Mac Dichoime, learning the King's abnormality, disarmed him. The King then agreed that if Mac Dichoime could keep the secret he could become permanent royal barber.

His knowledge so weighed upon Mac Dichoime that he became ill, finally falling to the ground and emitting three streams of blood from his mouth and nostrils. He was then healed. In time three saplings grew upon this spot. A noted satirist heard the saplings say to each other, "Eochiad, the man of the shield, has two horse's ears." The satirist took his news to court, where King Eochaid, after his initial anger had passed, agreed that it was difficult to keep any secret and exposed his deformity to the world.

This tenth-century tale appears to be later than any primitive Tristan story; certainly it is later than the time of Kynvarch of

53. See below, p. 69.

54. Kuno Meyer (ed. and trans.), "King Eochaid Has Horse's Ears," *Otia Merseiana,* III (Liverpool, 1903), 46–54.

Strathclyde, who, I have suggested, is the prototype of Mark's name. The fact that a king whose name means "horse" is suspicious of his wife and jealous of his accomplished and musical nephew is evidence that this tale is related to the Tristan cycle. And, as Miss Newstead says, it is chronologically impossible that the tale arose from any Continental rendition of the story.[55]

The second example also occurs in a tale of a jealous husband, a wandering wife, and an accomplished nephew. This is *The Pursuit after Diarmaid and Gráinne,*[56] which is old enough to have been referred to in the ninth century.[57] This particular incident is an interpolation in the main story, and one may reasonably ask how it got there. The story has usually been neglected as a curious [58] and presumably insignificant tale.

Diarmaid and Gráinne, having escaped from Gráinne's husband Fionn to the forest, were surprised by Aodh the son of Andala Mac Morna. In a long tale which Diarmaid told to Aodh, this incident occurred: Cian son of Oilioll Oluim was born with a caul across his head. As the boy grew, the caul grew, and when Cian was a man he habitually killed each barber who shaved him. Once when Cian was offended by Sgathan son of Scanlan, he invited Sgathan to shave him. Sgathan agreed and on loosening the binding on the head of Cian discovered the caul. Then Sgathan ripped open the caul with his knife so that a worm escaped. The rest of the story concerns the worm, which grew to be a monstrous serpent, and the attempts made to kill it.

The story of Cian is certainly a derivative of the horse's ears tale. The bindings around the head and the slaying of the barbers are sufficient proof. If the story were originally told about Mark or Kynvarch, it must have traveled wherever the Tristan story traveled and thus appeared later in the Diarmaid and Gráinne tale, which then must have been a derivative version and not a source, as has been said,[59] of the Tristan tale.

55. Newstead, "King Mark of Cornwall," p. 247.
56. Standish Hayes O'Grady (ed. and trans.), *Toruigheacht Dhiarmuda agus Ghrainne—The Pursuit after Diarmaid and Gráinne, Transactions of the Ossianic Society for the Year 1855,* III (Dublin, 1857), 122 ff.
57. Schoepperle, *Tristan and Isolt,* II, 399.
58. The word "curious" is Miss Schoepperle's: *ibid.,* II, 271, n. 3.
59. *Ibid.,* II, 397.

A third example of the horse's ears incident again involves a legendary Irish king, Labraid Loingsech.[60] The original text synopsized here was Middle Irish from *The Yellow Book of Lecan*, which is late fourteenth or early fifteenth century.[61] There are, however, references to Labraid Loingsech going back to the seventh century.[62] Two fragments from *The Yellow Book of Lecan* tell us that Labraid Loingsech was a powerful king who was loved by Moriath, daughter of Scoriath, although Moriath had never set eyes on him. Moriath sent as her messenger the harpist Craiftine, who persuaded Labraid (after some adventures) to marry Moriath. In other versions Craiftine the harpist was the servant of Labraid and wooed the lady for him.

Labraid had horse's ears, and every barber who shaved the King was slain immediately. Once when the King asked the son of a widow to shave him, the widow, aware of the fate of the royal barbers, begged the King to spare her son. The King said he would spare the boy if the boy would swear never to say what he saw, and so it was. But the news was too much for the boy, and he told the secret to a willow. Later the harpist Craiftine made a harp from that very willow, and when the harp was played it said, "Two horse's ears on Labraid Lorc." [63]

It should be added here that this king's traditional epithet *loingsech* is an etymological equivalent to the Welsh *llyghessavc*, which may mean "sea-farer," "pirate," "exile," or "fleet owner." This was the epithet given March son of Meirchiawn in the triads, although Mrs. Bromwich suggests that the similarity is a "remarkable coincidence." [64] I think not. Labraid Loingsech's horse's ears, a harpist serving as an ambassador of love, a lady who loved a man before she saw him [65]—all of these elements appear in the extant Tristan

---

60. Whitley Stokes (ed.), "Mythological Notes—VII. Labraid Lorc and his Ears," *RC*, II, 198. See also Geoffrey Keating, *The History of Ireland*, Vol. II, ed. P. S. Dinneen, *ITS*, No. VIII (1908), 172–74.

61. Myles Dillon, *Early Irish Literature* (Chicago, 1948), p. xviii.

62. Dillon, *The Cycles of the Kings*, p. 7.

63. This synopsis is taken from Dillon, *ibid.*, pp. 9–10.

64. Bromwich, *Trioedd Ynys Prydein*, p. 447.

65. The motif of the chosen lover is common to the Tristan story and to some allied tales. Thus in Eilhart Mark loved Isolt before he met her, and in Thomas Isolt desired Tristan to teach her to play the harp before she met him. See Eilhart von Oberge, *Tristant*, ed. Franz Lichtenstein, *Quellen und For-*

legends, and Labraid and Mark bear etymologically equivalent epithets. There are too many similarities to rely on coincidence. The Irish tradition of Labraid Loingsech and the Welsh traditions of Mark son of Meirchiawn certainly seem to be related.

In each of the three Irish complexes we have discussed, the tale of King Eochaid, *The Pursuit after Diarmaid and Gráinne,* and the tales about Labraid Loingsech, there are two common elements: (1) some incidents from the Tristan story; (2) the horse's ears story. First, King Eochaid's barber reminds us of Tristan; Diarmaid, who told the story of the caul, and Gráinne have been compared many times to Tristan and Isolt; Labraid, like Mark, had a harpist who was sent as an ambassador to woo a heretofore unseen loved one. And Labraid, like Mark in the triads, bore an epithet which meant among other things "fleet owner" or "seafarer." Second, Eochaid and Labraid concealed their horse's ears from all but their barbers, whom they customarily slew, and Cian son of Oilioll Oluim similarly concealed his caul.

A proposed reconstruction would be like this: The original Mark was Kynvarch, whose name meant "horse." Because of his name, a tale was told in which this king was afflicted with horse's ears. In all probability this story was suggested by the legend of Midas, which, like other classical myths, was apparently not unknown in Britain and Ireland. Mark's name might even be responsible for his inclusion into the Tristan story. In the Egyptian tales of Isis, Osiris, and Set, Isis, who was a healer among other things, was coveted by Set, who was often represented as an ass-eared god. This suggestion is reinforced by the relationship of the North British monasteries to both the Gaulish (there was a cult of Isis in fourth-century Gaul) and Coptic monasteries.

Two traditions, then, apparently evolved about the name *March:* one consisting of elements which we recognize in the Tristan legend and the other relating to the story of the horse's ears. Both descended with various alterations to the legends of King Eochaid of the Hui Failgi, Fionn of the Fianna, and Labraid Loingsech. How-

schungen zur Sprach- und Culturgeschichte, XIX (Strasbourg, 1877), ll. 1337 ff.; Loomis, *Tristram and Ysolt,* p. 83; Eugen Kölbing (ed.), *Die nordische und die englische Version der Tristan-sage,* 2 vols. (Heilbronn, 1882), I, 38; J. Bédier (ed.), *Le Roman de Tristan par Thomas, SATF,* No. LIII, 2 vols. (Paris, 1902–5), I, 94 f. For more about the chosen lover see below, Chap. Seven.

ever, in the Fenian tale the story of the horse's ears was altered and attached to a minor character. That the Tristan story is earlier than *Diarmaid and Gráinne* seems evident when we look at the development of the horse's ears legend—in the Tristan story it appears (in Béroul's version) about a king whose name meant "horse." In *Diarmaid and Gráinne* we have a degenerate version of the same story interpolated for no particular reason than that it had some relationship to an earlier form of the tale. The conclusion of the information given us by these Irish examples of the horse's ears tales is that the Irish tales are derivatives. The horse's ears story was associated, albeit loosely, with the Tristan tale from the time of the very beginnings of the Tristan legend. Since our Irish examples must be derivatives, we are left with the proposal that the original story was told not about Eochaid, Mac Dichoime, and Eochaid's queen; not about Fionn, Diarmaid, and Gráinne; and not about Labraid Loingsech, Craiftine, and Moriath. No, indeed: the original story was told about Mark, Tristan, and Isolt, or, as the Brythonic originators of the tale called them, Kynvarch son of Meirchiawn, Drystan son of Tallwch, and Essyllt.

KING MARCÁN ▓

Although Mark himself does not appear by name in any of the Irish tales which are similar to *Tristan and Isolt*,[66] there is one example in which the old king is named Marcán, and this name deserves some comment here. The example is *Scéla Cano Meic Gartnáin* or the *Story of Cano Son of Gartnán*,[67] in which Cano was loved by Créd, the young wife of old King Marcán, who in another tale is king of the Hy Many.[68] The love affair was ended when Cano approached Créd by ship. Créd mistakenly thought Cano was dead, and she killed herself by smashing her head on a rock. The story comes from *The Yellow Book of Lecan* (fasc. 128a46) and has been dated c. 900 by Thurneysen.[69]

66. A list of these tales and their proposed relationship to *Tristan and Isolt* has been offered by Carney, *Studies,* pp. 189 ff.
67. A convenient translation is in Dillon, *The Cycles of the Kings,* pp. 80 ff.
68. *Ibid.,* p. 87.
69. R. Thurneysen (trans.), "Eine irische Parallele zur Tristan-Sage," *ZRPh,* XLIII (1923), 385–88.

The parallels to the Tristan story include King Marcán, his young unfaithful wife, and the tragic ending. If *Diarmaid and Gráinne* or its type of tale represents the prototype of the Tristan story,[70] and if Mark came into the story only when it reached South Wales or Cornwall,[71] then how may one explain the presence of the name *Marcán* attached to this old king in this very parallel?

A sounder explanation than an Irish source for the Tristan triangle is this: there was a King Marcán of the Hy Many. The *Annals of the Four Masters* give his death as 649 and his father as Toimen.[72] In the *Annals of Ulster* 652 is the date of his death and his father is named Tomain.[73] However, in *Cormac's Glossary* there is mention of Marcán son of Aed son of Marcéine,[74] which O'Donovan, the translator, feels refers to King Marcán of the Hy Many.[75] There is a general similarity in formation between *Meirchiawn* and *Marcéine*. The Latin *Marcianus* is the name *Marcius* with an adjectival suffix; *Marcéine* is similarly the name *Marc* with a suffix -*éne*,[76] frequently used in forming derivative names. *Marcán* is a similar formation.[77] I know of no Marcán or Mark, son or grandson of an effective namesake, except Kynvarch son of Meirchiawn and story figures whose names were, I maintain, derived from the name of Kynvarch son of Meirchiawn. It is possible that the name *Marcán* reminded someone that a famous Mark was son of another Mark or the like, but since this Marcán was known to the story audience as the son of Aed, he became for the purposes of the story not the son but the grandson of his namesake. Thus from Marcán

70. Thus suggested Miss Schoepperle, *Tristan and Isolt*, II, p. 397: "[The Tristan story] seems to be a survival of an Old Irish elopement story." Professor Newstead agrees. See "The Origin and Growth of the Tristan Legend," *ALMA* p. 127.

71. Newstead, "Origin and Growth of the Tristan Legend"; "King Mark of Cornwall," p. 253. See also Bromwich, *Trioedd Ynys Prydein*, p. 446.

72. John O'Donovan (ed. and trans.), *Annals of the Four Masters* (Dublin, 1856), I, 265.

73. William M. Hennessy (ed. and trans.), *Annals of Ulster* (Dublin, 1887), I, 113.

74. John O'Donovan (trans.), and Whitley Stokes (ed.), *Sanas Chormaid* (Calcutta, 1868), p. 3.

75. *Ibid.*, p. 4.

76. R. Thurneysen, *A Grammar of Old Irish*, rev. ed., trans. D. A. Binchy and Osborn Bergin (Dublin, 1946), p. 175.

77. *Ibid.*, p. 173.

son of Tomain, Marcán son of Aed son of Marcéine was created. In a like manner, I believe, the story of the young unfaithful wife was attracted to this same Marcán: the familiar story was joined to the familiar name.

The Irish examples of the horse's ears episode demonstrate, to me, that an original figure named Mark (or horse) was the original cuckolded husband of the Tristan story. Unless Kynvarch son of Meirchiawn is postulated as having suggested the name of the original King Mark, the original wronged husband, there is no way, as far as I can see, to explain the appearance of Marcán in the *Story of Cano* and the reference to Marcán grandson of Marcéine in *Cormac's Glossary*. It does appear that the earliest Celtic prototype of King Mark and all figures like King Mark was Kynvarch son of Meirchiawn.[78]

THE TRISTAN LEGEND IN THE NORTH ▒

If the prototypes of Tristan and of Mark both come from the North, and if we find tales in a North British setting including the name *Drust* and such Tristan-like motifs as the killing of the giant in *The Wooing of Emer* and the bridal bed substitution in the tale of the conception of Lonan, is it not probable that a complete story of Drust and Kynvarch, much like the Tristan story even to the killing of the giant and the bridal bed substitution, was known in the North?[79] This is the argument of Professor Carney, and I believe it is supported by the findings here. What Mrs. Bromwich

---

78. One difficulty in this equation is that Kynvarch's son was the famous Urien Rheged, and it might seem improbable that Kynvarch could suggest King Mark with the latter never being mentioned as the father of such a famous son. I suggest that Urien was too famous for the story. His career and death were so well established that his intrusion into the tale would have been artistically inconsistent with the aim of a writer concerned with a love story. Thus the author of *The Pursuit after Diarmaid and Gráinne* was faced with the same problem and solved it by altering the traditional ending of the story to coincide with the known death of Diarmaid. See Carney, *Studies*, p. 219. After all, Urien's equally famous son, Owain, did not appear in all the tales about Urien.

79. In the sixteenth-century Welsh poem, *Ystoria Tristan*, Trystan son of Tallwch, and Esyllt, wife of March son of Meirchion, flee with their page and handmaid to the forest of Celyddon, which is, of course, in Scotland. See Loomis, *Tristram and Ysolt*, pp. xxi ff. and Williams, *Lectures on Early Welsh Poetry*, pp. 18 f.

calls the normal movement of early British heroic material, the localization in Wales of adventures of the heroes of the North,[80] may apply here as it did with other Welsh heroes such as Llywarch Hen,[81] Taliesin,[82] Myrddin,[83] Urien,[84] Owain,[85] and possibly even Arthur himself.[86]

80. "Celtic Sources of 'Tristan,'" p. 49; *Trioedd Ynys Prydein*, p. 431; "Scotland and the Arthurian Legend," *BBSIA*, XV (1963), 85–89; "The Celtic Inheritance of Medieval Literature," *MLQ*, XXVI, No. 1 (March, 1965), 203–27.

81. Williams, *Lectures on Early Welsh Poetry*, pp. 28 ff.

82. *Ibid.*, pp. 50 ff.

83. Kenneth Jackson, "The Motive of the Threefold Death in the Story of Suibhne Geilt," *Essays and Studies Presented to Professor Eoin Mac Neill*, ed. John Ryan (Dublin, 1940), pp. 547 ff.

84. Loomis, *Arthurian Tradition*, p. 269; Loth, *Les Mabinogion*, II, 1 ff., n. 1; Williams, *Lectures on Early Welsh Poetry*, pp. 63 ff.

85. Loomis, *Arthurian Tradition*, p. 269. John Mac Queen, "Yvain, Ewen, and Owein ap Urien," *TJDGNA*, 3d ser., XXXIII (1956).

86. When I began this study I had the most serious doubts about the genuine historicity of Arthur. But the convincing studies of Mrs. Chadwick and Mrs. Bromwich have persuaded me that he probably flourished in the early sixth century and was the first of those North British heroes whose reputation was later aggrandized in the South. See Chadwick, "The Lost Literature of Celtic Scotland," pp. 164 ff.; Bromwich, "Scotland and Arthurian Legend," p. 94; and "The Celtic Inheritance of Medieval Literature," pp. 218 ff.

Chapter Six

NORTH BRITISH NOMENCLATURE

HE THESIS of this chapter continues the argument that a number of names used in the Tristan story have association with North Britain. Having already argued that Tristan and Mark derived their names from the North, I now wish to suggest that Brangien was known by another name to the northern tellers of the tale, that Morgan (who in Thomas slew Tristan's father), the giant Urgen, and Isolt have names which may be associated with the North, and that certain place names also have northern derivations.

BRANGIEN

Brangien is Isolt's personal maid and as such plays the role of the confidante so necessary to any heroine engaged in a lifetime of subterfuge. In the Continental versions of the story Brangien first appears in Ireland, and according to Eilhart when Isolt went to prove for herself that the Irish dragon was dead, Brangien accompanied her and discovered the unconscious Tristan.[1] Thomas said that Isolt was accompanied by her mother; he gave Brangien her first appearance when she was entrusted with the vial which contained the love potion.[2] Both versions agree that on her wedding

---

1. Eilhart von Oberge, *Tristrant*, ed. Franz Lichtenstein, *Quellen und Forschungen zur Sprach- und Culturgeschichte*, XIX (Strasbourg, 1877), ll. 1766 ff.
2. Roger Sherman Loomis (ed. and trans.), *The Romance of Tristram and Ysolt*, new rev. ed. (New York, 1951), p. 130. Eugen Kölbing (ed.), *Die*

night Isolt implored Brangien to go to Mark's bed and thus deceive
the King into believing that his wife was a virgin.[3] Later, in both
versions, Isolt feared that Brangien would disclose the secret and
ordered some menials to take Brangien into the woods to slay her.
When Brangien saw what her fate was to be, she told her captors
that the only crime on her conscience was that she had lent Isolt
a white shirt because Isolt had soiled her own on the voyage between Ireland and Cornwall. This explanation was accepted, and
Brangien was released. An animal was slaughtered, and its blood
was brought to Isolt. But by this time Isolt had repented her cruelty.
She greeted the servants with curses and demanded that they bring
Brangien back to life. Of course they were able to do so, and the
two women embraced and vowed to be friends forever more.[4]

From that time on Brangien was Isolt's confidante and her go-
between with Tristan on many an assignation. Brangien's clever-
ness was second only to Tristan's; many times she guided the lovers
to each other and then faced King Mark with a plausible explanation for their conduct.

Eventually Tristan married Isolt of Brittany and returned secretly with his new brother-in-law, Kaherdin, to show him the
wonders of the Cornish court. In Eilhart's version Kaherdin admired Brangien but wooed Camille of Montrelles, Isolt's second
maid. Eilhart,[5] or his source, then killed off Brangien and advanced
Camille to the position of first lady in waiting. So Kaherdin still
wooed the principal servant of the heroine.[6] But we know from other
sources that it was Brangien whom Kaherdin loved, and Thomas
makes no mention of her death.[7]

nordische und die englische Version der Tristan-sage, 2 vols. (Heilbronn, 1882),
I, 56. Joseph Bédier (ed.), Le Roman de Tristan par Thomas, SATF, No. LIII,
2 vols. (Paris, 1902–5), I, 142.

3. Eilhart, Tristrant, ll. 2715 ff.; Loomis, Tristram and Ysolt, p. 134; Kölbing, Tristan-sage, I, 57; Bédier, Le Roman de Tristan par Thomas, I, 147, 156.

4. Eilhart, Tristrant, ll. 2863 ff.; Loomis, Tristram and Ysolt, pp. 135 ff.; Kölbing, Tristan-sage, I, 58 f.; Bédier, Le Roman de Tristan par Thomas, I, 157 ff.

5. Tristrant, ll. 7560 ff.

6. In the Welsh Ystoria Trystan, trans. Loomis, Tristram and Ysolt, pp.
xxi ff., Kae Hir (Kay the Tall) loved the handmaid of Essyllt. Evidently the
tradition was that Kay, Kae Hir, or Kaherdin (obviously different names for
the same person) loved the handmaid of Tristan's mistress.

7. In Thomas, according to Brother Robert, the adventure of the magic cush-
ion, which Eilhart allots to Camille, occurred with Brangien. See Loomis,

The confidante, is, of course, traditional in the love story. Both men and women have them: often a hero must show his more anguished side to some one, and the squire is so utilized. The heroine too must tell her troubles to someone, usually an old nurse or a personal maid. Examples are everywhere. Thus the position Brangien occupies is by no means unique. Nor is it particularly strange that in some of the versions she is wooed by Kaherdin, who at one point in the story serves as Tristan's companion. There is a widespread tradition in love stories that the retainers of the hero and heroine love each other. But who is Brangien? Where did she get her name and when did she get it? How long has she been in the story?

Mrs. Bromwich observes that Brangien's name is derived from an Old Welsh form of the name *Branwen*.[8] Now Branwen is the heroine of one of the tales of the *Mabinogion*,[9] but her adventures had little correspondence with those of Brangien. The name *Brangien* was borrowed from *Branwen* in its Old Welsh, or pre-twelfth-century,[10] form. On the other hand, there is some evidence, as I hope to explain shortly, that the character of the confidante to the heroine was established in the Tristan story before the tale moved south to pick up a name, and even some of the milieu,[11] of the Mabinogi *Branwen Daughter of Llŷr*.

Brangien was not always named Brangien, although she may be recognized without her name. In the sixteenth-century Welsh *Ystoria Trystan* she is named Golwg Hafddydd (aspect of a summer day), the handmaid of Essyllt, and is wooed by Kae Hir.[12]

Tristram and Ysolt, pp. 239 f.; Kölbing, *Tristan-sage*, I, 101 f.; Bédier, *Le Roman de Tristan par Thomas*, I, 340.

8. Rachel Bromwich, "Some Remarks on the Celtic Sources of 'Tristan,'" *THSC*, Session 1953 (London, 1955), p. 55.

9. Gwyn Jones and Thomas Jones (trans.), *The Mabinogion*, Everyman's Library No. 97 (London, 1949), pp. 25 ff. J. Loth, *Les Mabinogion*, 2 vols. (Paris, 1913), I, 119 ff.

10. Kenneth Jackson, *Language and History in Early Britain* (Edinburgh, 1953), pp. 5 f.

11. Bromwich, "Celtic Sources of 'Tristan,'" p. 55, demonstrates that there are some geographical parallels between the courts of King Mark and of Isolt's father and the courts of Bran and of Matholwch of Ireland in *Branwen Daughter of Llŷr*.

12. Sir Ifor Williams, "Trystan ac Esyllt," *BBCS*, V (Cardiff, 1930), pp. 115 ff. Loomis, *Tristram and Ysolt*, pp. xxi ff. See also Tom Peete Cross, "A Welsh Tristan Episode," *Studies in Philology*, XVII (1920), 93–110; J. Loth, "L'Ystoria Trystan et la question des archétypes," *RC*, XXXIV (1913), 366–96.

Golwg Hafddydd is a bardic metaphor indicating that what Kae Hir wishes is a bride with such an aspect: [13]

> For my tidings I require
> Nor maid of gold or other hire;
> Golwg Hafddydd I desire.[14]

Kae Hir (Kay the Tall) does no more in the *Ystoria Trystan* than exist and state his love for Essyllt's handmaid. Of course, in the French romances he is Kaherdin, the friend and confidant of Tristan.

The *Ystoria Trystan* consists of both verse and prose passages. The prose is in the nature of explanation and was written much later than the verse or *englynion*.[15] Thus when Kae Hir announces his love for Golwg Hafddydd in an *englyn*, we know that we are faced with an old relationship. But why was Kae Hir selected as the lover? Who is he? Certainly here he does not appear as the crude and overbearing Sir Kay that he is in the French Arthurian romances and in Malory. No, Kae in the early Welsh poems, along with Bedwyr, is a constant companion of Arthur [16] and almost as fabulous. Wherever Arthur appears, Kae usually does too. In the *Ystoria Trystan* Arthur is asked to mediate a dispute between March and Trystan. Kae's love for Essyllt's handmaid is part of the older and constant tradition that the confidante of a heroine must have an affair of her own.

Although the name *Brangien* probably came into the story in the South Welsh stage of its development, the activities of the go-between in the love story are obviously older. We have seen in the adventure of Drusticc that in the North British stage of the story the name *Drust* was associated with an adventure involving a substitution in a marriage bed.[17] Other tales, from the Irish traditions,

---

13. Bromwich, "Celtic Sources of 'Tristan,' " p. 55, n. 96.

14. Loomis, *Tristram and Ysolt*, p. xxiii.

15. Sir Ifor Williams, *Lectures on Early Welsh Poetry* (Dublin, 1954), p. 19.

16. Bromwich, "Celtic Sources of 'Tristan,' " p. 33, n. 8; *Trioedd Ynys Prydein—The Welsh Triads* (Cardiff, 1961), pp. 303 ff.

17. The marriage bed substitution is a widely-spread folktale, often a part of a Cinderella-type tale known as *The Forgotten Bride,* in which the maid who substitutes for the lady becomes the hero's long-lost love. See Gertrude Schoepperle, *Tristan and Isolt: A Study of the Sources of the Romance,* 2 vols. (Frankfurt and London, 1913; reprinted, New York, 1959), I, 206 ff., and cf. Middleton and Rowley, *The Changeling,* for a seventeenth-century example. This is Motif

reinforce our evidence that Brangien or a figure like her was part of the story from a time predating the South Welsh stage. These tales, which are apparently part of the Tristan complex,[18] include *Tochmarc Becfhola—The Wooing of Becfhola,* where the heroine discovered that her maid, whom she had assumed to be dead, still lived, and *Fingal Rónáin—How Ronan Slew His Son,* where a lascivious queen sought the son of her husband and pursued him by commanding her maid to be intimate with him. That these tales, in spite of their divergent plots, are related to the Tristan story I plan to demonstrate in the next chapter. If the reader will wait patiently for the proof of the relationship, I shall offer the following points which are common to the Tristan legend and these other tales:

1. The heroine has a maid.

2. At one point the heroine mistakenly believes that the maid is dead in *The Wooing of Becfhola.*

3. There is a marriage bed substitution, although in the case of the Preface to St. Mugint's *Hymn* it involves the substitution of man for hero rather than maid for heroine. In *Fingal Rónáin,* however, the substitution follows the more usual procedure.

A suggestion for a source of the bridal substitution was made by Professor Carney,[19] who cites *Ingen Ríg Gréc—The Daughter of the King of the Greeks* [20] as an old Oriental tale known early in Ireland.

The Daughter of the King of the Greeks lost her virginity prior to her wedding night. She deceived her groom by ordering her maid to act as a substitute on that night. The subterfuge was successful, and later the girl secretly murdered her maid.

This tale is a likely candidate for a source of the incident in the Tristan tale, although there is no evidence that it is the only candidate. There is a multiplicity of similar events in folklore.[21]

K.1911.2.1 in the Stith Thompson, *Motif-Index of Folk Literature,* rev. ed., 6 vols. (Bloomington, Ind., 1955–58).

18. For the relationship of these stories to the Tristan complex, discussions, and bibliographies see below, Chap. Seven, "The Reluctant Lover."

19. James Carney, *Studies in Irish Literature and History* (Dublin, 1955), pp. 230 ff.

20. Standish Hayes O'Grady (ed. and trans.), "Ingen Ríg Gréc: Iartaige na hIngine Colaige do Ghrécaib," *Silva Gadelica (I–XXXI),* 2 vols. (London, 1892), I, 413 ff.; II, 449 ff.

21. See Thompson, *Motif-Index of Folk Literature,* H.38.2.3, H.1558.4.3, K.1911, K.1223.

To the three points listed above another may be added, although the only evidence that it was present in the story prior to the South Welsh period is the northern name *Celyddon* (Caledonia) found in the *Ystoria Trystan*:

4. The maid herself has a love affair, as she did in the *Ystoria Trystan* with Kae Hir and in Thomas's *Tristan* with Kaherdin, whose name is a development of the name *Kae Hir*.

In summary this may be said about Brangien: from a very early pre-South Welsh, or northern, version of the Tristan story the heroine had a confidante who was a substitute in a bridal bed and was falsely believed to be dead. We know that the bridal substitution was known in North Britain (i.e., the Drusticc story) and that the false belief in the servant's death appeared in an Irish tale. Most likely before the story moved to South Wales this confidante was given an admirer of her own, a lover who was originally Kae but developed into Kaherdin, the confidant of Tristan. Then in the South Welsh stage, perhaps because of the audience's familiarity with Branwen, daughter of Llŷr, the confidante was named or renamed Brangien.

These investigations of Brangien suggest that whatever the link was between the Irish *aitheda* or elopement stories and the Tristan story, this link contained a figure much like Brangien although not necessarily bearing that name. The Brangien inquiries do not necessarily prove my thesis, that the link itself was located in North Britain. All that is established is that the link existed somewhere and that Brangien, by whatever name she was known, was part of this link.

MORGAN

A little more information appears when we consider the name *Morgan*. In Arthurian romance Morgan is usually a female figure and not a particularly nice one. She is Morgan la Fée, and although she "laid it over them all for variety," according to Mark Twain as quoted by Professor Loomis,[22] she does not appear as far as I know in the insular analogues of the Tristan story.

22. Loomis, "Morgain La Fée and the Celtic Goddesses," *Speculum*, XX (1945), 183–203, reprinted in *Wales and the Arthurian Legend* (Cardiff, 1956),

But there is another Morgan who must be considered, this time a male figure. Eilhart says nothing about him, but in Thomas's version, after King Mark had granted arms to young Tristan, Tristan begged permission to return to his homeland to avenge his father's death and win there his rightful heritage. At this time Tristan's father's dukedom was ruled by an usurper named Duke Morgan. In the battle that followed Tristan slew Morgan and conquered the dukedom.[23]

The name *Morgan* or *Morgant* as a male figure was associated by the Welsh bards with the North. A sixteenth-century version of the *Bonhed Gwyr Y Gogled* (MS. Peniarth 127, p. 95) mentions Morgant Mwynvawr (Morgan the Wealthy) among the Men of the North as a brother of Rydderch Hael and another son of Tutwal Tutclyt: "*Rydderch hael a Chynvyn glaer ac Iarderch drut a Morgant Mwynvawr brodorion, meibion tudwal tudclut ap kedic ap dyfnwal hen.*"[24] Mrs. Bromwich, discussing this relationship, comments that although Morgant Mwynvawr's blood connection with Rydderch Hael is probably not genuine, the statement of it suggests that in bardic tradition Morgant was known as one of the Men of the North. Secondly, Morgant's name is listed among the holders of the Thirteen Treasures of the Island of Britain, all the other identifiable holders bearing names that are associated with the North. Nennius in his *Historia Brittonum*[25] allied Morgant with other Men of the North and added that Urien, his ally, was assassinated by him. In *The Life of St. Kentigern* by Jocelyn of Furness[26] a North British tyrant named Morken harrassed St. Kentigern. Mrs. Bromwich[27] suggests that Morken was Nennius's Morgant, although

---

pp. 105–30. For more about Morgan la Fée see L. A. Paton, *Studies in the Fairy Mythology of Arthurian Romance*, Radcliffe College Monograph No. 13 (Cambridge, Mass., 1903; reprinted, 1960).

23. Loomis, *Tristram and Ysolt*, pp. 45 ff.; Kölbing, *Tristan-sage*, I, 27 f.; Bédier, *Le Roman de Tristan par Thomas*, I, 64 ff.

24. Bromwich, *Trioedd Ynys Prydein*, pp. 240 f., 466.

25. A. W. Wade-Evans (ed.), *Nennius's History of the Britons* (London, 1938), pp. 80 ff. F. Lot, *Nennius et l'historia Brittonum* (Paris, 1913), p. 202. See also A. O. Anderson, *Early Sources of Scottish History*, 2 vols. (Edinburgh, 1922), I, 13.

26. A. P. Forbes (ed.), *The Lives of S. Ninian and S. Kentigern*, The Historians of Scotland Series, V (Edinburgh, 1874), p. 69.

27. *Trioedd Ynys Prydein*, p. 466.

Professor Kenneth Jackson [28] is not completely persuaded. In the case of St. Kentigern we probably are dealing with fictional adventures attached to real people. If that is so, it does not matter whether Morken was Morgant. What does matter is that the name had attracted to it an unsavory reputation. To the North British audience, if a man bore the name of Morgan, Morgant, Morken, or something similar, he was expected to be a tyrannical overlord. Thus, when the name *Morgan* is attached to the name of the usurper who slew Tristan's father, one may well believe that the usurper was so named because the name would have meaning to a North British audience who knew that Morgant was the murderer of Urien and would expect the bearer of such a name to be a wicked person.

URGAN

Similar deductions may be drawn from the name *Urgan,* which was borne by a giant whom Tristan killed as a favor to the Welsh duke who gave him the dog Petit Crû. This passage appears only in Thomas [29] and his derivatives, Brother Robert [30] and Gottfried von Strassburg.[31] *Urgan* appears to be another form of the name Urien. According to Professor Jackson the name **Urgen* occupies an intermediary position between Old Welsh *Urbgen* and Modern Welsh *Urien.*[32] He says elsewhere that the spelling *Urgen* was used in Welsh in about the eleventh century.[33] The Urien who is mentioned by Nennius as an ally of Morgant and other Men of the North is not necessarily an antagonistic giant, although to his enemies he might have seemed so. But another figure derived from Urien supports this

28. Kenneth Jackson, "The Sources for the Life of St. Kentigern," *Studies in the Early British Church,* ed. Nora K. Chadwick (Cambridge, Eng., 1958), pp. 312–13.

29. Bédier, *Le Roman de Tristan par Thomas,* I, 217 ff.; *The Romance of Tristan and Iseult,* trans. Hilaire Belloc and Paul Rosenfeld (Garden City, N.Y., 1956; reprinted, New York, n.d.), pp. 132 ff.

30. Loomis, *Tristram and Ysolt,* pp. 171 ff.; Kölbing, *Tristan-sage,* Chaps. LXII–LXIII.

31. Gottfried von Strassburg, *Tristram und Isolt,* ed. A. Closs, 2d rev. ed. (Oxford, 1947), pp. 134 f. A. T. Hatto (ed. and trans.), *Gottfried von Strassburg Tristan with the Surviving Fragments of the Tristan of Thomas* (Harmondsworth, Middlesex, and Baltimore, 1960), pp. 249 ff.

32. Jackson, *Language and History in Early Britain,* p. 439.

33. Jackson, "The Sources for the Life of St. Kentigern," p. 285.

identification. In the *Didot Perceval*[34] Urbains guards the Perilous Ford and must be overcome by Perceval. The name *Urbains* has been identified as a form of *Urien*.[35] Although identification here is not positive, it seems probable that the name *Urgan*, as it appears in Thomas, is derived from an eleventh-century form of *Urien*, another name from the North.

ISOLT

As we have seen, the name *Isolt* is derived from the Welsh name *Essyllt*, which is mentioned in several triads and in the *Ystoria Trystan*, where she is the wife of March son of Meirchiawn and Trystan's mistress. The name, according to Professor Jackson, may be ultimately derived from the British or pre-Roman hypothetical **Adsiltia*, meaning "she who is gazed at."[36] It has appeared in a number of Welsh genealogies as *Etthil*. From this information there is little to connect the name with the environment of the North. But one triad gives us a clue, Triad 80 from MS. Peniarth 47:

> Three Faithless Wives of the Island of Britain. Three daughters of Culfanawyd of Britain:
> Essyllt Fair-Hair (Trystan's mistress),
> and Penarwan (wife of Owain son of Urien),
> and Bun, wife of Fflamddwyn.
> And one was more faithless than those three:
> Gwenhwyfar, Arthur's wife, since she shamed a better man than any (of the others).[37]

Owain son of Urien is, of course, one of the Men of the North. Speculation has been made of Fflamddwyn's identity. It is believed that the name, which means "Flamebearer," is a sobriquet attached to one of the English leaders slain by Owain.[38] If so, he too dwelt in the North, perhaps in Bernicia, an Anglo-Saxon kingdom on the northeast coast of England, a kingdom which historically provided

---

34. William Roach (ed.), *The Didot Perceval* (Philadelphia, 1941), pp. 195 ff. Dell Skeels, *The Romance of Perceval in Prose* (Seattle, 1961), pp. 38 ff.

35. Roger Sherman Loomis, "The Combat at the Ford in the 'Didot Perceval,'" *Modern Philology*, XLIII, No. 1 (1945), 63–71, reprinted in *Wales and the Arthurian Legend* (Cardiff, 1956), pp. 91–104.

36. *Language and History in Early Britain*, p. 709.

37. Bromwich, *Trioedd Ynys Prydein*, p. 200.

38. *Ibid.*, pp. 351 f.

antagonists for both Urien and Owain. Thus, with the exception of Arthur, whose actual identity is beyond the scope of this study, the men in the triads are of the North, albeit from different political entities: Trystan from Pictland, Owain from Rheged, and Fflam-ddwyn possibly from Bernicia.

The triad states that the three faithless ladies were the daughters of Culfanawyd of Britain or Kulvanawyt Prydein. Such relationships, certainly, have no historical meaning; they are probably little more than mnemonic conveniences. Still, the name *Kulvanawyt Prydein* is of interest because it too has northern associations. Mrs. Bromwich says that *Prydein,* which means "Britain," probably represents its homophone *Prydyn,* which means "Pictland." Furthermore, the name *Kulvanawyt* (that is *Kul—manawyt*) contains the element *manaw,* which appears in the name *Manau Guotodin,* which was given to a land in the vicinity of today's Edinburgh.[39] The exploits of the heroes of Manau Guotodin appeared in the *Gododdin,* a body of poems appearing in *The Book of Aneirin.*[40] Thus Mrs. Bromwich implies that the name of Essyllt's father, Kulvanawyt Prydein, has associations with the North.[41]

This is not to say that we know Essyllt was a Girl of the North. We know nothing for certain. But in the mind of someone and probably in the minds of his audience, the name *Essyllt* was associated with people like Owain and Fflamddwyn and a place like Manau Guotodin, all flourishing in the North about the year 600. Thus Essyllt, by association, joins Kynvarch, Drust, Morgant, and Urgen, all of whose names were borne by Northern heroes.

LOONOIS, MORROIS

Even some place names reflect the North. *Loonois,* the name of Tristan's traditional home, it is agreed, comes from the name *Lothian,* which was given to an area around Edinburgh, while *Mor-*

---

39. Nora K. Chadwick, "Early Learning and Culture in North Wales," *Studies in the Early British Church,* ed. Nora K. Chadwick (Cambridge, Eng., 1958), p. 77.
40. Sir Ifor Williams (ed.), *Canu Aneurin* (Cardiff, 1938), pp. xiv ff. Kenneth Jackson, "The Arthur of History," *ALMA,* p. 3.
41. *Trioedd Ynys Prydein,* p. 331.

rois, the name of the forest which sheltered Tristan and Isolt, may correspond to the Scottish place name *Moray.*[42]

In summary, many proper names of the story of Tristan have some association with the North. Whenever it was that these names came into the story, the audience must have been familiar with the heroic North British names. The conclusion presents itself that such an audience was made up of North British people. Thus is reinforced one argument of this study: that the story originated in North Britain and then moved to Ireland and to Wales. From Wales it moved to wherever the Tristan story was known.

42. Roger Sherman Loomis, "A Survey of Tristan Scholarship after 1911," appended to the 2d ed. of Gertrude Schoepperle's *Tristan and Isolt* (New York, 1959), II, 572.

Chapter Seven ✠ ✠

THE RELUC-
TANT LOVER

N THE LAST THREE CHAPTERS I have suggested that many proper names from the Tristan story had their origin in the heroic age of North Britain, the sixth century. As examples I have used forms of the names *Tristan, Mark, Morgan, Urgen, Isolt, Morrois,* and *Loonois.* In a previous chapter I said that the cultural centers of the North British during the heroic age and the several following centuries were the monasteries. The inference is that the story was first told in North Britain. I think it was, and as further evidence I offer now an examination of the major theme common to the Tristan story and to the majority of its known analogues: the reluctant lover. In this chapter I hope to demonstrate three points:

1. The reluctant lover theme appeared in the prototype of *Tristan and Isolt* and its Irish analogues.

2. The reluctant lover theme has a classical origin.

3. The best possible environment for adapting a classical or other pagan tale to local heroes and situations was provided during the monastic period of North Britain, where monasteries in the sixth, seventh, and eighth centuries contained people most likely to know such a tale and to refashion it with local heroes for local audiences.

THE SECOND ISOLT ▨

The reluctant lover is innocently unaware that he is loved by the heroine, who is usually the wife of one whom he respects and has no wish to injure. Disloyal to her husband, the heroine approaches the hero, and their liaison, whether it is real or supposed, invariably leads to tragedy. Usually the heroine elopes with the hesitant hero, often to a forest, where their union is consummated. But in other examples the hero is horrified by the lady's proposals and flees alone to the forest. In either case he chooses the forest because he is an accomplished woodsman.

Tristan and Isolt is a sophisticated development of this story. Many of the original elements are there: the disloyal wife, the union in the forest, and the tragedy. But the object of the hero's reluctance changes from Isolt the Queen to Isolt of the White Hands, a sub-heroine whose creation was necessary when Tristan became bound to the heroine not by her request but by a love potion. Tristan's relationship to the second Isolt, as well as to the first, shows a number of similarities to the many Celtic tales of the reluctant lover.

Let us, at the risk of being repetitious, recapitulate the part of the Tristan story dealing with the reluctant lover theme as it appears in Eilhart's version. Eilhart says [1] that Tristan traveled to the land of King Howel. There he learned that the King was under siege by a lord named Rivalin of Nantes, who wished to win King Howel's daughter by force. All of Howel's allies except his son Kaherdin had left him. Tristan offered his services to the King and as his first duty challenged Rivalin in single combat. Rivalin was defeated, and Tristan exacted from him a promise to abandon any future designs upon Howel's daughter. The grateful Howel and his son Kaherdin then offered the hand of the King's daughter to Tristan. The name of this prize was Isolt.

Tristan accepted his reward and lived with his bride for more than a year, but during this time she remained a virgin. His wife did not speak of her situation until once while riding across a stream she remarked in the presence of Kaherdin that the splashing water was more daring under her garments than had been the hand of any knight. Kaherdin was prepared to slay Tristan for insulting his sister, but Tristan convinced his brother-in-law that he loved another, the fairest woman on earth, and offered to show her to him.

---

1. Eilhart von Oberge, *Tristrant*, ed. Franz Lichtenstein, *Quellen und Forschungen zur Sprach- und Culturgeschichte*, XIX (Strasbourg, 1877), ll. 5488 ff. Gertrude Schoepperle, *Tristan and Isolt: A Study of the Sources of the Romance*, 2 vols. (Frankfurt and London, 1913; reprinted, New York, 1959), I, 38 ff.

Kaherdin and Tristan sailed to Cornwall, where Kaherdin saw Queen Isolt and understood Tristan's reluctance to touch Isolt, his wife. After some adventures they returned to the land of King Howel, and Tristan finally consummated his marriage with the second Isolt.

Marriage to a lady bearing the same name as the hero's loved one occurs in an Arabic story which Professor Loomis has offered as a source of this episode.[2] In this tale the hero, Kais, was forced by his father to abandon his wife, Lobna, because the marriage had been childless. Kais then married a second Lobna, at the insistence of her brother, but did not consummate his second marriage.

The Tristan story was not the only romance to be influenced by such a pattern. Miss Schoepperle[3] shows that in other romances the hero, separated from the heroine, is presented with a royal virgin as an award for his exploits. Usually the hero remains loyal to his mistress, and often the name of the royal virgin is the same as or suggestive of the heroine's name.

The second Isolt, then, is apparently a result of the introduction of the love potion and its accompanying need for a new heroine as the object of the hero's reluctance. The convention of courtly love, with its Arabic (or other Eastern) antecedents, its fidelity to the unobtainable mistress, and its wide dispersion among the eleventh- and twelfth-century European romances, is apparent.

Tristan, when he is confronted by the second Isolt, is a reluctant lover. That is, he is thrown into close association with a desirable young woman, yet contrary to normal expectation he refuses to touch her. Still this young woman is not the wife of the hero's lord, nor does the hero flee to the forest with or without her. Those elements are reserved for Tristan's relationship with the first Isolt. Tristan's reason for his actions with the second Isolt is fidelity to the mistress he left in Cornwall, and his behavior conforms to the requirements of

---

2. Roger Sherman Loomis (ed. and trans.), *The Romance of Tristram and Ysolt*, new rev. ed. (New York, 1951), p. xxviii. See also Roger Sherman Loomis, "Problems of the Tristan Legend," *Romania*, LIII (1927), 98 f. For more of the story of Kais and Lobna see Samuel Singer, "Arabische und europäische Poesie in Mittelalter," *Abhandlungen der Preussischen Akademie der Wissenschaften*, No. 13 (1918), pp. 8–10; J. van Dam, "Tristan-probleme II. Die Frage nach dem Urtristan," *Neophilologus* XV (1929–30), 97 f.

3. *Tristan and Isolt*, I, 162 ff.

courtly love. He is a reluctant lover but follows the courtly pattern in his combined relationships with the two Isolts. It seems reasonable that once there was only one Isolt and that the second is a doubling of the first.

Tristan's fidelity to his absent mistress is more fragile than is the fidelity of the ideal courtly love hero. According to Eilhart, after Tristan and Kaherdin returned from Cornwall, Tristan consummated his marriage with the second Isolt, and "Tristan's joy was untroubled." [4] Now such inconstancy was not unknown to the medieval hero. Consider for example the numerous adventures of the Lanzelet of Ulrich von Zatzikhoven; [5] the more familiar Lancelot, who was the unwilling lover of Elaine; [6] and the many adventures of Gawain.[7] Monogamy was rarely the most outstanding characteristic of either the primitive hero or the medieval hero derived from him. But the romance of Tristan is another matter. It is a love story of a man and a woman continually frustrated by the difficulties of their particular relationship; it is a story of two enchanted people bound by a love potion; [8] and with the exception of the one extra affair it is a tale of lifelong love and, on the part of Tristan,[9] lifelong fidelity.[10] Tristan is not Gawain or Lancelot. He exists to be Isolt's lover,

---

4. As quoted by Schoepperle, *Tristan and Isolt*, I, 49. The original is "sîne vroude die was stête." See Eilhart, *Tristrant*, l, 7079.

5. Roger Sherman Loomis (ed.), and K. G. T. Webster (trans.), *Lanzelet* by Ulrich von Zatzikhoven (New York, 1951), especially n. 85.

6. Eugène Vinaver (ed.), *The Works of Sir Thomas Malory*, 3 vols. (Oxford, 1954), Book XI, Chaps. ii ff.

7. Gawain's many adventures are too numerous to list here. It is enough to say that whenever the reputation of any hero was attached to the reputation of Gawain, the great love affair of that hero would also become an achievement of Gawain.

8. In Eilhart the potion lasts only for four years: *Tristrant*, l. 2283. In Thomas the potion is apparently for life: Loomis, *Tristram and Ysolt*, p. 133; Eugen Kölbing (ed.), *Die nordische und die englische Version der Tristan-sage*, 2 vols. (Heilbronn, 1882), I, 56 f.; Joseph Bédier (ed.), *Le Roman de Tristan par Thomas*, SATF, No. LIII, 2 vols. (Paris, 1902–5), I, 143 ff. The same with Gottfried: A. T. Hatto (trans.), *Gottfried von Strassburg Tristan with the Surviving Fragments of the Tristran of Thomas* (Harmondsworth, Middlesex, and Baltimore, 1960), p. 197.

9. Isolt's submission to Mark could hardly be called infidelity to her lover. Mark was her husband, and no medieval audience would have expected her to act in any other way.

10. Tristan's reputation for fidelity was legendary. The troubadour Cercamon

and infidelity becomes him less than it does other medieval heroes. Thomas omitted any reference to Tristan's consummation of his marriage. In doing so he created an orthodox tale in the Continental tradition of courtly love instead of in the insular Celtic tradition of the reluctant lover.

It has long been recognized that there exist in Ireland tales and fragments of tales with episodes similar to those found in the Continental Tristan. Chief among these and emphasized by Miss Schoepperle [11] is *The Pursuit after Diarmaid and Gráinne*.[12] Diarmaid was a hero who eloped with Gráinne, the wife of his uncle, Fionn, the chief of the Fianna. She had seen a "love spot" on Diarmaid's forehead and motivated by magic had fallen in love with him.[13] She put a sleeping charm on the assembled Fianna and persuaded the reluctant Diarmaid to flee with her to the forest. Tales about the Fianna, a band of Irish hunters and warriors, may have been told since the sixth century.[14] No evidence exists, however, that *Diarmaid and Gráinne* is any older than the ninth century.[15]

---

in the twelfth century contrasted his unfaithful mistress with the steadfast Tristan. See Alfred Jeanroy (ed. and trans.), *Les Poésies de Cercamon, Les Classiques français du moyen âge*, IV (1922), vs. 38. See also Rita Lejeune, "The Troubadours," *ALMA*, p. 396.

11. *Tristan and Isolt*, II, 395 ff.

12. The most complete edition is Standish Hayes O'Grady (ed. and trans.), *Toruigheacht Dhiarmuda agus Ghrainne—The Pursuit After Diarmaid and Gráinne, Transactions of the Ossianic Society for the Year 1855*, II (Dublin, 1857). Fragments of the story may be found in John G. Campbell, *The Fians, Waifs and Strays of Celtic Tradition, Argyllshire Series*, No. IV (London, 1891), 52 ff.; and J. H. Lloyd, O. J. Bergin, and Gertrude Schoepperle, "The Death of Diarmaid," *RC*, XXXIII (1912), 157–79. See also Tom Peete Cross and C. H. Slover (eds.), *Ancient Irish Tales* (London, n.d.), pp. 370 ff.

13. The "love spot" on Diarmaid's forehead caused all women who saw him to love him (see Campbell, *The Fians*, p. 52). Note that although Gráinne was motivated by magic to love Diarmaid, Diarmaid had no magical reason to love Gráinne. Tristan and Isolt, on the other hand, drank the magic potion together and were mutually enchanted. A magic inducement to love was common to the Irish, Roman, and other storytellers. Cf. Schoepperle, *Tristan and Isolt*, II, 401 ff.; Antti Aarne and Stith Thompson, *The Types of the Folktale*, FF Communications No. 184 (Helsinki, 1961), Type 580; Stith Thompson, *Motif-Index of Folk Literature*, rev. ed., 6 vols. (Bloomington, Ind., 1955–58), D.1355, D.1900.

14. Schoepperle, *Tristan and Isolt*, II, 395. For a summary of scholarship concerning the historical and legendary Fianna the reader is referred to T. F. O'Rahilly, *Early Irish History and Mythology* (Dublin, 1946), pp. 271–81.

15. James Carney, *Studies in Irish Literature and History* (Dublin, 1955), p.

Miss Schoepperle observed [16] that *Diarmaid and Gráinne* contains at least one major parallel to the Tristan legend. As Diarmaid and Gráinne were crossing a forest stream, Gráinne complained that as bold as Diarmaid was the splashing water was bolder than he. On being thus taunted, Diarmaid abandoned his restraint and slept for the first time with Gráinne.[17] Both Eilhart[18] and Thomas[19] use this incident which parallels the one involving Tristan, Isolt of the White Hands, and Kaherdin.

In the Continental versions of the story, Tristan neglected his wife because he was loyal to his mistress. But another situation exists in the Irish *Diarmaid and Gráinne*. In the latter, Diarmaid ignored Gráinne because of his loyalty to Fionn, who was Diarmaid's uncle and Gráinne's husband. The difference in the two situations is significant. Tristan was a reluctant lover because he was faithful to his mistress. Diarmaid was a reluctant lover because he was faithful to his uncle. But after being taunted, both Diarmaid and Tristan[20] lost their reluctance, although, as I remarked above, Tristan was stepping out of character when he did so. The incident of the splashing water, leading to a sexual union between the hero and a woman whom he had not desired, is much more at home in the Irish version, where the conflict is between self and lord, than in the Continental, where the conflict is between wife and mistress.

Because the incident of the splashing waters brings more meaning to the plot of *Diarmaid and Gráinne* than it does to the plot of the Continental Tristan, I think that the Diarmaid example represents the earlier tradition. Originally the hero was reluctant to seduce the wife of his uncle but did so when taunted. If, then, the Continental version contains a development of this situation, in an earlier version the splashing waters incident related not to Isolt of the White

---

195; Schoepperle, *Tristan and Isolt*, II, 398 f. Miss Schoepperle gives no evidence that the story is any older than the ninth century, although she assumes it is based on a much older Irish tradition.

16. *Tristan and Isolt*, II, 415 ff.

17. O'Grady, *The Pursuit After Diarmaid and Gráinne*, p. 108. O'Grady does not translate this passage.

18. *Tristrant*, ll. 6143 ff.

19. Loomis, *Tristram and Ysolt*, pp. 227 ff.; Kölbing, *Tristan-sage*, I, 95 f.; Bédier, *Le Roman de Tristan par Thomas*, I, 323 ff.

20. In Eilhart only, *Tristrant*, ll. 7070 ff.

Hands but to Isolt the Queen. Professor Carney [21] believes that the splashing waters incident and the hero's reluctance were transferred to the second Isolt when the love potion was introduced to the story. For if Tristan were bound to his mistress by magic, he could not be a reluctant lover. In fact, it seems probable that the second Isolt was created to receive the hero's reluctance, although her part in the story might well have been suggested by the Arabic *Kais and Lobna* and the other medieval tales in which a hero, absent from his mistress, is awarded a royal virgin who often bears a name like that of the absent heroine.

THE SEPARATING SWORD ✻

That the Tristan of the early version showed a coldness toward his Isolt is further indicated by the matter of the sword between the lovers. Eilhart [22] and Béroul [23] say that when Tristan and Isolt slept in the forest, they customarily placed a sword between them. Béroul does not explain this peculiar practice, and Eilhart wonders at its strangeness.[24] Thomas, as usual, rationalizes by saying that on one particular occasion when they returned exhausted to their forest dwelling, they threw themselves down to sleep. Tristan's sword happened to fall between them, and there it remained.[25] Eilhart wonders with good reason. The separating sword has no part in the story. Tristan and Isolt at the time of the incident were living as man and mistress, and even if they had expected Mark to spy on them on a given day there was no reason for them to sleep customarily with a sword between them.

Again, in *The Pursuit after Diarmaid and Gráinne* there is a similar incident, but in the Irish tale it is an organic part of the story, where in the Continental versions it is not. When Diarmaid eloped with Gráinne, he resolved not to touch her and kept his resolution until the incident of the splashing waters. Prior to that, however, it was his custom to sleep near her but separated from her

---

21. *Studies*, pp. 202 f.
22. *Tristrant*, ll. 4586 ff.
23. A. Ewert (ed.), *The Romance of Tristan by Beroul* (Oxford, 1953), p. 54, ll. 1805 f.
24. *Tristrant*, ll. 4586 ff.
25. Loomis, *Tristram and Ysolt*, pp. 180 f.; Kölbing, *Tristan-sage*, I, 81 f.; Bédier, *Le Roman de Tristan par Thomas*, I, 240 f.

by a large stone. Thus, he reasoned, if Fionn were to surprise them while they slept, he would see that their relationship was innocent.[26]

Like the incident of the splashing waters, the separation between the lovers is an integral part of the Irish story, where in the Continental romances it is either meaningless or rationalized.[27] Diarmaid slept apart from Gráinne in order to prove his innocence to the pursuing Fionn. Tristan had no innocence to prove, yet he maintained the tradition by utilizing a bare sword. Obviously *The Pursuit after Diarmaid and Gráinne* represents the older tradition, and in the older tradition the hero at this point was genuinely innocent. That is, he was a reluctant lover, and his reluctance was caused by his loyalty to the heroine's husband.

THE PRIMARY LOVE STORY

This, then, may be said about the reluctant lover. In an earlier version of the story, the hero was loyal to his lord although he fled to the forest with his lord's wife. Finally, however, he was taunted into accepting her as his mistress. But in the formation of the Continental versions the love potion made any restraint the hero had toward his uncle's wife impossible. Thus the hero's reluctance was transferred to a second Isolt created to receive it. The separating sword (or stone) was retained with the original heroine, where it has no meaning once the love potion has been drunk. The splashing waters incident moved on to be attached to the new heroine, the second Isolt. Originally the reluctant hero was an integral part of the primary love story, and this relationship is reflected in other analogous stories besides *Diarmaid and Gráinne*.

IRISH ANALOGUES

A number of these ninth-century Irish tales have been collected by Professor Carney.[28] Each contains some characteristic or incident

---

26. Campbell, *The Fians*, p. 56. In O'Grady's version, p. 28, the lovers sleep at a distance from each other; no mention of the stone is made.

27. As it is in the version by Gottfried von Strassburg, who introduces it as a device to deceive Mark. See A. T. Hatto (trans.), *Gottfried von Strassburg Tristan*, p. 272. See also Bédier, *Le Roman de Tristan par Thomas*, I, 245.

28. *Studies*, pp. 189 ff.

which has a parallel in the Tristan theme, suggesting that behind the ninth-century Irish tales and behind Tristan and Isolt lay a single source story which influenced in one way or another the Irish tales and the Tristan legend. All of these tales, and this is of primary importance, show some connection with the theme of the reluctant lover, the hero who was loved by a woman who belonged to another. Six tales which will be discussed now are *Baile Binnbérlach mac Buain—Baile of the Clear Voice Son of Buan*,[29] *Scéla Cano Meic Gartnáin—The Story of Cano Son of Gartnán*,[30] *Tochmarc Treblainne—The Wooing of Treblann*,[31] *Comracc Liadaine ocus Cuirithir—The Meeting of Liadan and Curithir*,[32] *Tochmarc Becfhola—The Wooing of Becfhola*,[33] and *Longes Mac n-Uislenn—The Exile of the Sons of Uisliu*.[34]

29. Summarized by Carney, *Studies*, pp. 223 ff.; and by Myles Dillon, *The Cycles of the Kings* (Oxford, 1946), pp. 27–29. See also Eugene O'Curry (ed.), *Lectures on the Manuscript Materials of Ancient Irish History* (Dublin, 1861), pp. 472–75; Kuno Meyer, "Baile Binnbérlach mac Buain—Baile of the Clear Voice Son of Buan," *RC*, XIII (1892), 220–27. Hereafter this story will be referred to as *Baile*.

30. Summarized by Carney, *Studies*, p. 215; and by Dillon, *The Cycles of the Kings*, pp. 79–83. See also D. A. Binchy, *Scéla Cano Meic Gartnáin*, ed. from *The Yellow Book of Lecan* with Introduction, Notes, Glossary, and Indexes, *Medieval and Modern Irish Series*, XVIII (Dublin, 1963); R. Thurneysen (trans.), "Eine irische Parallele zur Tristan-Sage," *ZRPh*, XLIII (1923), 388–402. Hereafter this story will be referred to as *Cano*.

31. Summarized by Carney, *Studies*, pp. 206 ff. A full text can be found in Kuno Meyer (ed.), "Tochmarc Treblainne," *ZCP*, XIII (1919–21), 166 ff. See also R. Thurneysen, *Die irische Helden- und Königsage bis zum siebzehnten Jahrhundert* (Halle, 1921), pp. 296 f. Hereafter this story will be referred to as *Treblann*.

32. Summarized by Carney, *Studies*, pp. 221 f. See also Kuno Meyer (ed. and trans.), *Liadain and Curithir, An Irish Love Story of the Ninth Century* (London, 1902). Cf. Schoepperle, *Tristan and Isolt*, II, 553 ff. Hereafter this story will be referred to as *Liadan*.

33. Summarized by Carney, *Studies*, p. 229; and by Dillon, *The Cycles of the Kings*, pp. 75–78. See also Standish Hayes O'Grady (ed.), *Silva Gadelica (I–XXXI)*, 2 vols. (London, 1892), I, 85 ff. Translations may be found in Cross and Slover, *Ancient Irish Tales*, pp. 533–37. Cf. Myles Dillon, "The Wooing of Becfhola and the Stories of Cano, Son of Gartnán," *Modern Philology*, XLIII, I (1945), 11 ff. A very readable and delightful rendition was made by James Stephens, *Irish Fairy Tales* (New York, 1920; reprinted, 1962), pp. 99 ff. Hereafter this story will be referred to as *Becfhola*.

34. Vernam Hull (ed. and trans.), *Longes Mac n-Uislenn—The Exile of the Sons of Uisliu* (New York, 1949).

The extant text of *Baile* is probably no older than the tenth or eleventh century,[35] although the language of the story is from the ninth century.[36] Baile Binnbérlach son of Buan was a delight to all who saw him and the chosen lover of Ailinn daughter of Lugain. He traveled from the North to the South to meet her but met a specter who informed him, falsely, that Ailinn was dead. As a result Baile died of grief. The specter then reported Baile's death to Ailinn, who also died of grief. They were buried separately, and trees grew from their graves. Tablets were made from the wood of these trees, and at the feast of Samain[37] these tablets sprang together so that no man could part them.

Baile, of course, is a garbled version of what I believe was the original story and contains echoes of the other tales. The hero Baile was the chosen lover of the heroine Ailinn. That is, he did not woo her but was wooed by her. This, naturally, is a characteristic of the reluctant lover, although from this particular version both the reason for reluctance (i.e. the old husband for whom the hero has loyalty) and the reluctance itself are missing. Like Diarmaid, who had a "love spot," Baile was beloved by all who saw him or heard of him.[38] He traveled from the North to the South like Cano and Cuirithir, heroes to be discussed shortly.[39] Like Tristan, Baile died of grief as the result of false information, although the linear distance between himself and his mistress was lessening.[40] Like Tristan and Isolt, Baile and Ailinn were buried in graves from which grew

35. Dillon, *The Cycles of the Kings,* p. 27.
36. Carney, *Studies,* p. 195.
37. Samain night or Halloween was traditionally a time of magic. Cf. below, p. 128, n. 32.
38. To be beloved just by those who saw him was not enough. Baile had to be loved because of his reputation so that Ailinn could choose him without having seen him. This motif recurs, of course, when Isolt chooses Tristan as her harp teacher without having seen him.
39. If Tristan was originally from Pictland and Isolt from or connected with Manau Guotodin on the south bank of the Firth of Forth, or even if Isolt was from Ireland, then Tristan too must have traveled to the South. See Map 7 below, p. 113.
40. Baile died while traveling toward Ailinn. In the extant versions of the Tristan story, Tristan died while Isolt was journeying to him. I maintain, however, that in an earlier version of the Tristan story it was Tristan who was traveling toward Isolt when the tragedy occurred. See below, p. 152.

magical trees which ultimately joined so that no man could part them.[41]

Most of the characters in *Cano* actually existed, but they were not historical contemporaries. For instance Aedán Mac Gabráin died in 606 and Cano himself in 688.

In the time of Aedán Mac Gabráin, King of Scottish Dalriada, Cano son of Gartnán and grandson of Aedán, was attacked by his grandfather and was forced to flee to Ireland. He went first to Ulster, where the Kings Diarmait and Bláthmac received him with honor. But the wrath of Aedán followed him; and warned by Diarmait's daughter (who had loved Cano before meeting him), Cano fled to Connacht, where he met Créd, wife of Marcán. Créd had heard tales about Cano and had fallen in love with him before she had met him. At a feast at the house of her father, Guaire, Créd put a sleeping charm into the wine of all those present except herself and Cano. Créd then begged Cano to be her lover, but he refused saying that he would send for her after he became king of Scotland. He entrusted her with a stone warning her never to break it, for he would live only as long as the stone remained whole. Years later when Cano was king of Scotland, he met annually with Créd. On one assignation Cano arrived by ship after having been so badly wounded that his face was covered with blood. Créd, watching from the land, was horrified at his appearance, dashed her head against a rock, and died. The stone broke when she fell; Cano himself died within three days.

A number of points here are paralleled in other Irish tales and in the Continental Tristan stories. Both Créd and the daughter of King Diarmait of Ulster loved the hero before seeing him, as did Ailinn and others. Cano, like Diarmaid the lover of Gráinne and like Tristan in Brittany, was a reluctant lover who first refused,

---

41. Professor Carney observes that the particular metaphor used for the joining of the wood—two wooden tablets joined like a vine around a branch—is unsuitable and is a remnant of an earlier story where a vine grew from one adjacent grave and a branch from the other. That is to say that *Baile* itself descends from an early form of the Tristan story. See *Studies*, pp. 224 f. For more about the tree and the vine see Peter Demetz, "The Elm and the Vine: Notes Toward the History of a Marriage Topos," *PMLA*, LXXIII, No. 5, Pt. 1 (Dec., 1958), 521–32.

then later accepted, the advances of the lady. Créd's husband was
Marcán, whose name apparently is related to the name of King
Mark of the Tristan stories.[42] The sleeping charm which Créd put
upon the company is paralleled by the charm which Gráinne, in
her pursuit of Diarmaid, also put on an assembled group.[43] The
death of Créd is similar, I believe, to the death of the original Isolt.[44]
Créd saw the apparently wounded Cano while she was on the land
and he was on the sea. The reason for her error was a color, not the
black of a sail but the blood red of Cano's face. On seeing his red-
dened face she was persuaded that he was mortally wounded and
dashed her head against a rock.

Treblann is a late [45] conglomeration which includes many motifs
besides those few which are relevant to the Tristan pattern. It is a
tale of Froech, one of the principals of the *Táin Bó Cúalnge*, the
great Irish epic. Treblann daughter of Froech son of Oengus loved
Froech son of Fidach Foltruad before she met him. She sent a
woman attendant to the younger Froech to say that she would elope
with him. In spite of the armed opposition of Treblann's foster
father, Coirpre, they did elope and after various adventures returned to Froech's home. There Froech discovered that his cattle
had been stolen. These were the very cattle he had promised Ailill
and Medb for the coming cattle raid of Cúalnge, and he was determined to retrieve them, even from as far away as the Alps.[46]
He left Treblann with a stone which he assured her would remain
whole as long as he lived. But the stone did not prove to be a faithful token. Enemies of Froech broke it by magic, although Froech
was not dead. Treblann was deceived and died of grief.

42. This is my own proposal. See above, pp. 70 ff. For a different opinion see
Binchy, *Scéla Cano.*
43. Professor Carney suggests that this motif of the sleeping charm is the
basic suggestion for the love potion of the Continental versions. See *Studies*, p.
216. I wonder. Love charms are extraordinarily prevalent in folklore.
44. Later in this study I shall maintain that the original Isolt was the watcher
on the shore who saw the black sails and in the belief that Tristan was dead
killed herself by smashing her head on rocks at the foot of a cliff. See below,
p. 152 ff.
45. The language of the tale, according to Professor Carney, implies that it
was composed between 1100 and 1250. See *Studies*, p. 211, n. 1.
46. That is, to attend to his career before his personal romance, as did the
heroes in *Cano* and *Becfhola* and the heroine in *Liadan.*

The combination of the chosen (i.e. reluctant) lover and the death based upon a deception suggests that *Treblann* is another example of an Irish tale related to the tradition which produced the story of Tristan. Froech, of course, cannot die in the tale, for the audience knew that he died in the *Táin Bó Cúalnge*.

Liadan is a reluctant lover story in reverse. That is, the heroine is reluctant. Still it must be related to the cycle here under consideration because, although the positions are reversed, the principals play their roles faithfully, conforming to the original parts in the legend. The story is old [47] and is close to the Tristan theme in that it presents the moral conflict between love and duty. Liadan, a poetess, was loved by Cuirithir. Cuirithir gave a feast for her and begged her to love him. Like the male heroes of similar stories, she asked him to wait while she attended to her career.[48] In time he traveled south to Munster, where she fled to the forest with him. After their forest idyll, they met a local saint and agreed to abide by his rule. He permitted them to sleep together but placed a young clerical student between them.[49] Eventually Cuirithir forswore any further union with Liadan and went on a pilgrimage. Liadan followed him, but he put to sea in a small boat and was never heard from again. Liadan discovered the flagstone upon which he customarily prayed and remained on it until she died. When she was buried, it was placed over her face.[50]

Becfhola appears in a fourteenth-century manuscript,[51] although the language of the story is as old as the year 900.[52] Becfhola was the wife of Diarmait son of Aed Sláine, King of Tara.[53] She loved Crimthand, a young hostage whom Diarmait treated like a foster son. Crimthand at first did not return her affection and considered

---

47. Carney dates the present form of the story about 850 (*Studies*, p. 220).

48. Thus did the heroes of *Cano* and *Becfhola*.

49. Carney says that this student is reminiscent of the dwarf sent by King Mark to spy on Tristan and Isolt. See *Studies*, p. 222. But I think the student is far more reminiscent of the separating sword. Like the sword he was placed between the lovers, while the dwarf was allowed to be any place in the room.

50. Cuirithir's flagstone placed over the grave of Liadan is reminiscent of the union in death, in which trees from the graves are entwined.

51. Dillon, *The Cycles of the Kings*, p. 75.

52. Carney, *Studies*, p. 195.

53. This Diarmait was a historical figure who is said to have died in 664. See Dillon, *The Cycles of the Kings*, p. 75.

fleeing to the forest to escape her. Eventually, however, he agreed to a tryst with her, and Becfhola set out, accompanied by her maid, to the forest. Becfhola and her maid did not meet Crimthand because they were attacked by wolves. Becfhola fled to the island of the warrior Fland, who spent the night with her but did not touch her. She asked him to marry her, but he begged a postponement because he had to win his inheritance. Becfhola returned to the place where she had been attacked by wolves and discovered to her surprise that her maid, whom she had believed to be dead, was alive. They returned to Diarmait, but when Fland did win his inheritance, Becfhola left her husband to go to him.

Becfhola contains not only one reluctant lover who considers escape to the forest but also a second who sleeps next to a lady throughout the night but contrary to expectation refuses to touch her. Again there are the idyll in the forest and the hero who requests a postponement of his liaison with the heroine until he proves himself. The supposed death and resurrection of the maid is important and is reminiscent of Isolt and Brangien.

More famous than any of these tales is the story of Deirdre in *The Exile of the Sons of Uisliu,* which, according to the language of its earliest manuscript, was probably composed in the eighth or ninth century.[54] Deirdre, the beautiful young ward and fiancée of the old King Conchobar Mac Nessa, fell in love with Noíse Mac n-Uislenn even before she saw him. Noíse was a musician of such ability that when he sang two-thirds more milk than usual was milked from each cow that heard him. He and his brothers hunted as swiftly as hounds. Noíse was loyal to King Conchobar and hesitated to return Deirdre's love until she pulled his ears and threatened to shame him unless he would elope with her.

They fled to Scotland with Noíse's brothers, the other sons of Uisliu. There Deirdre's beauty so impressed a Scottish steward who saw Noíse and Deirdre sleeping that he advised his king to kill the sons of Uisliu in order to obtain Deirdre as his own prize. Noíse, his brothers, and Deirdre were forced to flee. They returned to Ireland under a safe-conduct pass, but there the sons of Uisliu were treacherously slain. Deirdre was kept captive by King Conchobar for a full year, during which time she never smiled.

54. Hull, *Longes Mac n-Uislenn,* pp. 30 ff.

Eventually she committed suicide by smashing her head against a rock.

The following should be noted: The essential Tristan pattern of the old king, young wife, and young lover is repeated in this tale. Noíse is a reluctant lover. He has no desire to elope with the betrothed of King Conchobar until she threatens him. He is a famed musician and a famed hunter, as was Tristan. Noíse and Deirdre are watched as they sleep, as are Diarmaid and Gráinne in the incident of the separating stone and as are Tristan and Isolt in the incident of the separating sword. Although the manner of Deirdre's suicide does not appear in *Tristan and Isolt*, it is similar to the suicide of Créd in *Cano*.

THE MAGIC COMPULSION TO LOVE

All of these reluctant lover tales, from the fragments to *Tristan and Isolt* itself, contain someone who loves unwillingly. There exists in each story the necessity for causing the reluctant lover to love, since obviously, if he is reluctant to love, he will not go against his own inclinations unless forced to. In a like manner, all of the heroines of these stories love a man who is reluctant to return this love. Here too a similar problem in story construction exists: how is the narrator to make his audience believe that a lady could fall in love under such circumstances? A number of solutions to this problem exist; some appear to be more sophisticated than others, although lack of sophistication alone is not a guarantee of chronological priority. The simple solution is to say that she loves him and carry on from there. A more intriguing development of this same approach is to explain that she loved him before she met him: thus Deirdre in *The Exile of the Sons of Uisliu;* Ailenn in *Baile;* Créd in *Cano;* Treblann in *Treblann;* and even Isolt, who chose Tristan to teach her to play the harp before she met him. A further refinement is a magic compulsion for the lady's love of the man: thus Diarmaid had his "love spot," and Baile was beloved by everyone.

The next step, or it could be a simultaneous one, would be some sort of natural or supernatural power invoked by the heroine to cause the innocent hero to feel the way she does. Miss Schoepperle [55]

---

55. *Tristan and Isolt*, II, 403.

suggested that Deirdre employed the Irish *geis*[56] upon Noíse when she said to him while grasping his ears: "These [are] two ears of shame and of derision . . . unless you take me away with you."[57] I am not completely convinced that this passage represents an actual *geis,* but Miss Schoepperle's suggestion is not without merit. Gráinne, when she wished to be alone with Diarmaid, employed a sleeping potion to anesthetize the entire company except her hero. Créd in *Cano* did exactly the same. Neither Gráinne nor Créd used a supernatural medicine, but the idea of a drink to effect the heroine's plans must have been an integral part of the story, for it not only appears in the two versions mentioned above but reappears in an altered form in *Tristan and Isolt* as the charmed drink. Thus the magic potion of the Continental versions of the story has a dual ancestry. It owes its magic powers to the tradition that Diarmaid had a "love spot" and that the other heroines fell in love unexplainedly before meeting their heroes. It owes its form as a potion to the sleeping draft tradition, which was reflected in the actions of both Gráinne and Créd. It differs markedly from both of its ancestral traditions in that it is innocently drunk by both Tristan and Isolt, and here Miss Schoepperle offers a clue when she says:

In France as in other European countries in the twelfth century it was part of the wedding ceremony to offer a drink to the couple after the consummation of the marriage. They are brought to the bridal bed by their friends and, after they have been left to themselves for a while, the nearest relatives, sometimes the whole company, enter the room and bring them a strengthening drink.[58]

That is, the custom of a couple drinking together belonged to twelfth-century France, and it is not surprising that the insular traditions make no mention of it at all. So it must have been the Continental redactors of the story who introduced the love potion in its most known form. This innovation, of course, changed the entire tone of the Tristan story, for once Tristan had drunk the love potion he could no longer be a reluctant lover, and, accordingly,

56. A *geis* is a sort of a charm; the perpetrator of it uses it to work his will upon the victim, and the victim must obey or suffer unfortunate consequences.
57. Hull, *Longes Mac n-Uislenn,* p. 63.
58. *Tristan and Isolt,* II, 407, n. 1.

the entire second Isolt sequence had to be created so that the reluctant lover parts of the story could be retained.

RELATION OF IRISH ANALOGUES TO TRISTAN LEGEND ▓

In the above pages I have discussed seven Irish tales of a reluctant lover: *Diarmaid and Gráinne, Baile, Cano, Treblann, Liadan, Becfhola,* and the *Exile of the Sons of Uisliu.* That they are related to each other seems obvious. The problem now is what is their relationship to the Tristan story. Because *Diarmaid and Gráinne* is so closely paralleled by the Tristan story, Miss Schoepperle and others have said that the Irish tale is a source of the story of Tristan.[59] I question that it is. Items appearing in the Tristan legend appear in some of the Irish tales of the reluctant lover yet are not included in *Diarmaid and Gráinne*. The first item is the character of the hero himself. Tristan is a famed musician and hunter. Nothing is said about Diarmaid's musical abilities, and although Diarmaid is a hunter, his accomplishments in that area are no more noteworthy than those of any member of the Fianna. But Noíse in the *Exile of the Sons of Uisliu* sang so well he could increase the output of a cow's milk and hunted well enough to outrun his quarry. Second, in *Diarmaid and Gráinne* there is no mention of a king named Mark or something similar, yet in *Cano* the old king is named Marcán. Third, in *Tristan and Isolt* the heroine falls in love with the hero's reputation, as she does in *Baile, Cano, Treblann,* and the *Exile of the Sons of Uisliu*. In *Diarmaid and Gráinne* she decides, after seeing him, that she loves Diarmaid. Fourth, in *Baile, Cano,* and *Liadan,* the hero traveled from North to South to meet the heroine. If Drust originally came from Pictland, Isolt originally from Manau Guotodin, and Mark originally from or near Strathclyde, all of which having been suggested earlier, then Drust like the others must have traveled from North to South. See Map 7 on p. 113. Fifth, in *Tristan and Isolt* there is false information

---

59. *Ibid.*, II, 396 ff. See also Roger Sherman Loomis, "Problems of the Tristan Legend," *Romania,* LIII (1927), 82 ff.; *Tristram and Ysolt,* p. xxi; and H. Newstead, "The Origin and Growth of the Tristan Legend," *ALMA,* p. 127.

CHART 2
THE RELUCTANT LOVER MOTIFS

Characteristics and Incidents	Diarmaid and Gráinne	Baile	Cano	Treblann	Liadan	Becfhola	Exile of the Sons of Uisliu	Tristan and Isolt
Reluctant lover	X	X	X	X	X	X	X	X
Hero a famed musician and hunter							X	X
Old king named Mark			X					X
Old king uncle to hero	X							X
Love of heroine for hero before she meets him		X	X	X			X	X
Request for delay by hero			X	X	X	X		
Supposed death of maid						X		X
Journey from North to South		X	X		X			
Old king married or betrothed to young heroine	X		X			X	X	X

Characteristics and Incidents	Diarmaid and Gráinne	Baile	Cano	Treblann	Liadan	Becfhola	Exile of the Sons of Uisliu	Tristan and Isolt
Charmed drink or "love spot"	X	X						X
Elopement, usually to the forest	X				X	X	X	X
Separating sword or other object, either real or suggested	X				X		X	X
Splashing waters	X							X
False information leading to death		X	X	X				X
Death depending on a voyage			X		X			X
Death by dashing one's head against a rock			X				X	
Union in death		X			X			X

leading to the death of one of the protagonists, as there is in
Baile, Cano, and *Treblann.* Diarmaid's death, which will be discussed in Chapter Nine, is a somewhat different matter. Sixth,
Diarmaid's death does not depend on a voyage, although the death
of a protagonist does in *Tristan and Isolt, Cano,* and *Liadan.*
Seventh, in *Tristan and Isolt,* but not in *Diarmaid and Gráinne,*
there is a symbolic union in death, just as there is in *Baile* and, in a
sense, in *Liadan.* Chart 2 indicates the prevalence of these and
other motifs.

Carney [60] and Dillon [61] have noted that *Cano, Treblann, Liadan,*
and *Becfhola* form a group distinguished by the hero (or in the
case of *Liadan,* the heroine) who must attend to his career before
he permits himself to woo the heroine. Evidently together they
descend from a subgroup [62] not including *Diarmaid and Gráinne,*
The Exile of the Sons of Uisliu, and *Baile.* As close as *Diarmaid
and Gráinne* is to the story of Tristan, it does not include many
elements of the Tristan story found in the subgroup. We must conclude, then, that behind *Diarmaid and Gráinne* and behind the subgroup lay a common ancestor. This story was close in form to much
of the Tristan story that we know today. And because the Tristan
story and even *Cano* in the Irish analogues contain names known
in North Britain, it is my belief that this common ancestor was
first told to an audience familiar with North British names; that is,
it was first told in North Britain.

FINGAL RÓNÁIN AND THE MYTH OF *HIPPOLYTUS* 🔲

In many of these tales the reluctant lover was an accomplished
woodsman who met a tragic end. Often, as in *Diarmaid and Gráinne,*

---

60. *Studies,* pp. 194 f.

61. "The Wooing of Becfhola and the Stories of Cano, Son of Gartnán,"
p. 11.

62. *Táin Bó Fraích,* an Irish eleventh-century tale, seems to be influenced
by this subgroup. It contains the chosen lover and the hero who must make a
journey. See Carney, *Studies,* pp. 1 ff.; and J. F. Campbell, *The Celtic Dragon
Myth* with *The Geste of Fraoch and the Dragon,* trans. George Henderson,
(Edinburgh, 1911), 1 ff.

The Exile of the Sons of Uisliu, Liadan, and *Becfhola,* there is an elopement or the suggestion of an elopement to the forest. Before closing this chapter I wish to discuss one more Irish reluctant lover, another accomplished woodsman who meets a tragic end. This is Mael Fhothartaig of *Fingal Rónáin—How Ronan Slew His Son,*[63] a tale apparently from the tenth century,[64] a tale which is not in the same story group as the others yet is related in such a way as to show the link between the Celtic reluctant lover and his earlier counterpart.

Rónán, the old king of Leinster, married the young daughter of Echaid, king of Dunseverick. She, however, loved Rónán's son, Mael Fhothartaig. The young Queen wooed Mael Fhothartaig in this manner: she commanded her maid to lie with Mael Fhothartaig and tell him of her mistress's desire. Mael Fhothartaig accepted the servant but indignantly refused to dishonor his father. Instead he went with his warriors and hounds to Scotland, where his hounds were unsurpassed at bringing down game. But the men of Leinster demanded that he return, and he did so. Then the Queen told her maid that she would be killed if Mael Fhothartaig did not become the Queen's lover. Still Mael Fhothartaig refused the Queen, and finally she went to her husband, Rónán, and complained that Mael Fhothartaig was continually attempting to seduce her. The deceived King believed her and had his son slain. Just before his death, however, Mael Fhothartaig was able to prove his innocence. The young Queen then took her own life.

Rónán and his father-in-law Echaid actually lived in the seventh century, but since Rónán's death is recorded as some forty years before Echaid's, it is improbable that the relationship in the story was a factual one.[65]

The story, as I said above, has a number of similarities to the

---

63. David Greene (ed.), *Fingal Rónáin and Other Stories, Medieval and Modern Irish Series,* No. XVI (Dublin, 1955), 31–35. Synopsis by Myles Dillon, *The Cycles of the Kings,* pp. 42–48. See also Kuno Meyer (ed. and trans.), "Fingal Rónáin," *RC,* XIII (1892), 368–97; Cross and Slover, "How Ronan Slew His Son," *Ancient Irish Tales,* pp. 538 ff.

64. Greene, *Fingal Rónáin,* p. 2; Dillon, *The Cycles of the Kings,* p. 42.

65. Dillon, *The Cycles of the Kings,* p. 42, reports that the date of Rónán's death was recorded in various annals and chronicles as anywhere from 610 to 624. Echaid Iarlaithe, the king of Dál Araide, is said to have died in 665. See also Meyer, "Fingal Rónáin," p. 369.

other Irish reluctant lover stories: the young wife solicits her old husband's son, but he, contrary to the actions of the other reluctant lovers, never succumbs to her. Mael Fhothartaig is an accomplished hunter, but he does not take the heroine when he repairs to the forest. The principal difference is that in *Fingal Rónáin* the hero is steadfastly loyal, while in the other reluctant lover tales he is not.[66]

Kuno Meyer first pointed out the close similarity between *Fingal Rónáin* and the Greek myth of Hippolytus.[67] Theseus, king of Athens, late in life took Phaedra as his young bride. Unsatisfied with her husband, she sought Hippolytus, Theseus's grown son, who was horrified and stated plainly and often that he preferred his music and hunting, for he was skilled at both, to any entanglement with his father's wife. Phaedra was so insistent that Hippolytus fled to the forest, where he was more at home than he was at court. In disappointment Phaedra took her own life and left a note falsely accusing Hippolytus of seducing her. Theseus summoned Hippolytus, banished him, and prayed for his death. Because of the prayer, Hippolytus's chariot overturned, mortally wounding him; and he was brought back to Athens to die. Just before his death he convinced Theseus of his innocence. In remorse the King buried his wife and son in adjacent graves.[68]

---

66. Note too the similarity between the action of Rónán's wife's maid and Brangien. Both maids by command of their mistresses lie with a man who is far above them in rank and both are threatened by their mistresses with death.

67. "Fingal Rónáin," p. 371. See also Cross and Slover, *Ancient Irish Tales*, p. 538. David Greene, however, remains unconvinced that there is any connection between *Fingal Rónáin* and the Hippolytus story and has said so a number of times. See his *Fingal Rónáin;* "Early Irish Literature," *Early Irish Society,* ed. Myles Dillon, Irish Life and Culture Series, No. VIII (Dublin, 1954), 33; and "Fingal Rónáin," *Irish Sagas,* ed. Myles Dillon (Dublin, 1959), pp. 168 f. Greene's argument is that the story is a commonplace, but I think he is neglecting the similarities of both plot and character and the many classical tales which found their way into Irish legends.

68. Although many of the renditions of the Hippolytus myth would be adequate, here I have used the synopsis in Gustav Schwab, *Gods and Heroes,* trans. Olga Marx and Ernst Morwitz (London, 1950), pp. 222–26; Philip Vellacott's translation of Euripedes' *Hippolytus* in *Alcestis and Other Plays* (London, 1956); and the accounts by Robert Graves in *The Greek Myths,* 2 vols. (London, 1957), I, 356–60. For a study of the myth see Hazel E. Barnes, "The Hippolytus of Drama and Myth," *Hippolytus in Drama and Myth* (Lincoln, Nebr., 1960).

The parallels between the myth of Hippolytus and *Fingal Rónáin* are these: 1. An old King takes a young wife. 2. The young Queen loves her husband's son. 3. The son rejects her. 4. He flees to the forest, which he prefers to the court. 5. The Queen maligns him to his father. 6. The father has the son slain. 7. Before the son dies he convinces his father of his innocence. 8. The Queen takes her own life. The only major difference between *Fingal Rónáin* and the Hippolytus myth is the time of the Queen's suicide, which in the Greek version occurs before the father is told the calumny about his son.

I see no reason to question the influence of the Hippolytus story on the Irish *Fingal Rónáin*. Many classical stories were known in the British Isles during the Middle Ages, especially in the monasteries that flourished from Bangor in Ireland across North Britain to Lindisfarne.[69] The monasteries were staffed by some of the best scholars in Europe. The libraries of these religious centers were excellent. A Scottish or Irish monk of the sixth, seventh, or eighth century could read not only the histories of Ireland, Scotland, England, and the Church, but also Cato, Cicero, Horace, Juvenal, Lucretius, Martial, Ovid, Seneca, and evidence exists that these authors were known to users of the monastic libraries.[70] At Iona there was an extensive classical library, and Adamnán's *Life of Columba* shows classical knowledge.[71] Even Nennius is believed to have used a lost "Northern History" as the source of his *Historia Brittonum*.[72] Here were centers of learning which attracted scholars of the sixth, seventh, and eighth centuries, just as scholars today

69. See Map 7 below, p. 113. For more about these monasteries and the environment that produced them see Nora K. Chadwick, *The Age of the Saints in the Early Celtic Church* (London, 1961); Gareth W. Dunleavy, *Colum's Other Island* (Madison, Wis., 1960).

70. G. S. M. Walker (ed.), *Sancti Columbani Opera* (Dublin, 1957), pp. lxvi ff. and 221 f. For further information about these libraries see the following: Ramona Bressie, "Libraries of the British Isles in the Anglo-Saxon Period," *The Medieval Library*, ed. J. W. Thompson (New York, 1957), pp. 102–25; Rev. John Ryan, *Irish Monasticism* (Dublin, 1931), pp. 277 ff. and 369 ff.

71. James F. Kenney, *Sources for the Early History of Ireland*, 2 vols. (New York, 1929), I, 286 f., 431 ff.

72. Nora K. Chadwick, "The Conversion of Northumbria: A Comparison of Sources," *Celt and Saxon*, ed. Nora K. Chadwick (Cambridge, Eng., 1963), p. 160.

travel to leading universities. It is most likely that some scholar knew the story of Hippolytus and used his knowledge to construct a similar tale with a local setting.[73] This was either *Fingal Rónáin* or a nucleus which became *Fingal Rónáin*.

Another possible influence, older than the extant versions of the Hippolytus legend, is the Egyptian tale, *The Two Brothers*, assigned by Stith Thompson to the time of Pharoah Seti II.[74] This tale includes a version of the reluctant lover incident (Aarne-Thompson Type 870C*, Thompson Motif K. 2111: Potiphar's Wife) and love through the sight of a hair from the head of an unknown woman (Aarne-Thompson Type 516B, Thompson Motif I. 11.4.1). It is the combination of these motifs plus their occurence in an Egyptian tale, that suggests to me that here is another influence on the Tristan story, once again, like the ass-eared god, filtered down to the North British monasteries by way of the Coptic, Gaulish, and Irish monastic centers. The Potiphar's Wife motif also could have been an influence on the tale of Hippolytus, and indirectly on every reluctant lover story.

From the pattern of the reluctant lover tales, we can see, once we have accepted the possibility of a classical or earlier influence,

---

73. Perhaps he also knew the story of Peleus, the father of Achilles. The similarity of this tale and the elements which later were dovetailed into the Tristan pattern is interesting. Peleus was approached by his host's wife, whom he rebuffed. On two occasions she lied about the encounter. First she told Polymela, Peleus' wife, that Peleus intended to desert her to marry another. Polymela hanged herself. Second, she convinced her husband that Peleus had tried to seduce her. This husband challenged Peleus to a hunting contest, and Peleus appeared at it with a new sword provided by the gods. In time he proved himself to be the better hunter by producing the tongues of the slain beasts, just as Tristan on one occasion produced the tongue of a slain dragon. For accounts of these incidents see Graves, *Greek Myths,* I, 270. Of interest in this tale, or group of tales, is the placing together of those items which usually appear to have separate sources. That is, the reluctant lover, the gift of a sword, and the hero who must prove himself by producing a slain animal's tongue are here combined as they are in the Tristan story. Yet Hippolytus as a reluctant lover, because of his character as a hunter and musician, appears to be a closer parallel and thus a much more likely source for the Celtic tales than is the legend of Peleus. That Hippolytus' name contains a form of ἵππος, the Greek word for "horse" and that Mark's name is a Celtic word for "horse" might have suggested to someone that the tale of Hippolytus could be associated with local legends of Mark, just as Mark's name might have invited other legends.

74. Stith Thompson, *The Folktale* (New York, 1951), pp. 275 f.

the dependence of all of the reluctant lover tales on the Hippolytus story. Invariably the reluctant lover himself is an accomplished woodsman and hunter. In some cases he is a musician. The lady is the wife of a close and aging relative of the hero. She proposes a liaison with the young man, and he leaves for his beloved forest. But *Fingal Rónáin* stands apart from the others and is closer to the classical pattern. For in *Fingal Rónáin* the hero retains his innocence as he did in *Hippolytus*. In both *Diarmaid and Gráinne* and *Tristan and Isolt* he does not. Of course in the latter two he repairs to the forest, but something additional is added: the lady accompanies him. Where *Fingal Rónáin* is closely related to the original classical story, the other reluctant lover tales are a subdevelopment. The subdevelopment appears to be a descendant of the Hippolytus myth and an ancestor of *Diarmaid and Gráinne* and of *Tristan and Isolt*. It, obviously, was composed in the same environment: somebody in a North British monastery knew certain classical themes and recomposed them around local figures known to the local North British audiences. Other influences, which will be discussed subsequently, have been brought to bear upon this subdevelopment. It would be a convenience to give it a name, and because I think it was written about a Pictish hero named Drust, who was involved in adventures with other figures whose names were from the North, I shall call it the *Drustansaga*. Chart 3 shows the pattern that then emerges:

CHART 3
THE RELUCTANT LOVER TALES

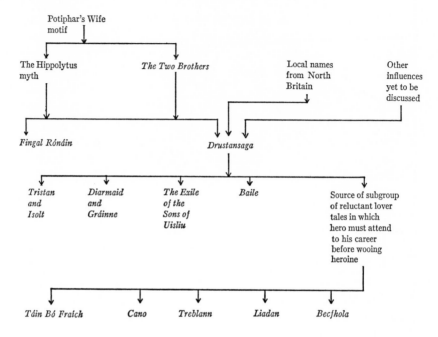

Map of part of Britain and Ireland c. 600–800 showing approximate political unities, some monasteries (†), and journeys taken by Baile, Cano, Cuirithir, and (presumably) Drust.

The approximate linguistic divisions are indicated as follows:

| Brythonic | Goidelic | English | Pictish |

Chapter Eight ※ ※

THE TRIBUTE GATHERERS

N THE previous chapter I proposed that the prototype of *Tristan and Isolt,* a prototype which for convenience' sake may be called the *Drustansaga,* was composed in a North British ecclesiastical center which contained a library of books some of which, most certainly, retold Greek myths. The author of the *Drustansaga* chose literary plots and personal characteristics and combined them with names of people and places known to a North British audience. This argument will be reinforced here by an analysis of two scenes involving tribute gatherers, a monster and a dragon conquered by the doughty Tristan. Although these two incidents appear to be a doubling of one adventure, I believe that they are separate episodes. Here I shall try to demonstrate that the Morholt sequence, like the reluctant lover triangle, is based on an adventure of Theseus and that the dragon-killing adventure is based on a completely separate motif, a world-wide dragon folktale.

THE MORHOLT AND DRAGON EPISODES ※

The action of *Tristan and Isolt* from the time Tristan is first aware of the menace of the Morholt until he presents Isolt to King Mark appears to be a series of duplications. Tristan kills two oppressors, the Morholt and the dragon; he makes two voyages to Ireland; and twice his identity is established by a token, once by his broken sword and once by the slain dragon's tongue.

It would seem, then, that one story has been duplicated.[1] An incognito hero slays a villain or monster and by means of a token is later identified. These two adventures, however, are not the same story, although there is every likelihood that they are distantly related. One episode appears to have been derived from the classical tale of Theseus and the Minotaur. The other shows evidence of belonging to a group of dragon-slaying adventures widely known in medieval Europe and remotely traceable to Perseus' adventure with Andromeda.

The Morholt and dragon episodes appear early in the tale, not long after Tristan had established himself at Mark's court.[2]

The king of Ireland's brother-in-law[3] had subdued many surrounding kingdoms to the King's rule. This oppressor, whose nature was more that of a monster than of a man, was named the Morholt. He was determined to add King Mark of Cornwall to his victims and accordingly sent messengers[4] announcing his arrival to claim a tribute of every third child born in Cornwall in the last fifteen years.[5]

1. As Mrs. Bromwich says in "Some Remarks on the Celtic Sources of 'Tristan,' " *THSC*, Session 1953 (London, 1955), pp. 40 f. See also A. G. Van Hamel, "Tristan's Combat with the Dragon," *RC*, XLI (1924), 331 ff.

2. The text of the following synopsis is based on Eilhart and differs somewhat from the version given on pp. 23–29. Where Thomas and Brother Robert differ will be indicated in the notes. For the Eilhart version see Eilhart von Oberge, *Tristrant*, ed. Franz Lichtenstein, *Quellen und Forschungen zur Sprach- und Culturgeschichte*, Vol. XIX (Strasbourg, 1877); see also Eilhart von Oberge, *Tristrant*, ed. K. Wagner, *Reinische Beiträge*, Vol. V (Bonn, 1924). For the Thomas and Brother Robert version see Roger Sherman Loomis (ed. and trans.), *The Romance of Tristram and Ysolt*, new rev. ed. (New York, 1951); Joseph Bédier (ed.), *Le Roman de Tristan par Thomas*, SATF, No. LIII, 2 vols. (Paris, 1902–5); Eugen Kölbing (ed.), *Die nordische und die englische Version der Tristan-sage*, 2 vols. (Heilbronn, 1882); A. T. Hatto (trans.), *Gottfried von Strassburg Tristan With the Surviving Fragments of the Tristan of Thomas* (Harmondsworth, Middlesex, and Baltimore, 1960).

3. In almost all versions except the synopsis by Miss Schoepperle he is specifically mentioned as the Queen's brother. Even in Eilhart, from whom Miss Schoepperle obtained her synopsis, the context makes it evident that the king of Ireland married the Morholt's sister. See Gertrude Schoepperle, *Tristan and Isolt: A Study of the Sources of the Romance*, 2 vols. (Frankfurt and London, 1913; reprinted, New York, 1959), I, 11–65. See also Eilhart, *Tristrant*, p. 41, ll. 351–65.

4. Thomas mentions no messengers.

5. Thomas says the tribute was three-score noble boys.

At this time Tristan was a very young man. He had recently been acknowledged as King Mark's nephew and was a popular favorite of the King. Thus when Tristan decided he must challenge the Morholt in personal combat, Mark at first ordered him not to face such a terrifying opponent. But eventually the King agreed to the combat, and he gave Tristan a new sword.[6] The Morholt arrived, and he and Tristan rowed separately to an island for their combat.

Tristan was victorious, but in the battle his sword broke, and he left a small piece of it in the Morholt's skull. The Morholt's corpse was taken to Ireland, where Princess Isolt, the King's beautiful daughter, took the fragment from his head before he was buried.[7]

The hero, however, was wounded, and only Princess Isolt,[8] who was extraordinarily adept at such matters, could cure him. Tristan, realizing that the stench of his wound was offensive to others, retired to a building away from the royal palace and later set to sea in a rudderless boat. The boat carried him to Ireland, where he gave his name as Pro of Iemsetir.[9] There he was healed by a servant of Princess Isolt,[10] but he did not meet her.[11]

When Tristan returned to Cornwall King Mark's barons, jealous because the young hero was now in effect Mark's heir, urged Mark to marry. A swallow then dropped a beautiful golden hair at Mark's feet, and the King swore that he would wed only the maiden from whose head the hair came.[12] Tristan was named to search for this lady. Again he set sail, and again he came to Ireland. On this trip he pretended to be a merchant named Tantris.[13]

At this time a dreadful dragon was harassing the people of Ire-

6. Called by Thomas one of the finest treasures in the realm.
7. In Thomas, Queen Isolt, the King's wife, removed the fragment.
8. In Thomas, Queen Isolt.
9. Tantris in Thomas. Bédier suggests that "Pro of Iemsetir" is an anagram for *Isot pro mire*. See *Le Roman de Tristan*, II, 211–12. See also Schoepperle, *Tristan and Isolt*, II, 376.
10. By Queen Isolt herself in Thomas.
11. In Thomas Tristan under the name Tantris gave the Princess Isolt lessons in the harp because she had been fascinated by his reputation and insisted on meeting him.
12. Neither the swallow nor the golden hair appears in Thomas, where Tristan, without amplifying explanation, simply sails to Ireland for the purpose of asking Isolt to become Mark's wife.
13. In Thomas he does not use any name on the second trip.

land, and the King had offered his daughter and half of the kingdom
to any hero who would slay the monster. Having armed himself,
Tristan, who was never one to turn down such an adventure, set out.
Although his lance broke, he was able to kill the dragon with the
very sword that had broken on the Morholt's head. He cut the
dragon's tongue from its head, and severely burned, he fell unconscious into a small brook.[14]

The King's seneschal, a coward who had long been frightened by
the dragon, now appeared. Seeing the dead monster and no one else,
he rushed back to court to claim the victory and demand the reward.

Princess Isolt did not believe him. She [15] went to the scene of the
battle where she found Tristan, whom she did not recognize because she had never seen him. Tristan was brought to the Princess'
chambers, where he was bathed and healed.[16] He opened his eyes
to see the Princess' golden hair and to know that his quest was
over.[17]

Princess Isolt then examined Tristan's sword [18] and noticed the
broken blade. She took the fragment which had been extracted
from the Morholt's skull and saw that it exactly fitted into the
blade. Then, recognizing him as the slayer of her uncle, the Morholt, she was angered and would have slain him had not Brangien,
her lady-in-waiting, reminded her that if she killed Tristan she
would have to marry the seneschal, whom she hated.

Approaching the King her father, Isolt said that she knew the
genuine slayer of the dragon and persuaded the King to absolve
him of his past misdeeds. She promised that on the next day he
would confront the seneschal.

On the following day, in the presence of Isolt's father and the

14. In Thomas he faints because of the poison in the dragon's tongue. Then
his face becomes swollen and blackened so that no one recognizes him.

15. Accompanied by her mother, Queen Isolt, in Thomas.

16. In Thomas, although Queen Isolt had previously healed him, he was also
unknown to her because his face was black and swollen. Nor does the Princess
recognize her harp teacher even after he is healed. However, in Gottfried both
ladies recognize him as Tantris as soon as they see him.

17. In some versions it is hinted that even before he sailed he knew that
Isolt was the Princess whom he sought. Thomas, of course, makes no mention
of the incident.

18. While he was bathing, according to Thomas.

assembled nobles, Tristan produced the dragon's tongue and thus confounded the seneschal. He requested from the King permission to take Isolt to Cornwall as King Mark's bride. This permission was granted, and preparations were made for a journey which terminated with Tristan presenting Isolt to King Mark as a bride.[19]

The above sequence of events contains two episodes which are separate yet overlap. The Morholt adventure occurs first. It is followed by the dragon-slaying incident. Then Tristan is positively identified as the hero of each adventure. First, Isolt recognizes him by his notched sword as the slayer of the Morholt. Second, Tristan identifies himself in the presence of Isolt's father and the assembled nobles as the possessor of the dragon's tongue and, accordingly, the slayer of the dragon. After all identities are satisfactorily unravelled, Tristan receives his prize, the Princess Isolt.

Although the Morholt and dragon episodes do overlap, they may be isolated into elements independent of each other. True, the two adventures have some points of similarity, but these are usually commonplace. It is the differences that matter. Here now is an event by event comparison of both adventures:

MORHOLT	TRISTAN DRAGON EPISODE
a. The heroine is the beautiful daughter of the king of Ireland.	a. The heroine is the beautiful daughter of the king of Ireland.
b. The Morholt is the brother of the heroine's mother.	b. The dragon is not related to the heroine.
c. The Morholt is the ally of the heroine's father.	c. The dragon is the enemy of the heroine's father.
d. The Morholt demands a periodic human tribute in the name of the King.	d. The dragon demands a human tribute for itself.
e. The Morholt crosses the sea to seek his tribute.	e. The dragon seeks his tribute near home.

19. It was on this journey that the magic love potion was accidently drunk by Tristan and Isolt, and whether they wished to or not they were obliged to love each other. But the magic potion is not the subject of this particular discussion and is accordingly omitted here.

MORHOLT	TRISTAN DRAGON EPISODE
f. The Morholt has no designs upon the King's daughter.	f. Presumably the dragon in time will demand the King's daughter.[20]
g. In spite of his uncle's protestations, Tristan, who is later to travel to the Morholt's home, challenges the Morholt.	g. Tristan comes from afar to challenge the dragon.
h. Since the action occurs in a land foreign to the Morholt, the daughter of the King has nothing to do with the outcome of the battle. But Mark gives Tristan a new sword.	h. The daughter of the King is the prize for whoever kills the dragon.
i. Tristan fights the Morholt on an island to and from which access is difficult.	i. Access to the scene of the battle presents no difficulty.
j. Tristan kills the Morholt.	j. Tristan kills the dragon.
k. The king of Ireland is angry.	k. The king of Ireland is grateful.
l. The identity of the slayer of the Morholt is obscured in Ireland because the combat occurs in Cornwall.	l. A false claimant says that he has slain the dragon.
m. (Later in Ireland) Tristan is identified in the bath as the slayer of the Morholt.	m. Tristan is identified by the dragon's tongue as the slayer of the dragon.

Clearly we have two stories, although they have these points in common: 1. A monster or villain demands tribute (d). 2. A hero who has traveled or is to travel challenges this oppressor (g). 3. The hero is victorious (j) but then must prove his identity (m). The differences between the two stories point to the existence of two tales, both demonstrably earlier than the first formation of the Tristan story.

It is the differences between these tales that are of interest. The

20. As dragons invariably do. See E. Sidney Hartland, *The Legend of Perseus*, 3 vols. (London, 1894), III, 1 ff.

Morholt is related by blood to Isolt; the dragon is not (b). The Morholt is an ally (c) and an agent (d) of Isolt's father; the dragon is an enemy (c) and his own master (d). The Princess' father is the oppressor in one episode and the oppressed in the other. If these differences are based on the doubling of one monster-killing episode, the alteration was a labored effort done with too many visible loose ends and irrelevancies. If the Morholt episode were a doubling of the dragon story, why should the Morholt be a man at all? Why is a man who was so bestial given a blood relationship to Isolt? Why does Mark give Tristan a new sword? Why does the battle occur on a small island? These matters do not come from the dragon story and they are not highly essential to *Tristan and Isolt*. Even Isolt's anger over the death of her uncle is not absolutely essential. She could have been just as angry over the death of a prize bull.

THE MINOTAUR AND THE MORHOLT

It has long been recognized that the dragon-killing episode has some relation to an old folktale in which a hero kills a dragon, is absent when an impostor takes credit for the deed, and then confounds the impostor by producing a token such as the dragon's tongue.[21] A second similarity between the Morholt episode and Theseus' slaying of the Minotaur has been observed [22] but never fully explored:

Aegeus,[23] the king of Athens, sent an annual tribute of seven young men and seven young women to King Minos of Crete, where they were placed in Minos' labyrinth to become victims of the dreaded Minotaur. This creature had been conceived by a bull upon Pasiphaë, the wife of King Minos, and was thus half man and half beast. The third time this tribute was due, Theseus, son of King

21. Bromwich, "Celtic Sources of 'Tristan,'" p. 38; Van Hamel, "Tristan's Combat with the Dragon," p. 332; Schoepperle, *Tristan and Isolt*, I, 203 ff. See also Hartland, *The Legend of Perseus*, III, 172 ff., 203 ff.
22. Bromwich, "Celtic Sources of 'Tristan,'" p. 38, n. 34. See also Bédier, *Le Roman de Tristan par Thomas*, II, 135.
23. Synopsis of the Minotaur myth taken from Robert Graves, *The Greek Myths*, 2 vols. (London, 1957), I, 293, 336 ff.; Gustav Schwab, *Gods and Heroes*, trans. Olga Marx and Ernst Morwitz (London, 1950), pp. 212 ff.

Aegeus, determined to put an end to the tribute and added his name to the list of young people bound for Crete. Before leaving, Theseus consulted the Oracle at Delphi, who advised him to pray to Aphrodite for guidance.

Theseus prayed as he was advised; and when he reached Crete, Ariadne, the beautiful daughter of Minos and Pasiphaë, fell so in love with him that she renounced allegiance to her father. She presented Theseus with a ball of thread which he was to unwind as he walked through the labyrinth and, more important, a magical sword with which he could overcome her hated half-brother, the Minotaur. Theseus succeeded in killing the Minotaur and, following the thread, led all of the Athenians to safety. Then, accompanied by Ariadne, he and the Athenians escaped to their ships and fled from the fury of Minos.

When they reached the Island of Dia or Naxos, the god Dionysius appeared to Theseus in a dream demanding that he leave Ariadne on the island. Theseus did so, and Ariadne became the bride of Dionysius.

Theseus had had an arrangement with his father, Aegeus, that were he successful in slaying the Minotaur his ship on the homeward journey would bear white sails instead of the black sails that customarily signified an unhappy mission. In his grief at losing Ariadne, Theseus neglected his promise, and the ship arrived with its usual black sails. King Aegeus, on being told that black sails were approaching, believed Theseus had failed. He threw himself from the Acropolis, fatally smashing his head on the rocks below.[24] Theseus then assumed the kingship of Athens.

The Morholt episode offers a closer comparison to the Minotaur story than to Tristan's dragon-slaying adventure. Here is a second event by event comparison, this time of the Morholt and Minotaur tales:

MORHOLT	MINOTAUR
a. The heroine is the beautiful daughter of the king of Ireland.	a. The heroine is the beautiful daughter of King Minos of Crete.

24. The obvious parallel of the black and white sails in the Tristan story will be discussed in the next chapter. See below, pp. 150 ff.

MORHOLT	MINOTAUR
b. The Morholt is the brother of the heroine's mother.	b. The Minotaur is the illicit issue of the heroine's mother.
c. The Morholt is the ally of the heroine's father.	c. The Minotaur is the ally of the heroine's father.
d. The Morholt demands a periodic human tribute in the name of the king of Ireland.	d. The king of Crete demands a periodic human tribute for the Minotaur.
e. The Morholt crosses the sea to seek his tribute.	e. The tribute must be brought to the Minotaur.
f. The Morholt has no designs upon the King's daughter.	f. The Minotaur has no designs upon the King's daughter.
g. In spite of his uncle's protestations, Tristan, who is later to travel to the Morholt's home, challenges the Morholt.	g. In spite of his father's protestations, Theseus comes from afar to challenge the Minotaur in its lair.
h. Since the action occurs in a land foreign to the Morholt, the daughter of the king of Ireland has nothing to do with the outcome of the battle. But Mark gives Tristan a new sword.	h. The daughter of King Minos is disloyal to her father and aids Theseus by giving him a new sword.
i. Tristan fights the Morholt on an island to and from which access is difficult.	i. Theseus fights the Minotaur in the labyrinth, to and from which access is difficult.
j. Tristan kills the Morholt.	j. Theseus kills the Minotaur.
k. The king of Ireland is angry.	k. King Minos of Crete is angry.
l. The identity of the slayer of the Morholt is obscured in Ireland because the combat occurs in Cornwall.	l. No false claimant steps forward.
m. (Later in Ireland) Tristan is identified in the bath by his sword as the slayer of the Morholt.	m. No identification of Theseus is necessary.

The Morholt tale is the Minotaur story with very slight changes. The Minotaur has become a man, albeit a beastlike one, and the action has been moved to the land of the potential victims for reasons which shall be offered in due course.[25] The Morholt, as was the Minotaur, is related by blood to the oppressing King's wife (b), and we still see a remnant of the labyrinth in the island where the battle occurs (i). Tristan, like Theseus, receives a gift of a new sword (h). When Tristan sees the daughter of the King, she recognizes the sword, and we are reminded that in the older story it was Ariadne who gave it to Theseus.[26] Tristan sails to the land of the Morholt after the battle instead of before it, as Theseus did in the Minotaur story (g).

If the parallel between the Morholt sequence and the Minotaur myth is acceptable, two more events must be added to the Morholt tale. After Tristan identified himself as the slayer of the dragon he received as his prize the Princess Isolt. He sailed away with her but presented her to another at his first port of call. After Theseus killed the Minotaur and escaped from the labyrinth, he sailed from Crete with Ariadne, the King's daughter, as his passenger. At his first port of call, however, he presented her to the god Dionysius. The removal of the Princess from her homeland and her subsequent presentation to another is part of the Minotaur tale. Because it occurs in the correct chronological position in the Tristan legend, separated from the rest of the Morholt episode only by the events of the dragon adventure, I believe that it may be assigned to the Morholt sequence rather than the dragon adventure, which it immediately follows. Winning the Princess is part of the dragon story, but sailing away with her and presenting her to another at the first port of call belongs to the Morholt-Minotaur pattern. Therefore I believe this much must be added:

MORHOLT	MINOTAUR
n. Isolt leaves Ireland with Tristan.	n. Ariadne leaves Crete with Theseus.

25. I think we are safe in saying that the action has been moved to King Mark's court from another court. Mark is perhaps the only king so oppressed who did not have as part of his household a beautiful nubile daughter or sister to present as an award to his deliverer.

26. More about this sword later. See below, pp. 149 f.

MORHOLT	MINOTAUR
o. At his first port of call Tristan gives Isolt to King Mark as a bride.	o. At his first port of call Theseus gives Ariadne to Dionysius as a bride.

THE DRAGON FOLKTALE ❋

Tristan's second combat, that with the dragon, was an episode similar not to the Morholt-Minotaur tale but to a worldwide folk-tale [27] in which a hero slays a dragon and then must prove his own identity before winning a princess.

In the folktale a dragon had been harassing the land of a given king demanding a human tribute. The desperate King offered the hand of his beautiful daughter and half of the kingdom to anyone who would slay the dragon. Everyone was frightened, and ultimately the King's daughter herself was scheduled to be the dragon's victim.

A hero now appeared in the kingdom to challenge the dragon. He was successful and cut out the beast's tongue as a token of victory.[28] Then, exhausted by the combat, he fell asleep.

While he was sleeping, there appeared a member of the court, usually one who had long since sought the hand of the King's daughter. Seeing only the dead dragon and assuming that the hero had been killed or had fled, he rushed back to the court claiming that he himself was the dragon slayer. The grateful King prepared to keep his promise, although the Princess felt that she would rather die than marry the false claimant. However, in the nick of time, usually at the wedding feast itself, the hero appeared with his token and publicly discredited the villain. The dragon slayer, then, amid great rejoicing married the princess.

Again with a close comparison it is easy to see that Tristan's victory over the dragon is still another example of this tale.

27. For more about this tale of the dragon slayer see Hartland, *The Legend of Perseus*, especially Chaps. XVI and XVII. See also Antti Aarne and Stith Thompson, *The Types of the Folktale*, FF Communications No. 184 (Helsinki, 1961), Type 300; Stith Thompson, *Motif-Index of Folk Literature*, rev. ed., 6 vols. (Bloomington, Ind., 1955–58), B.11, B.11.1, B.11.11.1, G.346, H.105.1, Q.112, T.68.1.

28. The tongue, of course, was not the only token, although it was the most popular one. See Hartland, *The Legend of Perseus*, III, 203 ff.

TRISTAN DRAGON EPISODE	DRAGON FOLKTALE
a. The heroine is the beautiful daughter of the king of Ireland.	a. The heroine is the beautiful daughter of a king.
b. The dragon is not related to the heroine.	b. The dragon is not related to the heroine.
c. The dragon is the enemy of the heroine's father.	c. The dragon is the enemy of the heroine's father.
d. The dragon demands a human tribute for itself.	d. The dragon demands a human tribute for itself.
e. The dragon seeks his tribute near home.	e. The dragon seeks his tribute near home.
f. Presumably the dragon in time will demand the King's daughter.	f. The dragon is about to demand the King's daughter.
g. Tristan comes from afar to challenge the dragon.	g. A hero comes from afar to challenge the dragon.
h. The daughter of the King is the prize for whoever kills the dragon.	h. The daughter of the King is the prize for whoever kills the dragon.
i. Access to the scene of the battle presents no difficulty.	i. Access to the scene of the battle presents no difficulty.
j. Tristan kills the dragon.	j. The hero kills the dragon.
k. The king of Ireland is grateful.	k. The king of the land is grateful.
l. A false claimant says that he has slain the dragon.	l. A false claimant says that he has slain the dragon.
m. Tristan is identified by the dragon's tongue as the slayer of the dragon.	m. The hero is identified by the dragon's tongue or another token as the slayer of the dragon.

The Tristan dragon episode is almost identical to the dragon folktale. The differences are slight: in the folktale the hero often confounds the impostor at the wedding feast and marries the girl. On the other hand the Morholt adventure is very dissimilar to the dragon folktale, as Tristan's dragon-slaying adventure is dissimilar to Theseus' adventure with the Minotaur.

Clearly in Tristan's Morholt and dragon adventures we have two separate episodes which exist outside the Tristan story, are older than the Tristan story,[29] and have been interwoven into the Tristan story. Still, in spite of their separate origins, the similarities in these episodes have given to the Tristan story a number of disturbing duplications.

Concerning the formation of the Tristan story, I have suggested that there was one original author and that he applied older tales, some from the classics, to known British historical figures. The two separate monster-killing episodes suggest that two source stories were used. The parallels just outlined indicate that one such source was part of the Theseus legend and that the other was the world-wide dragon folktale.

THE *WOOING OF EMER* AND THE TRISTAN LEGEND ▨

Of course the original tale of Drust, which for convenience's sake I have named the *Drustansaga*, is no longer extant. If it were, I think it would contain both the Morholt episode and the dragon-slaying adventure. Instead of a seventh- or eighth-century tale of Drust, there has survived a medieval Irish story in which the name *Drust* has been taken from the protagonist and reassigned to a minor character. This is the Dervorgil episode in the medieval Irish *Tochmarc Emire—The Wooing of Emer*,[30] which both Deutschbein and Thurneysen have said was originally a story about Drust and which also contains a few interesting points of comparison with both the dragon-slaying tale and the Morholt episode.[31] That is, it seems likely that the Dervorgil episode descends from a tale of

29. The Minotaur myth is obviously older than the Tristan legend, and the dragon folktale is related by Hartland, *The Legend of Perseus*, III, 1 ff., to the story of Perseus and Andromeda.

30. Kuno Meyer (ed.), "Tochmarc Emire la Coinculaind," *ZCP*, III (1901), 229 ff.; (trans.), "The Wooing of Emer," *Archaeological Review*, I (1888), 303 ff. See also Eleanor Hull, *The Cuchullin Saga* (London, 1898), pp. 81 f.; Tom Peete Cross and C. H. Slover (eds.), *Ancient Irish Tales* (London, n.d.), pp. 168 ff. In the latter two renditions, for *Durst* read *Drust*.

31. Max Deutschbein, "Eine irische Variante der Tristan-sage," *Beiblatt zur Anglia*, XV (1904), 16 ff. R. Thurneysen, *Die irische Helden- und Königsage bis zum siebzehnten Jahrhundert* (Halle, 1921), p. 392, n. 2.

Drust which included two combats, one with the equivalent of the Morholt and one with a dragon.

In the Dervorgil episode, during the days when King Conchobar ruled Ulster from Emain Macha, Cú Chulainn, traveling from Scotland to Ireland on his way to marry Emer, stopped on Samain night [32] at the house of Ruad, king of the Isles (Hebrides). Among the visitor's retainers was Drust son of Serb. Conall the Victorious and Loegaire the Triumphant had visited King Ruad before Cú Chulainn. They were collecting a tribute which in those days King Ruad customarily paid to the kingdom of Ulster. Cú Chulainn heard sounds of distress and asked why. He was told that Dervorgil, the daughter of Ruad, was about to be sacrificed to the Fomorians. The hero went to the waiting maiden, and when three Fomorians approached he slew them. He was wounded on his wrist, and Dervorgil gave him a strip of her garment as a bandage. He then departed without revealing his name. Later she told her father the whole story. Many warriors then boasted of having slain the Fomorians, and King Ruad had a bath prepared. Each was brought to the bath for the maiden's examination, Cú Chulainn among the others. In that way she recognized him. Ruad offered the hero his daughter, but Cú Chulainn was pledged to Emer and unable to accept. However, Dervorgil followed Cú Chulainn to Ireland, where he presented her to his companion, Lugaid of the Red Stripes.

The *Wooing of Emer* may be compared with both Tristan's Morholt and dragon-slaying episodes:

MORHOLT	WOOING OF EMER	TRISTAN DRAGON EPISODE
a. The heroine is the beautiful daughter of the king of Ireland.	a. The heroine is the beautiful daughter of King Ruad of the Isles.	a. The heroine is the beautiful daughter of the king of Ireland.
b. The Morholt is the brother of	b. The Fomorians are not related	b. The dragon is not related to

---

32. Samain night or Halloween was the traditional time when the Fomorians came to gather tribute. See H. d'Arbois de Jubainville, *The Irish Mythological Cycle*, trans., R. I. Best (Dublin, 1903), pp. 57 f.

MORHOLT	WOOING OF EMER	TRISTAN DRAGON EPISODE
the heroine's mother.	to the heroine.	the heroine.
c. The Morholt is the ally of the heroine's father.	c. The Fomorians are the enemies of the heroine's father.	c. The dragon is the enemy of the heroine's father.
d. The Morholt demands a periodic human tribute in the name of the king of Ireland.	d. The Fomorians demand human tribute for themselves, and King Ruad customarily pays tribute to King Conchobar of Ulster.	d. The dragon demands human tribute for itself.
e. The Morholt crosses the sea to seek his tribute.	e. The Fomorians cross the sea to seek their tribute.	e. The dragon seeks his tribute near home.
f. The Morholt has no designs upon the King's daughter.	f. The Fomorians demand the King's daughter.	f. Presumably in time the dragon will demand the King's daughter.
g. In spite of his uncle's protestations, Tristan, who is later to travel to the Morholt's home, challenges the Morholt.	g. Cú Chulainn comes from afar to challenge the Fomorians.	g. Tristan comes from afar to challenge the dragon.
h. Since the action occurs in a land foreign to the Morholt, the daughter of the king of Ireland has nothing to do	h. The daughter of the king is the prize for whoever kills the Fomorians.	h. The daughter of the king is the prize for whoever kills the dragon.

MORHOLT	WOOING OF EMER	TRISTAN DRAGON EPISODE
with the outcome of the battle. But Mark gives Tristan a new sword.		
i. Tristan fights the Morholt on an island to and from which access is difficult.	i. Access to the scene of the battle presents no difficulty.	i. Access to the scene of the battle presents no difficulty.
j. Tristan kills the Morholt.	j. Cú Chulainn kills the Fomorians.	j. Tristan kills the dragon.
k. The king of Ireland is angry.	k. King Ruad of the Isles is grateful.	k. The king of Ireland is grateful.
l. The identity of the slayer of the Morholt is obscured in Ireland because the combat occurs in Cornwall.	l. Many false claimants say that they have slain the Fomorians.	l. A false claimant says that he has slain the dragon.
m. Tristan is identified in the bath as the slayer of the Morholt.	m. Cú Chulainn is identified in the bath as the slayer of the Fomorians.	m. Tristan is identified by the dragon's tongue as the slayer of the dragon.
n. Isolt leaves Ireland with Tristan.	n. Dervorgil leaves the Hebrides in order to follow Cú Chulainn.	n. . . . .
o. At his first port of call, Tristan gives Isolt to King Mark as a bride.	o. At his first port of call, Cú Chulainn gives Dervorgil to Lugaid of the Red Stripes as a bride.	o. . . . .

The *Wooing of Emer* episode may be divided into three parts: 1. Those items which are common to it and to all the other tales under consideration here. 2. Those items common to it and to the two dragon stories. 3. Those items common to it and to the Morholt-Minotaur pattern.

The first group of this division includes the King's beautiful daughter (a), the demand for human tribute (d), the hero who travels (g), and the death of the monster (j). All are commonplace and may be found wherever there is a tale of a monster's death.[33]

The second group establishes much of Cú Chulainn's defeat of the Fomorians as another example of the worldwide dragon myth, just as is the episode in which Tristan slays the Irish dragon. In common there is the monster which has no blood relationship to the royal family (b) and which is harassing the king of the land (c), the demand for the King's daughter (f), the King's promise that his daughter shall go to the successful hero (h), the ease of access to the field of combat (i), the King's gratitude for the monster's death (k), the false claimants (l), and the identification by means of a token (m). Few of these items appear in the Morholt-Minotaur tradition, which includes the following: the monster/villain is related by blood to the royal family (b); the King with the beautiful daughter is the oppressor and not the oppressed (c); no one is demanding the King's daughter (f); the King does not promise his daughter (h); access to the field of combat presents great difficulty (i); the King is angered at the monster/villain's death (k) and there is no false claimant (l). The only items which seem similar are the villain who crosses the sea (e), which is not found in the Minotaur tale but is in the Morholt episode; the identification in the bath (m), related in part to the Morholt adventure; and the hero's surrender of the king's daughter (o).

The third group, the similarities between the Dervorgil incident and the Morholt episode, includes the tribute which is paid from one king to another (d), the villains who come from overseas (e), the recognition in the bath (m), the heroine who sails away from her homeland (n), and that parallel (o) in which Tristan wins Isolt to give her to Mark, while Cú Chulainn wins Dervorgil to

---

33. See Hartland, *Legend of Perseus*, III, passim.

give her to Lugaid of the Red Stripes. The tribute which passes from king to king has been relegated in the *Wooing of Emer* to a passing comment. Still, it is another mention of a request for tribute. That is, the Dervorgil incident contains two demands for tribute, one by the Fomorians reminiscent of the dragon-slaying folktale, and one by King Conchobar of Ulster reminiscent of the demand in the Morholt-Minotaur pattern. The parallel in which the hero wins the lady only to relinquish her to another is considered by Mrs. Bromwich to be peculiar to the Tristan and Dervorgil stories,[34] but it occurs in the Minotaur legend, which is older than either. The final similarity between the Dervorgil and Morholt incidents might occur in the proper names assigned to the villains themselves. The names of both the Morholt and the Fomorians contain the compound *mor*. Miss Schoepperle considered the possibility that the names might be related, but she rejected the theory upon advice from Kuno Meyer, whose personal letter she quotes.[35] Mrs. Bromwich does feel that a connection between the names is a strong possibility. Meyer himself, according to T. F. O'Rahilly, thought that the Fomorians might be historical people. O'Rahilly discusses the suggestion, but, agreeing with Thurneysen, rejects it.[36] De Jubainville observes a number of similarities between the legendary activities of the Fomorians and the myth of the Minotaur.[37]

The weight of the accumulated evidence discussed above demonstrates that the story pattern of the Dervorgil incident in the *Wooing of Emer* is related both to the worldwide dragon folktale and to the Morholt-Minotaur complex. The earlier conclusion, that this tale was originally told of Drust and was given to the more famous Cú Chulainn,[38] establishes that this particular amalgamation of the dragon and Minotaur tales was filtered through a story based on the reputation of a hero named Drust. This particular adventure of Drust appears, obviously later, both in the Tristan complex and in the Irish *Wooing of Emer*.

34. "Celtic Sources of 'Tristan,'" p. 39.
35. *Tristan and Isolt*, II, 331, n. 1.
36. T. F. O'Rahilly, *Early Irish History and Mythology* (Dublin, 1946), p. 524.
37. *The Irish Mythological Cycle*, pp. 57 f.
38. Deutschbein, "Eine irische Variante," pp. 16 ff.; and Thurneysen, *Die irische Helden- und Königsage*, p. 392, n. 2.

The problem is now one of timing. If the Morholt and dragon episodes were added at the same time to the reputation of Drust, then the source of the first part of the Dervorgil incident, up to Cú Chulainn's identification, would be the dragon-slaying adventure, and the source of the latter part of the Dervorgil incident, the heroine who sails from her own land with or after the hero and the hero's surrender of the heroine to another, would be derived from the Morholt-Minotaur pattern. Because the chronology of events is identical to the chronology in the Tristan legend, I believe that the primary source of the Dervorgil incident is the primitive Tristan legend itself, that is, the *Drustansaga,* beginning with the request for tribute made by one king to another and ending with Drust's surrender of the heroine to her husband. The secondary source of the Dervorgil incident is the primary source of this section of the *Drustansaga:* the dragon folktale and the Minotaur myth. Whoever it was who spun glorious tales about the old hero Drust knew a number of such stories and did not hesitate to combine them in this presentation of his hero. From the Theseus and dragon tales he wove two episodes into the fictionalized life of his hero. From this work of original genius has descended not only the Dervorgil incident but the *Tristan and Isolt* known today.

THE BATH

Although both Cú Chulainn,[39] after slaying the Fomorians, and Tristan,[40] after slaying the dragon, were recognized in the bath, and although I have proposed that a tale of Drust was the source of such an episode, there is still more to be said about this bath. Why should it have been necessary to bathe a hero to identify him? Cú Chulainn was wounded on his wrist, which was later bandaged with a strip

39. The exact quotation in English is: "Then the king had a bath prepared, and afterwards each one was brought to her separately. Cúchulainn came like all the rest, and the maiden recognized him" (from Hull, *The Cuchullin Saga,* p. 82; Cross and Slover, *Ancient Irish Tales,* p. 169). The Irish is: "Mosronad [Dorónad] fo*thraccud* don [lasin] rig 7 dobreta cach ar uair chuice. Tai*nic* Cucula*ind* dno cumai caich rorad [dorat] an ingen aithne [aichni] fair." See Meyer, "Tochmarc Emire la Coinculaind," p. 259.

40. In Thomas only. Eilhart mentions that he was bathed and then recognized, but no special attention was given to the bath.

torn from Dervorgil's clothing. Certainly there was no need for him
to be divested of his clothing to reveal a bandaged wrist. The bath
seems even more useless as a means of recognition in the Morholt
story, where Isolt might have examined Tristan's sword under any
of a variety of domestic conditions. Surely it was not necessary for
him to remove all his garments to permit her access to his sword.
Actually a bath alone is never used as a means of recognition outside
the Dervorgil story, although a wound or garment occasionally is. In
109 examples of this kind of tale Hartland says that a lady's garment
or part of one occurs as a token 18 times and a specific injury to the
hero seven times. But the dragon's tongue (or tongues) occurs 76
times.[41]

What then is the purpose of the bath? In both Eilhart's and
Thomas' versions Tristan is bathed as part of a healing process. In
Táin Bó Fraích, the hero is given a curative bath after combat with a
monster. In *Beowulf* Wiglaf bathes Beowulf after the dragon fight.[42]
Other examples of the curative bath may be found in such Irish
stories as *The First Battle of Moytura,*[43] *Eachtra Uilliam,*[44] and *Táin
Bó Cúalnge.*[45] Another common use of the bath is as a rite of hospitality, found in such Irish examples as *Tochmarc Ferbe,*[46] *The Violent Deaths of Goll and Garb,*[47] *The Martial Career of Conghal Cláir-*

41. *The Legend of Perseus,* III, 203 ff. Other means of recognition are as
follows: other parts of the monster's body with or without the tongue, 15 times;
a lady's ring (or rings), 12 times; a specific skill of the hero, three times; a possession of the hero, three times; and no token, three times.

42. *Beowulf and the Fight at Finnsburg,* ed. Fr. Klaeber, 3d ed. (New York,
1941), ll. 2720 ff. An excellent translation is by Charles W. Kennedy (New
York, 1940).

43. J. Fraser (ed. and trans.), "The First Battle of Moytura," *Ériu,* VIII
(1916), 34 f.

44. Cecile O'Rahilly (ed. and trans.), *Eachtra Uilliam* (Dublin, 1949), pp.
210, 225. On p. 196 of this seventeenth-century tale, however, a bath is used as
a means of recognition.

45. *Táin Bó Cúalnge,* ed. and trans. Ernst Windisch, *Irische Texte,* V (1905),
pp. 598 f.; trans. Joseph Dunn (London, 1914), p. 268. A recent and available
edition in both Irish and English is Cecile O'Rahilly (ed. and trans.), *Táin Bó
Cúalnge from the Book of Leinster* (Dublin, 1967).

46. Ernst Windisch (ed. and trans.), "Tochmarc Ferbe," *Irische Texte,* III
(1897), pp. 468 f.

47. Whitley Stokes (ed. and trans.), "The Violent Deaths of Goll and Garb,"
RC, XIV (1893), 416 f.

inghneach,[48] *The Battle of Magh Rath,*[49] *Comhrag Fir Diadh 7 Chon Culainn,*[50] and *The Feast of Bricriu.*[51] I think it may be said that the bath is customarily used for healing [52] or hospitality, not for identification.

Although the initial purpose of the bath was not recognition, the fact still remains that in both Thomas' version of *Tristan and Isolt* and the *Wooing of Emer* the hero while bathing was recognized by the heroine. Furthermore in both cases the bath occurred after the hero had been engaged in a combat frequently related in a worldwide dragon-killing folktale. Tristan identified himself as the slayer of the dragon by producing the dragon's tongue. This, according to Hartland, was the most common means of identification. It was so frequent that I propose that when the dragon-slaying adventure was attached to the story of Drust, thus forming the prototypes of dragon-slaying episodes in both the *Wooing of Emer* and *Tristan and Isolt,* the hero identified himself by means of the dragon's tongue as he did in 76 examples of Hartland's 109.[53]

This, then, may be said about the bath. In the original dragon adventure it was used to heal the hero. But when this adventure and the Minotaur story were attached to tales of Drust, the author saw a magnificent opportunity to dovetail his two stories. He thus caused the Princess to recognize the slayer of her uncle by recognizing the hero's sword while the hero was in his curative bath. This of course is the Tristan story, but I maintain it was also the Drust story and is reflected in the Dervorgil adventure. Remember the actual words of the Dervorgil episode: "Cúchulainn came [to the bath] like all the

48. Patrick M. MacSweeney, "Martial Career of Conghal Cláiringhneach," *ITS*, V (1904), 82 f.

49. John O'Donovan (ed. and trans.), *The Battle of Magh Rath* (Dublin, 1842), pp. 274 ff.

50. R. I. Best (ed.), "Comhrag Fir Diadh 7 Chon Culainn," *ZCP*, X (1915), 303.

51. George Henderson (ed. and trans.), "Fled Bricrend—The Feast of Bricriu," *ITS*, No. II (1899), 102 f. See also Cross and Slover, *Ancient Irish Tales*, pp. 254–80.

52. Cf. the Scottish tale "Fionn's Ransom," ed. John G. Campbell, *The Fians, Waifs and Strays of Celtic Tradition*, Argyllshire Series, IV (London, 1891), pp. 245 f.

53. Hartland, *Legend of Perseus*, III, 203 ff.

rest, and the maiden recognized him." Why did she recognize him? There is no reason why she should in the *Wooing of Emer,* but if we accept the proposal that this adventure descends from a tale of Drust very much like *Tristan and Isolt,* then her recognition itself descends from the Princess' recognition of Drust as the slayer of her uncle.[54]

The value of the Dervorgil story is that behind it lay a story of Drust which included adventures like Tristan's Morholt episode and combat with the dragon. Thus the prototype of the Dervorgil story is also the prototype of *Tristan and Isolt,* and it was told about Drust. Since the name *Drust* had changed to the name *Trystan* even in Welsh versions of the adventures of this figure, apparently these two tales, the Morholt and dragon, were assigned to one hero on British soil.

THE RECOGNITION PROBLEM

Unless there is evidence of a difference in story structure between the extant *Tristan and Isolt* and the hypothetical *Drustansaga,* my reconstruction of the *Drustansaga* follows the events of the extant *Tristan and Isolt.* Drust, therefore, after killing the Princess' uncle traveled to the land of the heroine, where he slew a dragon and then was twice recognized: as the slayer of the royal tribute gatherer because his sword was known and as the slayer of the dragon because he possessed the dragon's tongue. But if the Morholt adventure is based on the Minotaur episode, then the Irish Princess was the secret ally of Drust in the defeat of her uncle (or half brother), just as Ariadne was. Why, then, did she have trouble in recognizing him later? Van Hamel suggested that originally there was one recognition scene, when Tristan by means of his sword or another token was recognized as the slayer of the Morholt.[55] But if my reconstruction is valid, the Morholt episode, because its scene was shifted, demanded its own recognition scene; whereas the dragon folktale customarily offers a false claimant to be exposed.

I think that the explanation lies in the shifting of the Minotaur story from the land of the heroine to the land of the hero. The *Táin*

---

54. The equations of the Fomorians and the Morholt has been observed before. See Bromwich, "Celtic Sources of 'Tristan,'" pp. 39 f.

55. "Tristan's Combat With the Dragon," pp. 347 ff.

Bó Fraích offers a significant clue. In this eleventh-century Irish tale [56] the hero fights a monster in a barely accessible place, gains the enmity and then the friendship of the heroine's father, and has a second combat, this time with a dragon. The heroine of this story presents the hero with a sword just as he is going into combat with the first monster. The first of Tristan's two combats, that with the Morholt, was based, I believe, on Theseus' defeat of the Minotaur. In the Theseus myth, Ariadne presented the hero with a sword, as did the heroine of the *Táin Bó Fraích* in the corresponding combat. Therefore, I suggest that the heroine of the *Drustansaga* did the same. When the scene of the Morholt episode was moved to the land of the hero, the heroine, still the provider of the sword, *sent it to him*. This action was later dropped possibly because someone was more pleased by the drama of the sword fragment than by a heroine disloyal to her father.[57] However, a remnant survived: Isolt recognized Tristan because she recognized his sword. If the Morholt's skull exposed a flaw in the blade, what would the dragon, which could shatter a lance, have done to it? Heroes were not usually so tolerant of inferior craftsmanship. The answer appears to be that the original sword did not break, anyway not at that particular point of the story. Because the Princess recognized the sword but not its owner, she must have known the sword but not its owner. Therefore, she must have sent it to him. She was just as much a rebel as Ariadne.[58]

Why did she send a sword to the British (or Pictish) hero? In the Theseus myth Ariadne presented Theseus with the sword because she loved him. Very likely Isolt did the same. After the action of the Morholt episode was moved across the sea, she had to fall in love with the hero before she saw him. There is evidence that this is exactly what happened because in five Irish tales which show some

56. So dated by Carney, *Studies in Irish Literature and History* (Dublin, 1955), p. 24.
57. Also, as we shall see in the next chapter, the reconstruction of the death scene provided the broken sword for these incidents in the early part of the story. See below, p. 149.
58. This is not to say that the broken sword was the happy invention of the *Drustansaga* author. Usually when a hero breaks his sword, his death is near; and in the next chapter I hope to demonstrate that this particular broken sword episode was borrowed from Tristan's own death struggle.

relationship to the Tristan story—*Scéla Cano, Tochmarc Treblainne, Baile and Ailinn, The Exile of the Sons of Uisliu,* and *Táin Bó Fraích* —the heroine does just that. Even in Thomas' version Isolt at one point is eager to meet Tantris because she is fascinated by his reputation.

The reason for the necessity for two recognition scenes is now clear. Since the princess knew and loved the hero by reputation only, it was necessary that she identify him by his sword. Originally she was probably pleased to discover the killer of her hated relative. Her anger developed only after someone caused her to shift sides by inventing an affection for the Morholt. The fact that the recognition in one version occurred while the hero was bathing explains no more than that a bath was a part of the healing process; there is no evidence that the bath formed a necessary part of the identification.

The second recognition was part of the dragon folktale, in which the hero customarily identified himself by producing the dragon's tongue. There is no reason why the second recognition should be considered a redundancy. In one case the princess learned that the hero whom she had loved at a distance was actually with her, and in the other case the assembled court learned that this hero was the true slayer of the dragon.

The combination of the two monster-killing tales caused an ambivalent attitude on the part of the king, the heroine's father. His anger was based on that of King Minos and his pleasure on that of the harassed king in the dragon folktale. The abrupt change in his attitude is probably paralleled by a similar change in *Táin Bó Fraích* on the part of King Ailill toward Froech, who was also engaged against two monsters; the first a water beast which he overcame by means of a sword presented by the heroine; the second a serpent or dragon which dwelled overseas.[59]

The conclusion, then, is that the two episodes of the tribute gatherers, apparently a series of duplications, are not doublets. Each is its own story, and at an early date both were combined into the *Drustansaga.* The source of the Morholt episode, like the source of the reluctant lover theme, was an incident in the life of Theseus, which must have been very well known to the author of the *Drus-*

59. Carney, *Studies,* pp. 1–14.

tansaga. The source of the dragon-slaying episode was a worldwide dragon myth, also well known to this literate hypothetical author.

Because of the proper names in the story, the author of the *Drustansaga* must have been writing for a North-British audience. Because the *Drustansaga* utilized famous old names from the heroic age of the sixth century, it was probably composed no earlier than the seventh century. Because it obviously precedes the tenth-century [60] Dervorgil episode of the *Wooing of Emer* and because it was apparently composed during the period when the North British monasteries flourished, it probably was composed no later than the eighth century. The author, as I have shown in this chapter and the previous one, was dependent upon Greek and pan-European mythology. The most likely place in the North British seventh and eighth centuries for a literate man to have access to a library containing information about classical figures was the Columban monasteries. Therefore it must be concluded again that the author of the *Drustansaga* had access to a library in a North British monastery of the Columban Church, a library which would give him the information which he used.

Thus the argument of this entire study: a literate man, probably a cleric, associated with a North British Columban ecclesiastical center, combined incidents and motifs from his library with the known names of local heroes and in doing so produced the prototype of *Tristan and Isolt* and its analogues, a prototype which is called here the *Drustansaga.*

60. So dated by Helaine Newstead, "The Origin and Growth of the Tristan Legend," *ALMA,* p. 126.

Chapter Nine ✳ ✳

THE DEATH SCENE

WO VERSIONS of the death of Tristan appear in the Continental romances. According to Eilhart and Thomas, Tristan died as a result of the famous deception of the black and white sails. In the Prose Romances Tristan's death was caused directly by King Mark.

VARIOUS VERSIONS OF THE DEATH SCENE ✳

The version used by Eilhart and Thomas has become one of the famous scenes of literature. The wounded Tristan waits for Isolt the Queen to come over the seas and is told by Isolt of Brittany that the ship is approaching with black sails and therefore without his Isolt. After this duplicity by his wife Tristan turns his face to the wall and dies. Isolt then arrives and sweeps majestically through the streets to the house of the dead Tristan, where she too dies. King Mark, on hearing of the two deaths, has the famous lovers buried in adjacent graves.

The other version, found in the Prose Romances, is far more trite. In it King Mark surprised the unarmed Tristan and wounded him with a poisoned sword. Tristan knew he was mortally wounded and begged a last kiss from Isolt. She kissed him but was so grieved that her heart burst. They died in each other's arms. This rendition or something like it appears in the French *Prose Tristan*,[1] the Italian *Tavola Ritonda*,[2] and the English *Morte d'Arthur*.[3]

In this chapter I offer a conclusion of the tale as I believe it appeared in the North British *Drustansaga*. The reasons for the sequence of events in this conclusion are so complex that I shall present the conclusion itself first and then the discussion in the remainder of the chapter.

The incident of the black and white sails apparently appeared in my hypothetical *Drustansaga*, whose author, as I have suggested elsewhere, seems to have drawn upon the story of Theseus. Comparisons with cognate stories and with the events that followed Tristan's engagement with the Morholt suggest, however, that the parent version of Tristan's death must have contained certain incidents: Drustan was wounded by a poisoned weapon, as he was in all versions. In the course of his final battle he broke his sword, as he did in the extant versions of the Morholt episode. At the time of his fatal wound he was across a sea from Essyllt, as he was in Eilhart's and Thomas' versions. His wound was so noxious that he went into isolation, as he did after the Morholt battle. Still, he managed to send a message to Essyllt, who was the only one who could heal him. March sailed to Drustan's place of isolation in order to bring him to Essyllt. The black and white sails were agreed upon, but it was March who hoisted the black sails so as to deceive Essyllt. She, watching on a high cliff for the boat, saw the black sails and threw herself over the cliff, smashing her head on the rocks below. When Drustan landed, there was no one to heal him, and he died. March was thus morally responsible for both deaths.

In Eilhart these incidents occur:[4] Tristan, living in Brittany, was married to his virgin bride, Isolt of the White Hands. Her brother, Kaherdin, loved the wife of Nampêtenis. One day when Nampêtenis was away from home, Kaherdin, with Tristan's aid, gained admission to his mistress' chamber. When Nampêtenis returned, he forced her

---

1. E. Löseth (ed.), *Le Roman en prose de Tristan* (Paris, 1891), secs. 546 ff.

2. F. L. Polidori (ed.), *La Tavola Ritonda, Collezione di opere inedite o rare*, VIII (Bologna, 1864), I, 495 ff.

3. Eugène Vinaver (ed.), *The Works of Sir Thomas Malory*, 3 vols. (Oxford, 1954), Book XIX, Chap. xi.

4. Eilhart von Oberge, *Tristrant*, ed. Franz Lichtenstein, *Quellen und Forschungen zur Sprach- und Culturgeschichte*, XIX (Strasbourg, 1877), ll. 9033 ff.

to confess that she had been intimate with Kaherdin. Nampêtenis summoned an entourage and rushed in pursuit of Kaherdin and Tristan. In the subsequent battle Kaherdin was killed, and Tristan was wounded with a poisoned spear. As had happened before, no one could heal him but Isolt the Queen, wife of King Mark of Cornwall and sometime mistress of Tristan.

Tristan sent a messenger to Cornwall with a ring which Queen Isolt had long ago given Tristan. If the messenger returned with Queen Isolt, his ship was to bear white sails; if he failed, black sails. But Tristan's wife, Isolt of the White Hands, learned of this scheme. And when the ship returned bearing white sails, Isolt of the White Hands told Tristan that the sails were black. On hearing this news Tristan put his head down and died.

When Queen Isolt landed and learned of Tristan's death, she demanded to be taken to him. Then she lay down beside him and died.

King Mark had the two bodies brought to Cornwall and gave them a burial befitting their rank. From the grave of Isolt grew a rosebud, and from the grave of Tristan a vine. These met and could never be parted.

In Thomas' version the wife of a giant knight known as Tristan the Dwarf had been kidnapped. The giant asked Tristan to help him regain her. In the ensuing battle Tristan received his poisoned wound.[5]

Two versions of the death of a hero are included in the death of Tristan: first, the death from a poisoned wound which only one person could cure and, second, the death based on a misinterpretation of a message from the sea, a message signalled to the land by means of the color of the ship's sails.

THE POISONED WOUND ▒

The circumstances which lead to the poisoned wound have no parallel that I know of in the Celtic tales which have been associated

5. Roger Sherman Loomis (ed. and trans.), *The Romance of Tristram and Ysolt*, new rev. ed. (New York, 1951), pp. 263 ff. Eugen Kölbing (ed.), *Die nordische und die englische Version der Tristan-sage*, 2 vols. (Heilbronn, 1882), I, 107 ff. Joseph Bédier (ed.), *Le Roman de Tristan par Thomas*, SATF, No. LIII, 2 vols. (Paris, 1902–5), I, 378 ff.

with *Tristan and Isolt*. Evidently the author of the *estoire*[6] introduced matter that would appeal to his Continental audience.

The name *Nampêtenis,* used by Eilhart, is, according to Bédier, a
corruption of the form *le Nain Bedenis* or *Bedenis the Dwarf.*[7] This
name appears in the *Prose Tristan* as *Bedalis.*[8] Miss Schoepperle
accepts the derivation of the name *Nampêtenis* but does not believe
that either Bedenis or Thomas' Tristan the Dwarf were originally
dwarfs.[9] Harward, in his study of dwarfs, takes the opposite view,
maintaining that this figure was originally a ludicrous dwarf husband
who was created to be cuckolded.[10] No dwarf husband appears in
the related Irish *aitheda,* the Welsh fragments, or the classical stories
which I have proposed as antecedents to these tales.[11] Still the story,
or a form of it, was known to Thomas and Eilhart. Therefore the
incident was evidently in the *estoire,* but there is no evidence that it
was a part of the *Drustansaga.* I think Harward is correct when he
assigns such an incident to the world of the fabliau or the sophisticated Continental court. Tristan did receive a poisoned wound, and
in time the wound caused his death, but the original wound was not
given as a result of a Breton bedroom farce.

One characteristic of the death scene is common not only to most
of the versions of *Tristan and Isolt*[12] but also to the *Pursuit after*

6. The *estoire* was Bédier's and Miss Schoepperle's name for the hypothetical
twelfth-century Continental source of both Eilhart and Thomas. See Bédier,
Le Roman de Tristan, II, passim; Gertrude Schoepperle, *Tristan and Isolt: A
Study of the Sources of the Romance,* 2 vols. (Frankfurt and London, 1913;
reprinted, New York, 1959), I, 66 ff., and passim.
7. Bédier, *Le Roman de Tristan par Thomas,* II, 135 f.
8. Löseth, *Le Roman en prose de Tristan par Thomas,* secs. 535a, 540a, 541a.
9. Schoepperle, *Tristan and Isolt,* I, 249.
10. Vernon J. Harward, Jr., *The Dwarfs of Arthurian Romance and Celtic
Tradition* (Leiden, 1958), pp. 85 ff.
11. Bédier suggests that an ultimate source of the tale of the cuckolded dwarf
might be Theseus' descent into the regions of the dead, in which Theseus unsuc-
cessfully attempted to win Persephone, wife of Hades himself, for his friend
Pirithoüs. See *Le Roman de Tristan par Thomas,* II, 135 f. As much as I applaud
Bédier's instincts in searching for sources of *Tristan and Isolt* in classical mythology, I cannot endorse this particular comparison. Hades is not a dwarf; he
is not a ludicrous figure; and Theseus' mission failed in such a way that Theseus
became the ridiculous one.
12. All except the *Prose Tristan,* in which Tristan meets his death because
Mark stabs him in the back with a poisoned sword. See Löseth, *Le Roman en*

Diarmaid and Gráinne. This is the poisoned wound which could be cured by one person only, a person who fails to effect the cure. Isolt failed to heal Tristan because he died before she reached him. Diarmaid, too, died when he might have been saved.

It had been prophesied that Diarmaid, the lover of his uncle Fionn's wife, Gráinne, would be killed by a boar. In his last combat Diarmaid fought a boar and killed it, breaking his sword in the battle. However, he was wounded, according to some versions, by the poisoned bristles of the boar.[13] Fionn had the unique gift of healing anyone who drank water from his hands. Twice Fionn brought water in his hands to Diarmaid; and twice, remembering Diarmaid's relationship with Gráinne, he let the water slip through his fingers. The third time he held the water, but Diarmaid was dead.[14]

The similarity of the deaths of Diarmaid and Tristan suggests that in a common ancestor to both stories there was a hero who died because the one person who could save him from a poisoned wound failed him. The boar with the poisoned bristles was probably evolved in this way: Diarmaid existed as a folk hero before the love story was attached to his reputation. The tradition was that Diarmaid was killed by a boar. Men, even heroes, had died in such a way before. But in the love story the tradition was that the protagonist died from a poisoned wound which only one person could cure. The obvious combination of the two traditions would be a boar with poisoned bristles. Thus all traditions were adhered to and nobody's sensitivity was violated.

---

prose de Tristan, secs. 546 ff. Miss Schoepperle said that this version was more primitive and probably older than the incident of the black and white sails. See *Tristan and Isolt,* II, 439 f. But I hope to show here that such a death for Tristan is not a prototype but a degeneration of the better-known versions.

13. John G. Campbell, *The Fians, Waifs and Strays of Celtic Tradition,* Argyllshire Series, IV (London, 1891), pp. 56, 59, 62. See also J. H. Lloyd, O. J. Bergin, and Gertrude Schoepperle, "The Death of Diarmaid," *RC,* XXXIII (1912), 157–79.

14. Standish Hayes O'Grady (ed. and trans.), *Tqruigheacht Dhiarmuda agus Ghrainne—The Pursuit after Diarmaid and Gráinne, Transactions of the Ossianic Society for the Year 1855,* III (Dublin, 1857), pp. 180 f. Tom Peete Cross and C. H. Slover (eds.), *Ancient Irish Tales* (London, n.d.), pp. 411 ff. Campbell, *The Fians,* pp. 56, 59, 62.

THE VOYAGE FOR HEALING ▨

If death from a poisoned wound which only one person could cure is inherent in the Tristan story, the Voyage for Healing [15] must be considered, for it tells a story similar in all but the death itself.

When Tristan slew the Morholt he escaped with neither a whole sword nor a whole body. Part of his sword was left embedded in the Morholt's skull. And the Morholt had given him a poisoned wound which failed to heal. Eilhart says [16] that only Princess Isolt, the daughter of the King of Ireland, could heal Tristan's poisoned wound. No one in Cornwall could aid Tristan, and daily the stench of his wound became worse. He isolated himself in a little house by the sea, where he would offend no one. Finally he begged to be set adrift on the sea with only his sword and harp. His rudderless boat took him to Ireland, where he gave his name as Pro of Iemsetir and his profession as minstrel. He was cured by Isolt, who sent healing herbs with a messenger but did not see him. He then returned to Cornwall. Later he made a second voyage to Ireland, but he did not reveal that Pro of Iemsetir was Tristan.

Thomas' version of the Voyage for Healing [17] differs slightly from Eilhart's. According to Thomas, the one person who could heal the wound was Queen Isolt, the mother of Princess Isolt. Tristan was isolated and placed in a boat which by chance took him to Ireland. There he gave his name as Tantris, and although he was wounded he charmed the court with his harp. The Queen undertook to heal him; and the Princess Isolt demanded that he be presented to her and that he instruct her in the harp. He taught Isolt, and after he was completely healed he sailed back to Cornwall. Later he returned to Ireland, where in time he was recognized as both Tantris and Tristan.

Miss Schoepperle says that the Voyage for Healing was a foreign interpolation and that Eilhart's version is earlier than Thomas'

15. The Voyage for Healing is Miss Schoepperle's name for the series of incidents which followed the death of the Morholt. See *Tristan and Isolt*, I, 194 ff., II, 326 ff.

16. *Tristrant*, ll. 1012–1337.

17. Loomis, *Tristram and Ysolt*, pp. 80 ff.; Kölbing, *Tristan-sage*, I, 37 ff.; Bédier, *Le Roman de Tristan par Thomas*, I, 92 ff.

because the Voyage is less skillfully dovetailed with the rest of the story.[18] Thomas, she continues, eventually has his Tristan identified as the wounded minstrel, but Eilhart never mentions again the incidents of the Voyage for Healing. I agree with Miss Schoepperle that the Voyage for Healing was interpolated, but I do not believe that it was foreign to the story.

The essentials of the death scene are found in the Voyage for Healing: the poisoned wound, in both the deaths of Diarmaid and of Tristan; the broken sword in the death of Diarmaid; [19] the journey for healing in the death of Tristan; [20] and the one person who could cure the wound, in the death of Diarmaid and the death of Tristan.

Miss Schoepperle noted that the incident of the isolated hut, which precedes the Voyage for Healing and which I believe is a part of it, is similar to the classical story of Philoctetes, who also was isolated because he suffered from an offensive wound.[21] She also remarked, as had Golther previously,[22] that there was a similarity between the death of Tristan and the death of Paris, the Trojan War figure.[23] What Miss Schoepperle overlooked was that the Philoctetes incident led directly into the death of Paris, just as Tristan's isolation in a hut led directly into the Voyage for Healing.

PHILOCTETES AND THE DEATH OF PARIS

Philoctetes was the Greek archer who inherited Heracles' poisoned arrows. While traveling with the Greek army to Troy, Philoctetes wounded himself with one of these arrows. The wound festered, would not heal, and became so offensive that Philoctetes was exiled

18. *Tristan and Isolt,* I, 194 f.
19. Of course Tristan's sword was only chipped in the extant versions, but then he had to use it again. Note also that Beowulf broke his sword in his last battle. See Fr. Klaeber (ed.), *Beowulf and the Fight at Finnsburg,* 3d ed. (New York, 1941), ll. 2680 ff. Evidently in the minds of some there was a symbolic connection between the breaking of the sword and the last fight of a hero.
20. Transferred, of course, to Isolt, who makes the journey to heal the wounded Tristan.
21. *Tristan and Isolt,* II, 369 f.
22. W. Golther, *Tristan und Isolde in den Dichtungen des Mittelalters und der neuen Zeit* (Leipzig, 1907), pp. 20–23.
23. *Tristan and Isolt,* II, 437.

to a tiny island. Years later the Greek leaders learned that the Trojan Paris could be killed only by these same poisoned arrows. Odysseus went to the island and returned with Philoctetes and his arrows. Philoctetes fought with Paris and mortally wounded him. Paris had been told years before that if he received a poisoned wound he could be healed only by Oenone, the mistress whom he left for Helen. He was carried to Oenone's house, but she refused him aid as he had refused her love. After Paris was carried away to die, Oenone repented her action. When she reached Paris' side he was dead. She then killed herself, according to some versions by throwing herself on his funeral pyre.[24]

This sequence of events may be compared with the stories that have been presented. Philoctetes, before he shot Paris, received a poisoned wound which was so unpleasant that he had to be isolated on an island. Tristan, prior to the events of the Voyage for Healing, received from the Morholt a wound which was so unpleasant that he requested first a lonely hut and then a rudderless boat.[25] The same poison that had wounded Philoctetes wounded Paris. Only Oenone could cure Paris' wound, and she failed him. Only Isolt could cure Tristan's wound from the Morholt's poisoned sword, and only Isolt, who of course ultimately failed him, could cure the poisoned wound which caused Tristan's death. Only Fionn could cure the poisoned wound which caused Diarmaid's death, and like his counterparts in related stories, Fionn failed Diarmaid. For his cure Paris sought Oenone, just as Tristan sought Isolt in the Voyage for Healing, and just as Isolt sought Tristan at the time of their deaths.[26]

24. This synopsis is reconstructed from Gustav Schwab, *Gods and Heroes,* trans. Olga Marx and Ernst Morwitz (London, 1950), pp. 544 ff.; and Robert Graves, *The Greek Myths,* 2 vols. (London, 1957), II, 326 f.

25. The rudderless boat is another matter. Miss Schoepperle points out that it was a widely used tale in Old Irish and other literatures. See *Tristan and Isolt,* II, 370 ff. Cf. Rachel Bromwich, "Some Remarks on the Celtic Sources of 'Tristan,'" *THSC,* Session 1953 (London, 1955), pp. 41 f. The earlier tales of this type were a form of punishment in which God was to determine the fate of the victim. See Mary E. Byrne, "On the Punishment of Setting Adrift," *Ériu* XI (1932), 97–102.

26. Cf. the ending of *Oidhe Chloinne Tureann—The Fate of the Children of Tuireann,* ed. Richard O'Duffy (Dublin, 1888), pars. 64 ff. Cf. also the Egyptian myth in which the dead Osiris drifted in a chest from Egypt to Syria to be rescued and resurrected by Isis.

The similarities between the Voyage for Healing and the death scenes of Paris, Diarmaid, and Tristan are self-evident.

Before the Voyage for Healing Tristan fought the Morholt; and just before their deaths Paris fought Philoctetes, Diarmaid fought a boar, and Tristan fought an antagonist who bore a variety of names in the various versions. Tristan in the Voyage for Healing was suffering from a poisoned wound as were Paris, Diarmaid, and Tristan before their deaths. Tristan broke his sword on the Morholt, and Diarmaid broke his on the boar. Tristan's wound was so repulsive that he had to be isolated; so was Philoctetes' wound. Isolt was the only one who could cure Tristan of this wound, and Oenone, Fionn, and Isolt were similarly qualified. Tristan's journey to Isolt on the Voyage for Healing parallels Paris' journey to Oenone and Isolt's journey to the dying Tristan.

These comparisons certainly indicate that the Voyage for Healing is ultimately derived from the story of the isolation of Philoctetes and the death of Paris. Originally, then, it was the story of the death of a hero, and I think that in the *Drustansaga* it was part of the death scene of Tristan.

If the broken sword and the Voyage for Healing are removed from the early part of the story, the Morholt adventure is directly followed by the slaying of the dragon. This, I think, was the original sequence.[27] If, as I have proposed in Chapter Eight, the Isolt of the *Drustansaga* sent Tristan the sword with which he slew the Morholt (just as Ariadne gave Theseus the sword with which he slew the Minotaur), she would recognize the sword later without having to fit a broken chip to the blade. She did need some token by which she could recognize the hero, for she had never met him but was attracted to him from a distance, in the way that heroines of analogous Irish stories had of falling in love, sight unseen. There-

27. This particular sequence is reflected in *Táin Bó Fraích*. See James Carney, *Studies in Irish Literature and History* (Dublin, 1955), pp. 1 ff.; and J. F. Campbell, *The Celtic Dragon Myth* with *The Geste of Fraoch and the Dragon*, trans. George Henderson (Edinburgh, 1911), pp. 1 ff. In *Táin Bó Fraích* Fraích, the hero, received a sword from the heroine, killed a monster with it, received a healing bath, took a journey, and encountered a serpent. I suspect that this story was strongly influenced by the *Drustansaga*, and Carney in his discussion of it suggests that the *Táin Bó Fraích* was developed from North British sources, just as I am continually suggesting here that the *Drustansaga* was so developed. See Carney, *Studies*, Chaps. 1–3.

fore, she needed the sword, and even without its notch it served as a recognition token.

In summary, then, the Voyage for Healing originally did not immediately succeed the Morholt episode but was a part of the conclusion of the poem. The essence of this incident remained unchanged, although the voyage itself was transferred from the end of the story to an early part of it. Originally Tristan fought an antagonist, killed him of course, but broke his sword in the combat. He received a poisoned wound which festered and would not heal. He retired to isolation, and he knew that only Isolt could cure him. In time he sailed to her, and how she failed him when he arrived will be shown shortly.

THE BLACK AND WHITE SAILS

Traditionally in the Tristan legend the deaths of the protagonists depend on a misinterpretation of a message from the sea or the deception of the black and white sails. In the last chapter I suggested that Theseus' adventure with the Minotaur was the source of the Morholt episode. Theseus, in that adventure, returned home from Crete having promised that his ship would carry white sails if he had killed the Minotaur and black sails if he had been killed. But Theseus, grief-stricken at the loss of Ariadne, forgot his instructions. His ship appeared in the Athenian harbor bearing black sails; and old King Aegeus, Theseus' father, believing that Theseus was dead, hurled himself from the Acropolis, smashing his brains on the rocks below.[28]

Bédier suggested that whoever incorporated the story of the black and white sails into the Tristan story had read it in Servius' commentary on Vergil.[29] Miss Schoepperle also noticed the parallel to the Theseus story and added that one would expect to find such a story among any seafaring people.[30] That is to say, she felt that the story of the black and white sails was a worldwide commonplace, but I do not think the answer to the problem is quite so simple.

28. Schwab, *Gods and Heroes*, pp. 213 f.; Graves, *Greek Myths*, I, 337, 343.
29. *Le Roman de Tristan par Thomas*, II, 139.
30. *Tristan and Isolt*, II, 438.

The story has been told among seafarers, but not often enough, so far as I have discovered, to brand it a commonplace. In an early essay Miss Schoepperle listed several versions of an Irish example of the story,[31] the Fenian tale of *The Lad of the Skins,* which appears in a number of loosely similar retellings.[32] The story is long and full of material irrelevant to the questions at hand, but in certain versions of its climax Fionn returned in a ship bearing the corpse of the hero. Fionn had promised the hero's wife that he would signal her from the sea to tell her if her husband had survived the trip. In one case the signal was a certain color of sail, in another a flag. Fionn knew that the hero's wife would not permit the ship to land if she knew her husband was dead. He displayed the incorrect color and thus landed safely.

Miss Schoepperle[33] also cited a second example[34] from Irish folktales in which a black signal from the sea caused a hero to kill himself because he believed that his mistress, who was arriving in the ship, was dead. She offered this tale, however, with reservations because she could not trace it to older Irish literature. I endorse her suspicions. The tale she cited is too much like extant tales of the death of Tristan. That is, it appears to be a development not of the insular *Drustansaga* but the Continental *estoire.*

Another example of death following false news from the sea was mentioned by Professor Carney.[35] In *Cano*[36] the heroine looked to the sea and received false news of the hero's death. She then smashed her head against a rock, just as Deirdre did in *The Exile of the Sons of Uisliu.* In still other stories of elopement either the sea motif or the false information persists alone.[37]

---

31. A. Kelleher and G. Schoepperle, "Finn dans le pays des géants," *RC* XXXII (1911), 185–86, nn. 3, 4.

32. Campbell, *The Fians,* pp. 228, 266 f. Jeremiah Curtin, *Myths and Folk-Lore of Ireland* (Boston, 1890), pp. 244 ff. W. Larminie, *West Irish Folktales* (London, 1893), pp. 64 ff. G. Dottin, *Contes et légendes d'Irlande* (Le Havre, 1901), pp. 47 ff.

33. *Tristan and Isolt,* II, 438, n. 2.

34. J. G. Campbell, *Clan Traditions and Popular Tales of the Western Highlands and Islands, Waifs and Strays of Celtic Tradition,* V, Argyllshire Series (London, 1895), p. 76.

35. *Studies,* pp. 215 ff.

36. Ed. Dillon, *The Cycles of the Kings* (Oxford, 1946), pp. 80 ff.

37. Cf. Chart 2 above, pp. 104–5.

In these death stories, whenever false information from the sea leads to a death, it is the land watcher who believes that the sea-borne hero is dead and thus commits suicide, usually in the unique manner of self-destruction upon jagged rocks. The story of Theseus contained such a scene, and I believe it was passed forward to all these other tales.

What then is the original version of the deaths of Tristan and Isolt? I have already suggested that Tristan originally received a poisoned wound and journeyed to Isolt and that Isolt failed to heal him. Now if this sequence is combined with the motif of the black and white sails, it appears that it was not Tristan but Isolt who was awaiting the ship and who died because she received false information from the sea.[38] That is, Tristan, like Theseus, was in the ship; Isolt, like Aegeus, was the land watcher.

If Isolt did die because she was deceived by news from the sea, how did she learn her news, and what did she do when she learned it? I think that the manner of her death is obvious. Like Aegeus in the story of Theseus, like Créd in *Cano,* and like Deirdre in *The Exile of the Sons of Uisliu,* Isolt too must have thrown herself on rocks and smashed her head. This type of death appears in the Theseus story, which I propose as an ancestor to the *Drustansaga,* and the two Irish tales, *Cano* and *The Exile of the Sons of Uisliu,* which were apparently descendants of the Theseus story and of the *Drustansaga* too. Now if Isolt died by throwing herself on to rocks, the messenger who reported black sails must be eliminated from this part of the story.[39] In order to effect such a suicide, Isolt must have been standing in a place where she could throw herself down a cliff. That is, I believe that Isolt knew that Tristan was coming to her, that he was wounded, and that the sails on the boat were to announce whether he had or had not survived the trip.

In most of the cognate tales the wronged husband was morally or actually responsible for the hero's death. In the story of Phaedra he ordered the hero to be killed; in *Diarmaid and Gráinne* he purposefully neglected to resuscitate the hero; in *The Exile of the Sons of Uisliu* he ordered Noíse's death; and in the *Prose Tristan* he

---

38. So agrees Professor Carney, *Studies,* p. 202.

39. Here I disagree with Professor Carney, who in his reconstruction retains the messenger as King Mark.

killed the hero. From the last three of these death scenes Miss Schoepperle deduced that in an early version of the story King Mark was responsible for the lovers' deaths.[40] I agree with her in that Mark was responsible but wish to add Professor Carney's corollary that he was only morally and not physically responsible for the deaths. Carney sees Mark as the messenger, but there is no messenger in any insular version. I do not see why Isolt would throw herself over the cliff unless she were watching for the ship. Rather, I think we can take a suggestion from the very late tale of *The Lad of the Skins*. We remember that in one version of that story Fionn was in the ship with the hero and raised the incorrect sail, thus deceiving a lady on the shore. Also, in one version, Fionn was the hero's uncle. With that late tale as a hint, we can propose a reconstruction in which Mark was morally responsible for the deaths of the lovers and Isolt watched from the cliff for the black or white sails. The solution is that Mark was in the ship with the wounded Tristan.[41] He probably rescued Tristan from his place of isolation much as Odysseus rescued Philoctetes. Mark, knowing that only Isolt could cure Tristan's wound, raised the black sail so that Isolt would be deceived into believing that Tristan had not survived the trip. He knew she would then kill herself and knew that without her aid Tristan, too, would die. Thus, as it was in the Theseus story, the source of the misconception was a black sail which reported false information and not, as in the present stories, a white sail incorrectly reported as black. Isolt, when she saw the black sail, threw herself from the cliff, dying just as Aegeus had died. Tristan, on arriving at the house of the one person who could cure his wound, found her dead and of course unable to help him. Then he died in the same manner Paris died.

This, of course, is not the ending which we all know. The criticism

---

40. *Tristan and Isolt*, II, 437 ff.

41. Although Mark is not a seafarer and hardly ever leaves his kingdom in the extant versions of the legend, he was known in Welsh lore as one of the three fleet owners of the Island of Prydein and was associated with the men of Llychlyn, who were sea raiders. See William F. Skene, *The Four Ancient Books of Wales*, 2 vols. (Edinburgh, 1868), II, 458 f.; J. Loth, *Les Mabinogion*, 2 vols. (Paris, 1913), I, 361; and Rachel Bromwich, *Trioedd Ynys Prydein—The Welsh Triads* (Cardiff, 1961), Triad 14, p. 25, and pp. 82–83. See also W. J. Gruffydd, *Rhiannon* (Cardiff, 1953), p. 26, n. 2.

may be raised that such a version is based on what is not in the extant *Tristan and Isolt* rather than what is. In a sense this is a fair criticism. My insular reconstruction is based on elements in the Voyage for Healing, elements in other insular tales declared by others to be related to the Tristan story, and elements from the myth of Theseus. The familiar ending to the story, I think, is a Breton contribution, as is much of the extant *Tristan and Isolt*.[42] J. Loth [43] and Professor Loomis [44] cite a Breton tale which Professor M. Cuillandre of the College of Vannes heard during his childhood early in this century and wrote to Loth:

> Il s'agissait, je crois, d'un voyage d'épreuve en pays lointain; le héros devait en revenir vainqueur avant d'épouser la fille du roi dont il était épris et qui l'aimait elle aussi. Il fut convenu entre les deux jeunes gens que si l'entreprise réussissait, le vaisseau qui ramènerait le héros porterait une voile blanche; dans le cas contraire, ce serait une voile noire. L'attente fut longue, semble-t-il. La jeune princesse languit et tomba gravement malade. Elle envoyait souvent une compagne au sommet d'une tour pour voir si quelque voile n'apparaissait pas à l'horison. Un matin une voile se montra. La malade demanda: *"Du pe wenn eo gweliou al lestr?"* "Noires ou blanches sont les voiles du bateau?" Sa compagne répondit que la voile était *sombre comme la nuit (tenval evel an noz)*. Et la fille du roi mourut, désespérée. Ce fut le châtiment du père qui détestait le héros et qui avait dicté la réponse à la compagne de sa fille.

Here we see a close Breton parallel to the conventional ending of the Tristan story. The Princess, lying ill, waits for a report from the sea. When the hero does appear, with the anticipated white sails, a female companion, following orders from the Princess' father, brings the false information that the sails are black. As a result the Princess dies in despair. Unlike the insular and the classic versions, this tale depends upon the female messenger, who is apparently one of the many Breton contributions to the *estoire* and accordingly to the Continental versions of the story.

42. So agrees Professor Newstead. See "The Origin and Growth of the Tristan Legend," *ALMA*, p. 129.

43. J. Loth, "Contributions à l'étude des romans de la Table Ronde—XIII La voile blanche et la voile noire à l'île Molènes," *RC*, XXXVII (1917–19), 323.

44. Roger Sherman Loomis, "Breton Folklore and Arthurian Romance," *Comparative Literature*, II (1950), 293.

But every bit of evidence which may be gathered leads to the conclusion that the black and white sails story existed in the insular version of the tale, although it differed appreciably from the Continental ending. The prototype of the insular version, or *Drustansaga,* as I prefer to call it here, if it corresponded at all to the tales discussed above, must have had the heroine as the shore watcher killing herself on the rocks below when she saw the deceptive black sails. Such an ending is artistically satisfying and conforms to every version except the Continental ones.

DEATH IN THE *PROSE TRISTAN*

If the *Drustansaga* was constructed as I propose, it becomes impossible to accept Miss Schoepperle's suggestion that the scene of the *Prose Tristan* in which Mark fatally stabs Tristan is more primitive. Miss Schoepperle, looking at the death of Noíse in *The Exile of the Sons of Uisliu,* believed that in whatever original death scene preceded *The Exile of the Sons of Uisliu* and *Tristan and Isolt* the hero was killed directly by the wronged husband.[45] But a number of matters in both *The Sons of Uisliu* and the *Prose Tristan* point to an original such as the one I have reconstructed in this chapter. First, Deirdre, like Aegeus and also Créd in *Cano,* died by smashing her head on a rock. Although Deirdre dived no further than from a chariot, it still appears to me that death in such a manner is difficult unless the suicide chooses a high place to dive from. And the high place brings us right back to the high cliff of the black and white sails, which, as we have seen, were not unknown in Irish tales. Second, the death of Diarmaid, which includes the broken sword of the Voyage for Healing and the poisoned wound which only one person could cure, tells us that these elements too were in an earlier prototype. Third, we see that even in the degenerate *Prose Tristan* Mark used a poisoned sword when he killed Tristan. This poisoned sword, too, is reminiscent of the construction in this chapter. Fourth, the name *Bedalis,* associated by Bédier [46] and Miss Schoepperle [47] with Nampêtenis and Tristram the Dwarf,

45. *Tristan and Isolt,* II, 442 ff.
46. *Le Roman de Tristan par Thomas,* II, 135 f.
47. *Tristan and Isolt,* I, 249.

who figured in Tristan's death scene, appears in the *Prose Tristan*,[48] making it appear that the author knew of the conventional death scene of Tristan.

Miss Schoepperle agrees that the *Prose Tristan* is a "late and hopelessly corrupt redaction." [49] She is quite right, of course, when she says that it may contain older material than the extant poems. But in the particular case of the death scene, the evidence is that it does not. The problem of all the sources of the *Prose Tristan* is too involved for this study. I suggest that its author drew from any number of current popular romances in an effort to create a conglomeration including something for everybody. Possibly he knew that in an earlier version Mark was responsible for the deaths of the lovers—and possibly he did not but simply felt that a wronged husband should take his own vengeance. Either way, it does seem to me, after examining all of the evidence, that the death scene in the *Prose Tristan* is a later construction and that it supplanted, in that version, the more widely known and evidently earlier scene of the black and white sails.

THE ORIGINAL DEATH SCENE

The conclusion resulting from this argument is that the original death scene of Tristan was much closer to the story of Theseus than is the death scene in the extant versions. The wounded Tristan, after suffering a period of isolation because of his noxious wound, was in the boat, and Isolt was the watcher on the land. Mark, also in the boat, had raised black sails so that Isolt incorrectly thought Tristan was dead. She killed herself by smashing her head on the rocks below the cliff where she was standing. Tristan, who was counting on Isolt to cure him, arrived too late and also died. Mark, consequently, was morally responsible for both deaths. This version conforms with existing analogues and also with the proposed source. If there was a *Drustansaga* or source story, and the evidence is that there was; if this *Drustansaga* was composed by a North British ecclesiastical person familiar with local names and classical myths, and the evidence is that it was; if this *Drustansaga* was the

48. Löseth, *Le Roman en prose de Tristan*, secs. 535a, 540a, 541a.
49. *Tristan and Isolt*, I, 9.

ancestor of the extant tales, both *Tristan and Isolt* and analogues, and again the evidence is that it was; then it follows that the death scene outlined above must have been the source of all the death scenes in the extant tales.

Now let us turn to an examination of this *Drustansaga*.

Chapter Ten ▨ ▨

THE DRUSTAN-SAGA

 POPULAR STORY, one that appears widely in many versions, must have a source, an originator who first put the components of the story together and told it to whoever would listen. To explain that the source of such a story is "lost in antiquity" is merely to say that we do not know who the original storyteller was, not, of course, to say that he did not exist. But when the source of a story is hidden in a known historical period rather than in antiquity, then with a little investigation we should be able to discover something about its origin. To say that *Tristan and Isolt* developed from early medieval Irish tales such as *Diarmaid and Gráinne* and that the source of *Diarmaid and Gráinne* is "lost in antiquity" is neither sufficient nor, as far as I can see, true. *Tristan and Isolt* is related to *Diarmaid and Gráinne* in that they both descended from the work of a highly literate person, undoubtedly religious, who probably was associated with a North British monastery in about the seventh century.

SUMMARY OF FINDINGS ▨

In summary, my reasons for this conclusion are as follows:
1. The Irish Columban monasteries were a likely seventh-century place for sophisticated literary composition.

    a. There were Irish Columban monasteries in North Britain during the seventh and eighth centuries. The most renowned were Iona, Lindisfarne, and Whithorn, but others existed.

b. The tradition within the Irish Columban monastery was one of scholarship. The invasions of the fourth and fifth-century barbarians into western Europe caused many Gaulish scholars to flee to Ireland, where they brought a knowledge of the classics, the Latin language, and the Greek language. Ecclesiastical leaders like St. Columba and those who followed him were able to have an understandable classical background which they took to North Britain.

2. The proper names in the Tristan legend have some association with the North Britain of about the sixth century.

a. The name *Tristan* is acknowledged to be a development of the Pictish name *Drust,* and although the name was common among Pictish kings, for reasons given above I believe that this particular Drust lived in the sixth century.

b. The name *Tallwch,* which was given to Tristan's father in the Welsh fragments of the tale, is a homonym of the Pictish name *Talorc.*

c. The name *Mark* is a form of the name *Kynvarch,* which was borne by a North British king of the sixth century, and I have suggested that the Mark of the Tristan legend received his name from this Kynvarch.

d. The name *Morgan,* which in Thomas' version of the Tristan story was the name of a usurper slain by Tristan, is a name generally associated in North Britain with a male figure who commits a villainy.

e. The name *Urgan,* assigned by Thomas to a giant slain by Tristan, is a form of the name *Urien,* borne by one of the kings in North Britain during the sixth century.

f. In the Welsh Triad 80 in MS. Peniarth 47 the name *Essyllt Fair-Hair* is assigned to Tristan's mistress and is associated in the triad with Owain, a historical figure from sixth-century North Britain; Fflamddwyn, whose name was borne by one of this Owain's antagonists; and Culfanawyd of Britain, whose name contains a form of the element *Manaw,* which itself is associated with the place name *Manau Guotodin,* a sixth-century name for land which is today near Edinburgh.

g. The name of Tristan's traditional home is *Loonois,* a name agreed to be related to the name *Lothian,* an area near Edinburgh.

h. The name of the forest which sheltered Tristan and Isolt is *Morrois,* a name which may be related to the Scottish place name *Moray.*

Thus it seems apparent that whoever first set down the story of Tristan and Isolt was writing for an audience familiar with both the personal and place names of North Britain.

3. The Tristan legend contains a number of elements reminiscent of the myths known to the Greeks and Romans.

a. Tristan's character and some of his adventures are similar to the character and adventures of Hippolytus, the tragic hero of the Greek myth of Phaedra, as it was dramatized by Euripedes.

b. Tristan's adventure with the Morholt is reminiscent of Theseus' conquest of the Minotaur.

c. Tristan's death contains elements of the deaths of Aegeus, the father of Theseus, and Paris, the son of the Trojan king Priam.

d. Tristan's voyage to Ireland to be healed by Isolt appears to be related to an illness and voyage of Philoctetes, a hero associated with the Trojan war.

The story of Tristan and Isolt has come far from what I believe was its original telling in an Irish Columban monastery located in North Britain during the seventh or eighth century. For convenience I have labeled this Columban version the *Drustansaga.*

SYNOPSIS OF THE *DRUSTANSAGA*

Perhaps as a *tour de force* I have attempted a reconstruction of the *Drustansaga* in synopsis form. This reconstruction is exactly the same as the extant versions of the legend except that the findings listed above have been incorporated. Thus it serves, as I hope this book does, as a useful link between what I believe are the sources of the story and the tale as everyone knows it.

A long time ago, perhaps a hundred years ago, a powerful king named March or Kynvarch ab Meirchawn lived here in Strathclyde. Early in his reign he promised his sister in marriage to Talorc ab Muircholach, king of the neighboring Picts. The marriage duly took place, and in time the couple had a male child whom they named, according to the traditions of the Pictish kings, Drust, or as they came to call him, Drustan. The child grew to be a young man distinguished for his love of hunting and of music. He was not known to be especially interested in women.

To the south in Strathclyde still dwelled March, Drustan's uncle. It was decided that the boy should visit his uncle and perhaps learn at the Strathclyde court the niceties of being a British or Pictish prince. At the court of March, Drustan was admired as a princely hunter and musician from Pictland, or as some said, Loonois. He learned swordsmanship and in time became a friend of Cai Hir (Cai the Tall), who, when he was not at the court of March, was a companion of the renowned Arthur and Bedwyr.

Not only did Drustan learn his swordsmanship, but he also had the opportunity to hear the four languages of March's land: Brythonic or British, which he had learned from his mother; Goidelic or Irish, from the monks who were spreading across the land from Iona; some English from those who had wandered in or been captured from Bernicia and Deire; and Pictish, the language of his father.

Curious stories were told about Drustan's uncle. It was said that he had refused to give a bell to a holy man or saint, yet he changed his decision on discovering that the bell rang only for that holy man, that he had a powerful fleet, and (most curious) that under his headgear he concealed horse's ears. Long ago he had had to murder his barbers to prevent them from divulging his deformity. But after one barber proved to be physically incapable of keeping the secret, March ceased his murderous ways and let the secret be known to whoever wished to know it. Drustan never saw this deformity, but more than once he had heard the tale.

In time Drustan grew to be very much a hero and the King's favorite. He subdued at least two of March's antagonists: a political usurper named Morgant and a giant of a man called Urbgen. (Many years later March named his own son Urbgen, but that is another story.) Drustan's fame was becoming widespread beyond March's borders, to Manau Guotodin, among other places.

There the king Culfanawyd and his daughter Essyllt heard of Drustan's prowess, and so great was Drustan's fame that Essyllt, perhaps spurred by magic, fell in love with Drustan, even before she had ever met him. As a sign of her love she sent him a gift: a beautiful jeweled sword.

The land of Manau Guotodin was not completely at peace with March's kingdom. Years before, March had lost a battle with King Culfanawyd, and ever since he had been forced to send Culfanawyd a periodic tribute of some of the choice young people of the kingdom. The one who insisted on this tribute and who personally saw that it was carried out was known as the Morholt, a monster of a man and the brother of Culfanawyd's queen. Essyllt detested her brutal uncle but had never been able to demonstrate her hatred.

Drustan too hated the very name of the Morholt, and as the time grew near for the periodic tribute, he begged March to include him among the young people to go. March immediately denied Drustan's request. The boys and girls who made up the tribute were slated for slavery, and March could not think of so losing his nephew. Eventually, after much persuasion, March relented: Drustan was allowed to join the people designated as the tribute.

No one at Manau Guotodin knew that the group from Strathclyde included March's own nephew. Great was the amazement of all when one of the Strathclyde captives loudly proclaimed that he would challenge the Morholt in single combat. The Morholt himself was amused at the challenge and designated a small island where the battle would be held. He and the unknown challenger rowed to the island in individual boats. Drustan on arriving kicked his boat off the shore announcing that since only one of them was returning, only one boat was necessary.

Drustan fought boldly against the Morholt, who certainly was much more of an antagonist than Morgant or Urbgen had ever been. With a prodigious display of strength the stranger slew the Morholt. The Pictish hero, however, was sorely wounded in the battle. In spite of his wound, Drustan rowed back to the others and collapsed on the beach.

The Morholt was not beloved even among his own people. They hailed the unknown hero and then, noticing that he was wounded, sent word of his injuries to the best physician in the land. This healer was none other than the Princess Essyllt, who had inherited her curative powers from her mother, also a great healer. Although

she did not know who the hero was, Essyllt had a curative bath
prepared and filled it with strange drugs known only to her. Then he
was brought to her, and she had his gear put aside while he was
placed in the bath. After she had assured herself that he would
recover, she turned to see what kind of equipment such a great hero
would own. And she noticed his sword. It was the very one she had
sent Drustan, and she was overjoyed that the person who had slain
the Morholt was the very hero whom she had loved.[1]

Although Essyllt loved Drustan, he cared no more for her than
for anyone else who would have healed him. As soon as he was fit
and able, he concerned himself with forcing King Culfanawyd to
agree that now that the Morholt was dead the tribute should be
abolished. Then with the other young people from Strathclyde, he
returned to March's court.

Drustan was now more of a court favorite than ever. The other
courtiers were jealous and feared that March would make Drustan
his heir. They came in a group to March and suggested that he
marry and beget a son who would be the uncontested heir to the
throne. March was thinking of how to stall them when a swallow
flew in the open window bearing in its beak a single strand of
golden human hair. The King seized this single hair and announced
that he would certainly marry, but he would marry only whatever
beautiful woman had been the original owner of that striking strand
of hair. One of the courtiers then suggested that the hero Drustan
be sent to find this mysterious woman. Once again March demurred
at placing Drustan under such an impossible obligation, but Drustan
had no objections. Essyllt, the Princess of Manau Guotodin, he
silently recalled, had hair that would match the single strand.

So once again Drustan set off for Manau Guotodin, and once
again March felt to himself that he was sending his nephew on a
fruitless quest.

Now things had changed in Manau Guotodin: a dangerous
dragon had taken up a lair not far from the King's palace. Periodically it emerged, laid waste the countryside, and carried off citizens
to be devoured. The King was desperate. No local hero had been

---

1. The curative bath and accompanying recognition are placed directly after
the Morholt episode on the evidence that the bath and recognition occurred
directly after Cú Chulainn's victory over the Fomorians.

able to kill the dragon or even to frighten it into ceasing its dreadful depredations. A gloom had settled over the land, and the King had offered his daughter and half of the kingdom to any hero who would slay the monster.

On arriving Drustan learned this information before he even had a chance to present himself at court. Without hesitation he turned his horse directly to the dragon's lair. On hearing Drustan's challenge, the monster appeared. Drustan, wielding the sword Essyllt had given him, charged into the battle.

Again the hero was victorious. He slew the dragon, severed its head, and as a token of victory cut out the monster's tongue. Then being exhausted he retired behind a hill and slept.

A courtier from Manau Guotodin then appeared. He saw the slain dragon and the severed head. No one was around, and the courtier, who had long wished to marry the Princess Essyllt, took the head back to the palace and claimed to have been the one who slew the dragon.

Immediately preparations for the wedding were made amidst great rejoicing. And when Drustan appeared claiming to have slain the dragon, no one believed him except perhaps the Princess, who was evidently indulging in wishful thinking. Drustan waited until the very hour before the appointed wedding. Then, holding the dragon's tongue aloft so that all could see, he rode into the assemblage and loudly accused the intended bridegroom of being a liar, a cheat, and a false claimant. The court was thrown into confusion. Some sided with Drustan, some against him. But the evidence of the tongue was irrefutable. The King had to agree that Drustan had won Essyllt and half of the kingdom fairly. The false claimant was hauled away for punishment, and Drustan was proclaimed to be the bridegroom and possessor of half of the kingdom.

Then, to the surprise of all, Drustan announced that he did not wish half of the kingdom. He was the servant of March ab Meirchawn and had neither time nor use for a kingdom. Secondly, although he would claim Essyllt, he would not claim her for himself. He displayed the single strand of golden hair and explained King March's desire to wed its owner. All agreed that the strand could have come only from Essyllt's head. Thus, with the King's permission, Essyllt was to be the bride of none other than March himself. Drustan's only mission was to conduct her to his uncle.

So it was agreed: Drustan and Essyllt made preparations for the return journey.

Essyllt, so she confessed to Golwg Hafddydd, her personal maid, was delighted to make a journey with Drustan. Her love for him had not lessened, and she welcomed the opportunities afforded by the close associations inevitable on such a journey. But Drustan had no intention of being disloyal to his uncle. Each night when they slept, he placed his jeweled sword between them, announcing his loyalty to all and aggravating Essyllt's frustrations. But as they were riding their horses over a stream, Essyllt broke into laughter. When asked why, she replied that the horses' hooves had kicked some water up on her leg, and that that water was bolder than Drustan ever had been. Drustan was overcome. He abandoned his loyalty to King March. From that day on Essyllt was Drustan's mistress.

Essyllt now had this problem: it would never do to let March know that Drustan had preceded him as her lover. She discussed the situation with her maid, Golwg Hafddydd, and she persuaded her maid to take her place on the nuptial couch.

So it was. March, on seeing Essyllt's golden hair, married her with much ceremony. And that night, under cover of darkness, March, thinking that he was with his bride, slept with Golwg Hafddydd.

Essyllt knew that her secret was safe with Drustan, but she was not sure about her attendant. The answer was to have her slain. Accordingly Essyllt hired some local people to take Golwg Hafddydd into the woods and kill her. But Golwg Hafddydd was eloquent. She persuaded her captors to kill a pig, bloody their swords on it, and show the bloodied swords to Essyllt. All this was done, and Essyllt to her surprise discovered that she regretted having her attendant killed. After this news was brought to Golwg Hafddydd, she reappeared. Queen and attendant fell into each other's arms vowing never again to have a disagreement.

Drustan too had to have a confidant. He selected Cai, the friend of Arthur and Bedwyr. Cai and Golwg Hafddydd not only were privy to the secrets of Drustan and Essyllt but became lovers themselves.

In time, of course, the secret came out. The courtiers, Drustan's enemies from before, were the first to know; March was the last. Essyllt never did know that March knew as much as he did, as we shall see. Ultimately the courtiers persuaded March against his will to banish Drustan and Essyllt. The lovers fled to the Forest of Morrois, at the extreme end of Drustan's native Pictland. Drustan as usual was more at home in a forest than at court.

In time March missed his wife and allowed the lovers to return. But spurred by his courtiers and honestly suspicious, he soon ordered Drustan to leave the court forever. Before leaving, Drustan bid a long farewell to Essyllt. They agreed that should he ever become ill and need her renowned curative powers, he would send her a message, and she would do what she could.

Drustan left, journeyed over the sea, and entered the service of a foreign king, probably in Ireland. There in battle, although he broke his sword, he slew his adversary (as usual) and received a poisoned and noxious wound which festered and would not heal. The wound became so offensive that Drustan was isolated in a small hut. He knew that only Essyllt could cure the wound and sent a message to her explaining the straits he was in. Essyllt, unaware that her husband March knew of her intrigue with Drustan, received Drustan's message and went straight to March with it. March pretended to show the concern for his nephew that Essyllt had. He told Essyllt that he himself would take one of the ships of his renowned fleet, sail to his nephew's place of isolation, and return with Drustan. If the hero survived the trip, March's ship would display a white sail—if not, a black sail. Essyllt promised that every day she would watch for March's ship. Her observation point was to be a high cliff overlooking the rocky coast. March knew that if he returned with a black sail Essyllt would be so distraught that she would throw herself from the cliff. March, true to his word, sailed to Drustan's place of isolation. He took the wounded hero on his ship and sailed toward home. But secretly knowing of Essyllt's intrigue with his nephew, he sailed with black sails. Every day Essyllt went to the cliff. Then one day she saw March's ship, and it had black sails. As March knew she would, she threw herself from the cliff, smashing her head on the rocks below. When Drustan arrived she was dead, and there was no one to cure his wound. He too died, and March had the lovers buried side by side. From the grave of Essyllt grew a rosebush, and from the grave of Drustan a vine. These met, and no man could ever part them.

BIBLIOGRAPHY

I. MAJOR VERSIONS OF THE TRISTAN LEGEND 🔲

As an aid to the reader, the versions are listed according to the way or ways in which they are most commonly known. For explanation and discussion of the versions and their derivatives, see pp. 29 ff.

Bédier, Joseph. *Le Roman de Tristan et Iseut*. Paris, 1918.
———. *The Romance of Tristan and Iseult*. Translated by Hilaire Belloc and Paul Rosenfeld. Garden City, N. Y., 1956; reprinted, New York, n.d.
Berne *Folie Tristan*. Edited by Joseph Bédier. *Les Deux Poèms de la folie Tristan*. *SATF*. No. LIV. Paris, 1907.
———. Edited by Ernest Hoepffner. *Folie Tristan de Berne*. 2d ed. Paris, 1949.
Béroul. *Le Roman de Tristan par Béroul*. Edited by E. Muret. *SATF*. No. LII. Paris, 1903. Revised by L. M. Defourques. *Les Classiques français du moyen âge*. Paris, 1947.
———. *The Romance of Tristran by Beroul*. Edited by A. Ewert. Oxford, 1953.
Eilhart von Oberge. *Tristrant*. Edited by Franz Lichtenstein. *Quellen und Forschungen zur Sprach- und Culturgeschichte*. Vol. XIX. Strasbourg, 1877.
———. *Tristrant*. Edited by K. Wagner. *Reinische Beiträge*. Vol. V (Bonn, 1924).
———. *Tristrant*. Synopsized by Gertrude Schoepperle. *Tristan and Isolt: A Study of the Sources of the Romance*. 2 vols. Frankfurt and London, 1913; reprinted New York, 1959. I, 11–65.
Gottfried von Strassburg. *Tristram und Isolt*. Edited by A. Closs. 2d rev. ed. Oxford, 1947.
———. *Tristram and Isolt*. Translated by A. T. Hatto. *Gottfried von Strassburg Tristan with the Surviving Fragments of the Tristan of Thomas*. Harmondsworth, Middlesex, and Baltimore, 1960.
———. *Tristan und Isolde*. Edited and translated by Wilhelm Hertz.

Tristan und Isolde von Gottfried von Strassburg. 3d ed. Stuttgart and Berlin, 1901.

———. *Tristram und Isolt.* Edited by F. Ranke. Berlin, 1930.

Marie de France. *Le Chèvrefeuil.* Edited by A. Ewert. *Lais.* Oxford, 1944. Pp. 123–26.

———. *Le Chèvrefeuil.* Edited by Ernest Hoepffner. *Lais.* Strasbourg, 1921.

———. *Le Chèvrefeuil.* Edited by Karl Warnke. *Die Lais der Marie de France.* 3d ed. Halle, 1925. Pp. 181–85.

Oxford *Folie Tristan.* Edited by Joseph Bédier. *Les Deux Poèms de la folie Tristan. SATF.* No. LIV. Paris, 1907.

———. Edited by Ernest Hoepffner. *Folie Tristan d'Oxford.* 2d ed. Paris, 1943.

Prose *Tristan.* Edited by E. Löseth. *Le Roman en prose de Tristan.* Paris, 1891.

Sir Tristrem. Edited by Eugen Kölbing. *Die nordische und die englische Version der Tristan-sage.* 2 vols. Heilbronn, 1882.

Thomas of Britain. Edited by Joseph Bédier. *Le Roman de Tristan par Thomas. SATF.* No. LIII. 2 vols. Paris, 1902–5.

———. Translated by A. T. Hatto. *Gottfried von Strassburg Tristan with the Surviving Fragments of the Tristan of Thomas.* Harmondsworth, Middlesex, and Baltimore, 1960.

———. Translated by Brother Robert of Norway. Edited by Eugen Kölbing. *Die nordische und die englische Version der Tristan-sage.* 2 vols. Heilbronn, 1882.

———. Edited and translated by Roger Sherman Loomis. *The Romance of Tristram and Ysolt.* Rev. ed. New York, 1951.

———. Edited by B. H. Wind. *Fragments du Tristan de Thomas.* Leiden, 1950.

Ystoria Tristan. Edited and translated by Tom Peete Cross. "A Welsh Tristan Episode," *Studies in Philology,* XVII (1920), 93–110.

———. Edited and translated by Roger Sherman Loomis. *The Romance of Tristram and Ysolt.* Rev. ed. New York, 1951. Pp. xxi–xxvi.

———. Edited and translated by J. Loth. "L'Ystoria Trystan et la question des archétypes." *RC,* XXXIV (1913), 366–96.

———. Edited by Sir Ifor Williams. "Trystan ac Esyllt." *BBCS,* V (1930), 115–29.

II. OTHER WORKS ▩

Aarne, Antii, and Stith Thompson. *The Types of the Folktale.* FF Communications No. 184. Helsinki, 1961.

Adamnán. *The Life of St. Columba.* Edited by Williams Reeves. Dublin, 1857.

Anderson, A. O. *Early Sources of Scottish History*. 2 vols. Edinburgh, 1922.

Aneurin. *The Gododdin of Aneurin Gwawdrydd*. Translated by Thomas Stephens. Printed for the Honourable Society of Cymmrodorion. London, 1888.

―――. "Canu Aneurin." Translated by Gwynn Jones. *Cymmrodor*, XXXII (1922), 4–47.

―――. *Canu Aneurin*. Edited by Sir Ifor Williams. Cardiff, 1938.

Barnes, Hazel E. "The Hippolytus of Drama and Myth," *Hippolytus in Drama and Myth*. Lincoln, Nebr., 1960.

Bede. *Venerabilis Baedae*. Edited by Carolus Plummer. 2 vols. Oxford, 1896.

Bernard, J. H., and R. Atkinson. *The Irish Liber Hymnorum*. 2 vols. London, 1898.

Best, R. I. (ed.). "Comhag Fir Diadh 7 Chon Culainn." *ZCP*, X (1915), 303.

Binchy, D. A. *Scéla Cano Meic Gartnáin*. Edited from *The Yellow Book of Lecan* with Introd., Notes, Glossary, and Indexes. Vol. XVIII of the *Medieval and Modern Irish Series*. Dublin, 1963.

Bressie, Ramona. "Libraries of the British Isles in the Anglo-Saxon Period." *The Medieval Library*. Edited by J. W. Thompson. New York, 1957. Pp. 102–25.

Brodeur, Arthur G. "Arthur, Dux Bellorum." *University of California Publications in English*, III (1939), 237–83.

Brogan, Olwen. *Roman Gaul*. London, 1953.

Bromwich, Rachel. "The Celtic Inheritance of Medieval Literature." *MLQ*, XXVI, No. 1 (March, 1965), 203–27.

―――. "The Character of Early Welsh Tradition." *Studies in Early British History*. Edited by Nora K. Chadwick. Cambridge, Eng., 1954; reprinted, 1959. Pp. 83–136.

―――. "Scotland and the Arthurian Legend." *BBSIA*, XV (1963), 85–95.

―――. "Some Remarks on the Celtic Sources of 'Tristan.'" *THSC*, Session 1953 (London, 1955), pp. 32–60.

―――. *Trioedd Ynys Prydein—The Welsh Triads*. Cardiff, 1961.

―――. "The Welsh Triads." *ALMA*. Pp. 44–51.

Bruce, J. D. *Evolution of Arthurian Romance*. 2d ed. 2 vols. Baltimore, 1928.

Brugger, E. "Ueber die Bedeutung von Bretagne, Breton in mittelalterlichen Texten." *ZFSL*, XXI (1898), 79–162.

Byrne, Mary E. "On the Punishment of Setting Adrift." *Ériu*, XI (1932), 97–102.

Campbell, John F. *The Celtic Dragon Myth* with *The Geste of Fraoch and the Dragon*. Translated by George Henderson. Edinburgh, 1911.

―――. *Popular Tales of the Western Highlands*. 4 vols. London, 1890–93.

Campbell, John G. *Clan Traditions and Popular Tales of the Western Highlands and Islands. Waifs and Strays of Celtic Tradition.* Argyllshire Series V. London, 1895.

———. *The Fians. Waifs and Strays of Celtic Tradition.* Argyllshire Series IV. London, 1891.

Carney, James P. "Comments on the Present State of the Patrician Problem." *Irish Ecclesiastical Record,* 5th Series XCII. (July, 1959).

———. *The Problem of St. Patrick.* Dublin, 1961.

———. *Studies in Irish Literature and History.* Dublin, 1955.

———. " 'Suibne Geilt' and 'The Children of Lir.' " *Éigse,* VI, Pt. II (1950), 83–110, later reprinted in *Studies in Irish Literature and History,* pp. 129–64.

Chadwick, H. M. *Early Scotland.* Cambridge, Eng., 1949.

Chadwick, Nora K. *The Age of the Saints in the Early Celtic Church.* London, 1961.

———. (ed.). *Celt and Saxon.* Cambridge, Eng., 1963.

———. "The Conversion of Northumbria: A Comparison of Sources." *Celt and Saxon.* Edited by Nora K. Chadwick. Cambridge, Eng., 1963. Pp. 138–66.

———. "Early Culture and Learning in North Wales." *Studies in the Early British Church.* Edited by Nora K. Chadwick. Cambridge, Eng., 1958. Pp. 29–120.

———. "The Lost Literature of Celtic Scotland." *Scottish Gaelic Studies,* VII (1953), 115–83.

———. "The Name Pict." *Scottish Gaelic Studies,* VIII, Pt. 2 (1958), 172.

———. "St. Ninian: A Preliminary Study of Sources." *TJDGNA,* Whithorn Volume, 3d ser., XXVII (1950), 36 f.

——— (ed.). *Studies in Early British History.* Cambridge, Eng., 1959.

Chambers, E. K. *Arthur of Britain.* London, 1927.

Clark, J. M. *The Abbey of St. Gall.* Cambridge, Eng., 1926.

Crooke, W. "King Midas and his Ass's Ears." *Folk-Lore,* XXII (1911), 183–202.

Cross, Tom Peete. *Motif-Index of Early Irish Literature.* Bloomington, Ind., 1952.

———, and C. H. Slover (eds.). *Ancient Irish Tales.* London, n.d.

Cuissard, Ch. (ed.). "Vie de Saint Paul de Léon." *RC,* V (1881–83), 413–60.

Curtin, Jeremiah. *Myths and Folk-Lore of Ireland.* Boston, 1890.

D'Arbois de Jubainville, H. *The Irish Mythological Cycle.* Translated by R. I. Best. Dublin, 1903.

Demetz, Peter. "The Elm and the Vine: Notes Toward the History of a Marriage Topos." *PMLA,* LXXIII, No. 5, Pt. 1 (Dec., 1958), 521–32.

Deutschbein, Max, "Eine irische Variante der Tristan-sage." *Beiblatt zur Anglia,* XV (1904), 16–21.

Dillon, Myles. *The Cycles of the Kings.* Oxford, 1946.

Dillon, Myles. *Early Irish Literature*. Chicago, 1948.

———. "The Wooing of Becfhola and the Stories of Cano, Son of Gartnán." *Modern Philology*, XLIII, I (1945), 11 ff.

Dottin, G. *Contes et légendes d'Irlande*. Le Havre, 1901.

Duke, John A. *The Columban Church*. Edinburgh and London, 1932; reprinted, 1957.

Dunleavy, Gareth W. *Colum's Other Island*. Madison, Wis., 1960.

Dunn, Joseph (trans.). *The Ancient Irish Epic Tale—Táin Bó Cúalnge*. London, 1914.

Eisner, Sigmund. *A Tale of Wonder—A Source Study of the Wife of Bath's Tale*. Wexford, Ire., 1957.

Euripedes. *Alcestis and Other Plays*. Translated by Philip Vellacott. London, 1956.

Evans, J. Gwenogvryn, and John Rhŷs. *The Text of the Book of Llan Dâv*. Oxford, 1893.

Everett, Dorothy. *Essays on Middle English Literature*. Oxford, 1955.

Faral, E. *La Légende arthurienne*. Pt. 1. *Bibliothèque de l'école des hautes études*. Nos. CCLV–CCLVII. Paris, 1929.

Fletcher, Robert Huntingdon. *Arthurian Material in the Chronicles*. Boston, 1906; reprinted, New York, 1958.

Forbes, A. P. (ed.). *The Lives of S. Ninian and S. Kentigern*. The Historians of Scotland Series, No. V. Edinburgh, 1874.

Foster, Idris Llewelyn. "*Culhwch and Olwen* and *Rhonabwy's Dream*." *ALMA*. Pp. 31–43.

Foulon, Charles. "Wace." *ALMA*. Pp. 94–103.

Fraser, J. (ed. and trans.). "The First Battle of Moytura." *Ériu*, VIII (1916), 34 f.

Geoffrey of Monmouth. *Historia Regum Britanniae*. Edited by A. Griscom. London and New York, 1929.

———. *History of the Kings of Britain*. Translated by Sebastian Evans. Revised by Charles W. Dunn. New York, 1958.

———. *Vita Merlini*. Edited by John J. Parry. *University of Illinois Studies in Language and Literature*, Vol. X, No. 3. Urbana, Ill., 1925.

Gillespy, F. L. "Layamon's *Brut:* A Comparative Study in Narrative Art." *University of California Publications in Modern Philology*, III, (1916), 361–510.

Golther, W. *Tristan und Isolde in den Dichtungen des Mittelalters und der neuen Zeit*. Leipzig, 1907.

Graves, Robert. *The Greek Myths*. 2 vols. London, 1957.

Greene, David. "Early Irish Literature." *Early Irish Society*. Edited by Myles Dillon. Irish Life and Culture Series. No. VIII. Dublin, 1954. Pp. 22–35.

———. *Fingal Rónáin and Other Stories*. Medieval and Modern Irish Series. Vol. XVI. Dublin, 1955.

———. "Fingal Rónáin." *Irish Sagas*. Edited by Myles Dillon. Dublin, 1959. Pp. 167–81.

Gruffydd, W. J. *Math vab Mathonwy*. Cardiff, 1928.

———. *Rhiannon*. Cardiff, 1953.

Gwynn, E. J., and W. J. Purton. "The Monastery of Tallaght." *Proceedings of the Royal Irish Academy*, XXIX, Sec. C., No. 5. Dublin, 1911.

Hartland, E. Sidney. *The Legend of Perseus*. 3 vols. London, 1894.

Harward, Vernon J., Jr. *The Dwarfs of Arthurian Romance and Celtic Tradition*. Leiden, 1958.

Henderson, George (ed. and trans.). "Fled Bricrend—The Feast of Bricriu." *ITS*, Vol. II (1899).

Hennessy, William M. (ed. and trans.). *Annals of Ulster*. Dublin, 1887.

Henry, Françoise. *Early Christian Irish Art*. Translated by Máire Mac Dermott. Dublin, 1954–55.

Hoepffner, E. "The Breton Lais." *ALMA*. Pp. 112–21.

———. *Les Lais de Marie de France*. Paris, 1955.

Huet, G. "Le Témoignage de Wace sur les 'fables' arthuriennes." *Le Moyen Âge*, XXVIII (1915), 234–49.

Hull, Eleanor. *The Cuchullin Saga*. London, 1898.

Hull, Vernam (ed. and trans.). *Longes Mac n-Uislenn—The Exile of the Sons of Uisliu*. New York, 1949.

Jackson, Kenneth. "Arthur in Early Welsh Verse." *ALMA*. Pp. 12–19.

———. "The Arthur of History." *ALMA*. Pp. 1–11.

———. "A Further Note on Suibhne Geilt and Merlin." *Éigse*, VII (1954), 112–16.

———. *Language and History in Early Britain*. Edinburgh, 1953.

———. "The Motive of the Threefold Death in the Story of Suibhne Geilt." *Essays and Studies Presented to Professor Eoin Mac Neill*. Edited by John Ryan. Dublin, 1940. Pp. 547 ff.

———. "Once Again Arthur's Battles." *Modern Philology*, XLIII (1945), 44–57.

———. "The Pictish Language." *The Problem of the Picts*. Edited by F. T. Wainwright. Edinburgh, 1955. Pp. 129–66.

———. Review of *Canu Aneurin*, by Sir Ifor Williams. *Antiquity*, XIII (1939), 25–34.

———. "The Sources for the Life of St. Kentigern." *Studies in the Early British Church*. Edited by Nora K. Chadwick. Cambridge, Eng., 1958. Pp. 273–357.

Jackson, W. T. H. "Gottfried von Strassburg." *ALMA*. Pp. 145–56.

Jarman, A. O. H. *The Legend of Merlin*. Cardiff, 1960.

Jeanroy, Alfred (ed. and trans.). *Les Poésies de Cercamon, Les Classiques français du moyen âge*. Vol. IV (1922).

Jones, Gwyn, and Thomas Jones (trans.). *The Mabinogion*. Everyman's Library No. 97. London, 1949.

Jones, J. J. "March ap Meirchion, A Study in Celtic Folklore." *Aberystwyth Studies*, XII (1932), 21–33.

Keating, Geoffrey. *The History of Ireland*, Vol. II. Edited by P. S. Dinneen. *ITS*, No. VIII (1908).

Kelleher, A., and G. Schoepperle. "Finn dans le pays des géants." *RC*, XXXII (1911), 185–86.

Kennedy, Charles W. (trans.). *Beowulf*. New York, 1940.

Kenney, James F. *Sources for the Early History of Ireland*. Vol. I: *Ecclesiastical*. 2 vols. New York, 1929.

Klaeber, Fr. (ed.). *Beowulf and the Fight at Finnsburg*. 3d ed. New York, 1941.

Langdon, Arthur G., and J. Romilly Allen. "Catalogue of the Early Christian Inscribed Monuments in Cornwall." *Archaeologia Cambrensis*, 5th ser., XII, No. 45 (1895), 50 ff.

Larminie, William. *West Irish Folktales*. London, 1893.

Layamon's Brut. Edited by J. Hall. Oxford, 1924.

Layamon. *Brut*. Edited by Sir Frederic Madden. London, 1847.

Lejeune, Rita. "The Troubadours." *ALMA*. Pp. 393–99.

Lloyd, J. H., O. J. Bergin, and Gertrude Schoepperle. "The Death of Diarmaid." *RC*, XXXIII (1912), 157–79.

Loomis, Roger Sherman. "The Arthurian Legend before 1139." *Romanic Review*, XXXII (1941), 3–38. Reprinted in *Wales and the Arthurian Legend*. Cardiff, 1956. Pp. 179–220.

———— (ed.). *Arthurian Literature in the Middle Ages*. Oxford, 1959.

————. *Arthurian Tradition and Chrétien de Troyes*. New York, 1949.

————. "A Bibliography of Tristan Scholarship after 1911." Appended to 2d edition of Gertrude Schoepperle's *Tristan and Isolt*. New York, 1959, II, 588–92.

————. "Breton Folklore and Arthurian Romance." *Comparative Literature*. II (1950), 293.

————. "The Combat at the Ford in the 'Didot Perceval.'" *Modern Philology*, XLIII, No. 1 (1945), 63–71. Reprinted in *Wales and the Arthurian Legend*. Cardiff, 1956. Pp. 91–104.

————. "The Descent of Lancelot from Lug." *BBSIA*, III (Paris, 1951), 67 ff.

————. "Layamon's *Brut*." *ALMA*. Pp. 104–11.

————. "The Legend of Arthur's Survival." *ALMA*. Pp. 64–71.

————. "Morgain la Fée and the Celtic Goddesses." *Speculum*, XX (1945), 183–203. Reprinted in *Wales and the Arthurian Legend*. Cardiff, 1956. Pp. 105–30.

————. "The Oral Diffusion of the Arthurian Legend." *ALMA*. Pp. 52–63.

————. "The Origin of the Grail Legend." *ALMA*. Pp. 274–94.

————. "Problems of the Tristan Legend." *Romania*, LIII (1927), 82–102.

————. "*The Spoils of Annwn*, An Early Welsh Poem." *PMLA*, LVI (1941), 887–936. Reprinted in *Wales and the Arthurian Legend*. Cardiff, 1956. Pp. 131–78.

————. "A Survey of Scholarship on the Fairy Mythology of Arthurian

Romance since 1903," with Bibliography. Appended to 2d edition of *Studies in the Fairy Mythology of Arthurian Romance* by Lucy Allen Paton. New York, 1960. Pp. 280–307.

———. "A Survey of Tristan Scholarship after 1911." Appended to 2d edition of Gertrude Schoepperle's *Tristan and Isolt*. New York, 1959, II, 565–87.

———. *Wales and the Arthurian Legend*. Cardiff, 1956.

Loth, J. "Contributions à l'étude des romans de la Table Ronde—XIII La voile blanch et la voile noire à l'ile Molènes." *RC*, XXXVII (1917–19), 323.

———. *Les Mabinogion*. 2 vols. Paris, 1913.

———. "Le Noms des Tristan et Iseut." *RC*, XXXII (1911), 407 ff.

Macalister, R. A. S. *Archaeologia Cambrensis*, LXXXIV (1929), 181.

———. *Corpus Inscriptionum Insularum Celticarum*. Dublin, 1945–49. I, 465 f.

Mackay, William. "Saints Associated with the Valley of the Ness." *Transactions of the Gaelic Society of Inverness*, XXVII (1908–11), pp. 145–62.

Mac Queen, John. "Yvain, Ewen, and Owein ap Urien." *TJDGNA*, 3d ser., XXXIII (1956), 107–31.

MacSweeney, Patrick M. (ed. and trans.). "Martial Career of Conghal Cláiringhneach." *ITS*, No. V (1904), 82 ff.

Malory, Thomas. *Le Morte d'Arthur*. Introd. by John Rhŷs. Everyman's Library Nos. 45 and 46. 2 vols. New York and London, 1906; reprinted, 1941.

———. *The Works of Sir Thomas Malory*. Edited by Eugène Vinaver. 3 vols. Oxford, 1954.

Meyer, Kuno (ed.). "Baile Binnbérlach mac Buain—Baile of the Clear Voice Son of Buan." *RC*, XIII (1892), 220–27.

——— (ed. and trans.). "Fingal Rónáin." *RC*, XIII (1892), 368–97.

——— (ed. and trans.). "King Eochaid Has Horse's Ears." *Otia Merseiana*. Liverpool, 1903. III, 46–54.

———. *Learning in Ireland in the Fifth Century*. Dublin, 1913.

——— (ed. and trans.). *Liadain and Curithir, An Irish Love Story of the Ninth Century*. London, 1902.

——— (ed.). "Tochmarc Emire la Coinculaind." *ZCP*, III (1901), 229 ff.

——— (ed.). "Tochmarc Treblainne." *ZCP*, XIII (1919–21), 166 ff.

——— (trans.). "The Wooing of Emer." *Archaeological Review*, I (1888), 68–75, 150–55, 231–35, 298–307.

Nennius. *Nennius et l'historia Brittonum*. Edited and translated by F. Lot. Paris, 1913.

———. *History of the Britons*. Edited and translated by A. W. Wade-Evans. London, 1938.

Newstead, Helaine. *Bran the Blessed in Arthurian Romance*. New York, 1939.

———. "King Mark of Cornwall." *RP*, XI, No. 3 (1958), 240–53.

Newstead, Helaine. "The Origin and Growth of the Tristan Legend." *ALMA*. Pp. 122–33.

O'Curry, Eugene. *Lectures on the Manuscript Materials of Ancient Irish History*. Dublin, 1861.

O'Donovan, John (ed. and trans.). *Annala Rioghachta Eireann—The Annals of the Four Masters*. 7 vols. Dublin, 1851.

———— (ed. and trans.). *The Battle of Magh Rath*. Dublin, 1842.

———— (trans.), and Whitley Stokes (ed.). *Sanas Chormaic*. Calcutta, 1868.

O'Duffy, Richard (ed.). *Oidhe Chloinne Tureann—The Fate of the Children of Tuireann*. Dublin, 1888.

O'Grady, Standish Hayes (ed.). *Silva Gadelica (I–XXXI)*. 2 vols. London, 1892.

———— (ed. and trans.). *Toruigheacht Dhiarmuda agus Ghrainne—The Pursuit After Diarmaid and Gráinne*. *Transactions of the Ossianic Society for the Year 1855*. Vol. III. Dublin, 1857.

O'Rahilly, Cecile (ed. and trans.). *Eachtra Uilliam*. Dublin, 1949.

————. *Ireland and Wales*. London, 1924.

———— (ed. and trans.). *Táin Bó Cúalnge from the Book of Leinster*. Dublin, 1967.

O'Rahilly, T. F. *Early Irish History and Mythology*. Dublin, 1946.

————. *The Two Patricks*. Dublin, 1942.

Paris, Gaston. "Comptes-rendus." *Romania*, IX (1880), 592–614.

Parry, John J., and Robert A. Caldwell. "Geoffrey of Monmouth." *ALMA*. Pp. 72–93.

Parry, Thomas. *A History of Welsh Literature*. Translated by H. Idris Bell. Oxford, 1955.

Paton, Lucy Allen. *Studies in the Fairy Mythology of Arthurian Romance*. Radcliffe College Monograph No. 13. Cambridge, Mass., 1903; reprinted, New York, 1960.

Philpot, J. H. *Maistre Wace*. London, 1925.

Polidori, F. L. (ed.). *La Tavola Ritonda. Collezione di opere inedite o rare*, VIII (Bologna, 1864).

Radford, Ralegh. *Journal of the Royal Institution of Cornwall*. N.s., I (1951), Appendix.

Reid, R. C. "Trusty's Hill Fort." *TJDGNA*, XIV (1930), 366–72.

Rhŷs, J. *Archaeologia Cambrensis*. 4th ser., V (1875), 369.

————. *Celtic Folklore, Welsh and Manx*. 2 vols. Oxford, 1901.

————. *The Hibbert Lectures, 1886*. London and Edinburgh, 1888.

————. *Studies in the Arthurian Legend*. Oxford, 1891.

————, and J. Gwenogvryn Evans. *Text of the Mabinogion from the Red Book of Hergest*. Oxford, 1887.

Roach, William (ed.). *The Didot Perceval*. Philadelphia, 1941.

Ryan, Rev. John. *Irish Monasticism*. Dublin, 1931.

————. *Saint Patrick*. The Thomas Davis Lecture Series, No. 4. Dublin, 1958.

Schirmir, W. F. *Die frühen Darstellungen des Arthurstoffes.* Cologne, 1958.

Schoepperle, Gertrude. *Tristan and Isolt: A Study of the Sources of the Romance.* 2 vols. Frankfurt and London, 1913; reprinted, New York, 1959.

Schwab, Gustav. *Gods and Heroes.* Translated by Olga Marx and Ernst Morwitz. London, 1950.

Scott, Alexander B. "S. Drostan of Buchan and Caithness." *Transactions of the Gaelic Society of Inverness,* XXVII (1908–11), 110–25.

Simpson, W. Douglas. *The Historical Saint Columba.* 3d ed. Edinburgh and London, 1963.

Singer, Samuel. "Arabische und europäische Poesie in Mittelalter." *Abhandlungen der Preussischen Akademie der Wissenschaften,* No. 13 (1918), pp. 8–10.

Skeels, Dell. *The Romance of Perceval in Prose.* Seattle, 1961.

Skene, William F. *Celtic Scotland.* 3 vols. 2d ed. Edinburgh, 1886–90.

———. *The Four Ancient Books of Wales.* 2 vols. Edinburgh, 1868.

Stephens, James. *Irish Fairy Tales.* New York, 1920; reprinted, 1962.

Stokes, Whitley (ed. and trans.). *The Martyrology of Oengus.* London, 1905.

——— . "Mythological Notes—VII. Labraid Lorc and His Ears." *RC,* II (1873–75), 198.

——— (ed.). *The Tripartite Life of St. Patrick.* 2 vols. London, 1887.

——— (ed. and trans.). "The Violent Deaths of Goll and Garb." *RC,* XIV (1893), 396–449.

Tatlock, J. S. P. "The Dates of the Arthurian Saints' Legends." *Speculum,* XIV (1939), 345–65.

———. *Legendary History of Britain.* Berkeley and Los Angeles, 1950.

Thompson, Stith. *The Folktale.* New York, 1951.

———. *Motif-Index of Folk Literature.* Rev. ed. 6 vols. Bloomington, Ind., 1955–58.

Thurneysen, R. *A Grammar of Old Irish.* Rev. ed. Translated by D. A. Binchy and Osborn Bergin. Dublin, 1946.

———. *Die irische Helden- und Königsage bis zum siebzehnten Jahrhundert.* Halle, 1921.

——— (trans.). "Eine irische Parallele zur Tristan-Sage." *ZRPh,* XLIII (1923), 385–402.

Todd, James H. *The Book of Hymns of the Ancient Church of Ireland.* 2 vols. Dublin, 1855–69.

Ulrich von Zatzikhoven. *Lanzelet.* Edited by Roger Sherman Loomis. Translated by K. G. T. Webster. New York, 1951.

Van Dam, J. "Tristanprobleme II: Die Frage nach dem Urtristan." *Neophilologus,* XV (1929–30), 88–105.

Van Hamel, A. G. "Tristan's Combat with the Dragon." *RC,* XLI (1924), 331–49.

Vinaver, Eugène. *Études sur le Tristan en prose, les sources, les manuscrits, bibliographie critique.* Paris, 1925.

———. "The Prose Tristan." *ALMA*. Pp. 339–47.

———. "Sir Thomas Malory." *ALMA*. Pp. 541–54.

———. *The Tale of the Death of King Arthur by Sir Thomas Malory.* Oxford, 1955.

Wace. *Le Roman de Brut.* 2 vols. Edited by Ivor Arnold. *SATF*. No. LXXXIII. (Paris, 1938–40).

Wade-Evans, A. W. *The Emergence of England and Wales.* Cambridge, Eng., 1959.

———. "Prolegomena to a Study of the Lowlands." *TJDGNA*, Whithorn Volume, 3d ser., XXVII (1950), 54–84.

——— (ed.). *Vitae Sanctorum Britanniae et Genealogiae.* Cardiff, 1944.

Wainwright, F. T. (ed.). *The Problem of the Picts.* Edinburgh, 1955.

Walker, G. S. M. (ed.). *Sancti Columbani Opera.* Dublin, 1957.

White, Jon Manchip. "Tristan and Isolt." *History Today*, III, No. 4 (April, 1953, 233–39. Reprinted in *Myth or Legend*. Edited by G. E. Daniel. London, 1955. Pp. 69 ff.

Whitehead, Frederick. "The Early Tristan Poems." *ALMA*. Pp. 134–44.

William of Malmesbury. *De Gestis Regum Anglorum.* Edited by William Stubbs. 2 vols. London, 1887–89.

Williams, Sir Ifor. *Lectures on Early Welsh Poetry.* Dublin, 1954.

Williams ab Ithel, John (ed.). *Annales Cambriae.* London, 1860.

Windisch, Ernst (ed. and trans.). "Táin Bó Cúalnge." *Irische Texte*, V (1905).

——— (ed. and trans.). "Tochmarc Ferbe." *Irische Texte*, III (1897).

Wyld, H. C. "Layamon as an English Poet." *Review of English Studies*, VI (1930), 1–30.

———. "Studies in the Diction of Layamon's *Brut*." *Language*, IX (1933), 47–71, 171–91; X (1934), 149–201.

Zimmer, H. "Beitrage zur Namenforschung in den altfranz Arthurepen, 'Tristan, Isolt, Marc.' " *ZFSL*, XIII (1891), 58–86.

INDEX

The text of this book is composed in eleven-point Old Style No. 7, two points leaded. Display typography is Goudy Old Style. Composition, printing by letterpress on Warren Olde Style paper, and binding in a G. S. B. fabric, are by Kingsport Press, Inc. The typography and binding design are by Elizabeth G. Stout.